Many sociologists have maintained that trust is the glue of social life. Trudy Govier confirms this view in a sustained discussion of the concept and contexts of trust, showing that trust is more significant and more prevalent than is usually assumed. She argues that social bonding is built on trust and maintains that trust is essential if we are to live ethically, responsibly, and well.

Govier offers a general account of trust in a variety of social contexts and explores the negative effects of distrust on society. For example, she examines the role of trust in relationships between doctors and patients and between politicians and constituents. With well-chosen examples ranging from the Oka crisis to Meech Lake, Govier points out that distrust in politics has been especially prevalent and, while it may be well-founded, can have pernicious effects.

Social Trust and Human Communities will be of great interest to students and scholars in the areas of applied ethics, social theory, and politics.

TRUDY GOVIER is an independent philosopher who lives and works in Calgary, Alberta. She is the author of numerous articles and several books.

Social Trust and Human Communities

TRUDY GOVIER

McGill-Queen's University Press
Montreal & Kingston · London · Buffalo

HM
291
.G65
1997

© McGill-Queen's University Press 1997
ISBN 0-7735-1662-X
ISBN 0-7735-1680-8

Legal deposit fourth quarter 1997
Bibliothèque nationale du Québec

Printed in Canada on acid-free paper

This book has been published with the help of a grant from the Humanities and Social Sciences Federation of Canada, using funds provided by the Social Sciences and Humanities Research Council of Canada.

McGill-Queen's University Press acknowledges the support received for its publishing program from the Canada Council's Block Grants program.

Canadian Cataloguing in Publication Data

Govier, Trudy
    Social trust and human communities
    Includes bibliographical references and index.
    ISBN 0-7735-1662-X (bound)-
    ISBN 0-7735-1680-8 (pbk.)
    1. Trust (Psychology). 2. Community. I. Title.
    HM291.G649 1997   302   C97-900598-1

Contents

Preface

My appreciation of the profound importance of trust began nearly thirty years when I was involved with a man who was a compulsive liar. His accounts of even relatively mundane daily events were unreliable to point of absurdity. I did my loyal best to believe him, struggling to see him in a positive light and regard events his way. I deceived both him and myself about how I felt and thought. When the inevitable moment of crisis arrived, I admitted to myself how little I could trust him. Coming to understand the web of falsehoods that had surrounded our intimate conversations, our hopes, and our goals for the future, I felt betrayed and insecure, but at the same time I was immensely relieved. I no longer had to try to believe things that I knew in my heart were not true. I had learned some painful lessons. The most important was never to establish intimate relationships with untrustworthy people.

Although I never forgot this lesson about the importance of trust, it was many years before I tried to reflect on its meaning seriously. When the topic again became central in my interests, the context was more political than personal. In the early and mid-1980s I debated the topic of nuclear disarmament before various university and public groups. One theme nearly always came up: trusting the Russians. Nuclear-arms control or disarmament might be all very well, people said, but how could you trust those Russians? The regime was communist, the leaders brutal tyrants. "Those people" had no conscience and were un-Christian, had no morality, would trick, lie, and deceive whenever it suited their purposes. They were to be feared, never to be trusted. Capable of anything at all, they were a brutal force and could only be confronted with force.

In Cold War days these beliefs about the Russians were held by most ordinary people and many academics, especially in the fields of strategic studies and foreign policy. Their words differed, their styles of thought differed, but their conclusion was the same: we cannot trust the Russians. However, these people who expressed such intense fear of the Russians were distinctly un-worried about the risks of getting into a nuclear war. Though they said they did not trust the Russians, they apparently had tremendous trust in the safety of nuclear-weapons systems in the United States and the Soviet Union. They had considerable confidence in the accuracy and safety of nuclear technology, the reliability of technicians and military personnel, and the rationality of political leaders – including those Russian leaders whom they "could not trust."

I found this combination of attitudes strange and suspected that it was counter-productive and based on double standards. But the official line on the problem of trust offered by peace groups was also open to question. On our view, trust was not necessary because treaty compliance could be verified. The verification of arms-control and disarmament treaties depended on procedures that could be reliably carried out by honest and competent people working in sound institutions. Given this verification, it would not be possible to cheat. So trust was not an issue, we said; you do not have to trust the Russians. The problem was this pat solution is that verification itself presumes co-operation and thus some degree of trust. Our view was simplistic, and we had our own double standard. We were willing to trust the Russians, the United Nations, and those in charge of monitoring treaties. But we were not willing to trust nuclear technicians, Western strategic experts, policy analysts, our national defence ministry, or our own governments.

This situation of contending double standards of trust and distrust puzzled me. It led to my interest in trust and distrust as topics in their own right. The dilemma of trust and disarmament still interests me, although events have altered its practical terms. The nuclear-weapons scene is transformed; the Soviet Union is no more; and the Russians are recipients of aid from Western countries and (usually) our official friends.

Even when abstractions like the Cold War are not involved, people have quite different ideas about trust and distrust. They start from different assumptions about human nature and culture, and interpret human communities in different ways.

A spectacular crisis of trust in politics was Canada's Meech Lake affair. In 1987 Canadian Prime Minister Brian Mulroney had worked out a controversial constitutional arrangement that would have decentralized governmental power and granted to the province of Quebec special status as a "distinct society" within Canada. The so-called Meech Lake Accord was approved tentatively by representatives of the provincial governments, but by the spring of 1990, after provincial elections had produced several new governments, it seemed unlikely that the accord would receive the necessary unanimous approval before the 23 June deadline at which it was due to expire. With less than six weeks remaining, Mulroney called all the provincial premiers to Ottawa for a week of intensive closed meetings.

Enraged citizens picketed the meeting, carrying signs saying, "It's a matter of trust." They were suspicious about what was going on behind closed doors, resented a system in which eleven white men appeared to have the power to determine the future legal framework of the country, and felt excluded and powerless. Dissenting premiers later described the pressure and fatigue of the meetings as unbearable. Some weeks later Mulroney casually admitted that he had deliberately left little time between the meeting and the deadline to put maximal pressure on the premiers. He was "rolling the dice," he told columnist Jeffrey Simpson. When Simpson reported the remark in the *Toronto Globe and Mail*, everyone involved was furious. People felt utterly betrayed at such deliberate and unnecessary risk-taking and manipulation. Mulroney's confidence ratings, plummeted, never to recover. The accord did not get the necessary approval, and the country was left in a state of constitutional crisis.

During Meech Lake I was working away on my research on the attitudes of trust and distrust and their significance in epistemology and social philosophy. I was assiduously reading a wide variety of papers in philosophy, sociology, and social psychology, becoming ever more fascinated with the subject, though somewhat confused and overwhelmed by the breadth of it all.

There were so many related notions. Trust and distrust. Faith, belief, expectation, and confidence. Hope, optimism. Self-trust. Self-confidence. Doubt, scepticism, pessimism. Cynicism. Despair. People's instincts on trust, their conceptions of trust, and their sense of what might be important about the subject seemed to vary enormously. The same variety appeared in books and articles on the topic. Different disciplines took different approaches; definitions varied considerably, and many researchers and authors explored specific subtopics without offering any general account.

In a book on the philosophy of money, the author explained how money presupposes trust and went on to argue that such trust will not easily survive government attempts to control exchange rates. A sociological paper described how marijuana users try to determine who is a trustworthy source of the drug. A rhetorician had studied the comparative credibility of psychiatrists and psychologists. A medical article maintained that the hostile ideas accompanying extreme distrust could be a factor causing heart attacks. A humanist psychologist criticized as absurdly superficial the understanding of trust implied by the encounter-group trust technique. In this exercise one is to fall back, assuming that another will catch him. Supposedly, by letting himself fall, a person indicates trust, and by catching the falling person, the other helps to establish it.

A sociologist used his experience as a cab driver to offer an account of what it means to trust someone as a passenger. A philosopher argued that we largely construct the social world and could construct a better world for ourselves if we were willing to trust other people more than we do. Less interesting were seemingly endless papers describing laboratory experiments based on Prisoner's Dilemma games. In a cell with buttons to push, subjects indicated whether they would make a co-operative move towards an unidentified "opponent." Such a move was assumed to indicate trust in the other party.

Peace researcher and philosopher Sissela Bok claimed that an atmosphere of trust was essential for human thriving and peace, both within a single society and in international life. Annette Baier, another philosopher, suggested that trust was more important to women than men and that men philosophers tend to misrepresent human relationships by overestimating the significance of rules and contracts. (I found three doctoral dissertations on trust, all by women, and heard from two graduate students wanting to write on the subject – both women.) Erik Erikson, a developmental psychologist, spoke of "basic trust" as an attitude a secure infant has in depending on its mother. For philosopher Laurence Thomas basic trust was something else entirely: a confidence that unknown other people do not intend to harm us.

I have tried in this book to incorporate some of these accounts, although I could not possibly discuss all of them. In this book I offer a general account of trust and distrust, one I intend to be applicable to a variety of contexts in personal, social, political life. This book is primarily about social trust and deals only peripherally with issues of self-trust and personal trust, which I have explored elsewhere.

As a matter of verbal usage, trust is not limited even to human beings. We speak of trusting or not trusting all kinds of things, including animals, machines, the human senses, the forces of history, and God himself. My interest, however, has been in *people* trusting or distrusting *other people* in social contexts, and in the significance of these attitudes for our social and political life.

What fascinates me is our boundless interdependence as human beings, our mutual vulnerability, and our ability to ignore or cope with so many risks and latent possibilities because we trust each other. Social trust and distrust are attitudes of people who live together and are boundlessly interdependent and vulnerable to each other. As sociologists have maintained, trust is the glue of social life. As I hope to show, it is more prevalent and more significant than most of us appreciate. When it diminishes, society and community are diminished as well.

In preparing this book I have benefited greatly from the work of others who have helped me through conversation, correspondence, and writing. Especially significant have been the published works of Annette Baier, Sissela Bok, Laurence Thomas, John Hardwig, C.A.J. Coady, Martin Buber, Erving Goffman, Niklas Luhmann, Nel Noddings, Haim Gordon, and Harold Garfinkel. David Gallop, Bob Carter, Janet Sisson, Janet Keeping, and my husband, Anton Colijn, have been generous in giving personal support. In the early years of this project I was fortunate to have research assistance from James D.D. Smith and Donald Conrad. The Social Sciences and Humanities Research Council of Canada gave me generous support between 1989 and 1994, for which I am deeply grateful.

The topic of trust is a difficult and elusive one, and I make no pretence of offering a complete or definitive account. If this book can make a contribution by indicating the nature and importance of social trust, and serving as a resource for further thought, I will be well satisfied.

Social Trust and Human Communities

1 Trust, Precarious Treasure

The human capacity for trust is amazing. When we trust, we move from limited evidence to expectations and actions culminating in a complex web of emotions, beliefs, and attitudes. Those attitudes structure our interpretations of other people, situations, and human nature as such. Despite the vicissitudes of our sometimes fractured social order, most of us maintain considerable trust much of the time. Overall, we have positive expectations about what other people will do; we are open to other people, and feel a basic confidence and security about how the world works. We count on other people fearlessly and confidently; we allow ourselves to depend on other people, often other people whom we know not at all. To a far greater extent than we normally realize, trust is implicit in our daily lives and our social world. Most of the time it does not betray us.

Human institutions are constructed by human beings and founded on human roles, norms, and decisions. Our boundless interdependence and mutual vulnerability in societies is fascinating. To a large extent we cope with complexity, ambiguity, and risk because we trust each other. Life is a boundless set of social interactions made possible by trust between and among people and, because that trust is precarious, sometimes made desperately complicated and tense by distrust and a lack of trustworthiness.

As a matter of verbal usage, trust and distrust are not restricted to human beings. We speak of trusting or not trusting many kinds of things: other people, the government, leaders, foreign leaders, other countries, the postal service, our senses, forces of nature, forces of history, pets, cars, computers, brakes, and banking machines. However, this book is not about trusting God, animals, or machines. It is about people trusting other people, whether friends and intimates or strangers, whether as individuals or in groups.

WHAT IS TRUST?

Trust is fundamentally an attitude, based on beliefs and feelings and implying expectations and dispositions. Consider, for instance, what is involved in trusting a friend. When we trust a friend, we believe that she is likely to act kindly and benevolently towards us, that she is unlikely to harm us, certainly would not deliberately harm us, that she is well-disposed toward us. We expect our friend to lend a sympathetic ear, to co-operate in making joint arrangements, to help out in time of crisis. There are many terrible things people can do to each other, and when we trust a friend we assume confidently – without thinking of it – that she will not do any of these things. We assume that she will not break confidences, tell our secrets, abuse our children, or try to steal our job. To trust a friend is to believe that her motivations (towards ourselves) emerge from affection, care, and concern, and not from dislike, ambition, or egoism.

Trust also involves a sense of the other's competence. If we trust a friend to give advice, or care for our house or pet, we believe that she is capable of doing these tasks. If we trust her to give us comments on an essay, we believe that she is competent to do the job and that she will do it with integrity, with our best interests at heart.

Trust is typically founded on a sense of the sort of person the other is, with regard to motivations and to competence. To trust a friend is to regard her as a person of integrity, one who is sincere, caring, and dependable, both in general and in the context of this particular relationship. Trust implies expectations that have an open-ended character. When we trust a friend, we do not have a list of all the things she is supposed to do; we trust her to do what is fitting and appropriate to the circumstances and to our relationship, as situations change and issues and needs arise. When we trust, we take risks and are vulnerable. There are no guarantees, and it would be an indication of lack of trust to look for them.

Trusting another, we are willing to go ahead without a guarantee. We feel that we can rely or depend on the other, even though there is always some possibility that he or she will act in unexpected ways, or even betray us. Trust affects our interpretations of other people, our sense of what they are doing. For example, if we hear that a trusted friend has been disloyal, callous, or cruel, we will not at first be inclined to take the story at face value. If, however, we hear such things about someone we distrust, we are likely to believe them and to regard them as manifestations of serious flaws of character.

Trust is not an all-or-nothing thing. We may trust or distrust to various degrees (we may trust some people more than others). Furthermore, trust and distrust are often relativized to specific roles or contexts. We will typically trust friends to care for us, to respond in emergencies, to be fairly reliable about arrangements and appointments, and to keep confidences. But even good friends we may not trust in every respect. Suppose, for example, we know that a good friend is somewhat unreliable about money; though trusting her in general, we might not trust her to repay small loans. We are likely to regard her as a good friend, one who is trustworthy overall but not likely to repay us. We should not give her money unless we are prepared to see it as, in effect, a gift. Trust on the whole does not mean trust in every context.

Logically, contexts can be separated, and in practice we sometimes do this, as the previous example shows. Repaying money is different from driving; babysitting is different from giving competent advice about an examination. But often contexts are not fully separate, especially so far as distrust is concerned. Distrust readily seeps from one context to others. If a friend lies about a small matter or lets us down on a holiday arrangement, we may begin to distrust her in other contexts, wondering whether she has a dishonest streak or does not care enough about us to make sure our plans work. Such seepage of distrust is quite natural, but easily destructive to relationships.

Though the word "trust" is often used vaguely and has a kind of warm, fuzzy aura about it, there is nevertheless a kind of logic or epistemology to trust. It is not entirely a matter of feeling and emotion. Trust presupposes beliefs, and often those beliefs are based on evidence. The case of trusting people "immediately" or "instinctively" is a special one, and even here we probably have evidence – we just do not reflect on what it is, or articulate it. There are good reasons for deeming people trustworthy or untrustworthy in various respects, and there seems to be considerable agreement on these. People who are honest, reliable, and caring are trustworthy. People who are dishonest, manipulative, and uncaring are untrustworthy. We make ethical and epistemic judgments about trust, saying that we trusted "too much" or "too little" in given cases, referring to people as too trusting (gullible) or too suspicious (paranoid). Often there are reasonable grounds for such judgments.[1]

As exemplified in the case of trusting a friend, the attitude of trust involves the following features:

A expectations of benign, not harmful, behaviour based on beliefs
   about the trusted person's motivation and competence;
B an attribution or assumption of general integrity on the part of the
   other, a sense that the trusted person is a good person;
C a willingness to rely or depend on the trusted person, an acceptance of risk and vulnerability; and
D a general disposition to interpret the trusted person's actions
   favorably.

Trust exists in various degrees: we may, for instance, trust someone
only a little, but more than we used to. And trust is often relative to
particular contexts and ranges of action: we might trust someone in
the role of snow-shoveller but not that of baby-sitter. Sometimes we
trust absolutely – but that is not every case.

In trusting another person whom we know, our expectations are
typically based on our experience with him or her and what we know
from that experience. But when there is trust, our expectations go
beyond what evidence proves: in new situations, from trusted agents
whom we believe to have a capacity to initiate actions, we expect
decent and caring behaviour. We have not encountered these people
in such situations before; they could act badly, but we confidently
believe that they will not. This kind of trust has been called thick
trust.

Trust may exist not only between intimates, lovers, friends, and
colleagues who know each other well and share many experiences,
feelings, and problems but also between people who we have only a
slight personal relationship. This kind of trust has been called thin
trust. We trust many people to whom we relate in the context of social
roles: the dentist, the hairdresser, the school principal, and so on. And
we may implicitly trust people we know not at all – as when we buy
and eat meat from a supermarket, take an airplane, or enter a hospital for surgery. Needless to say, trust in such contexts has less emotional depth and richness than trust in contexts of sexual and personal intimacy, friendship, or collegiality. Trust in these more distanced contexts is based on a relatively restricted range of experience
with the other person or even – as in the cases of supermarket shopping and driving – on no relationship with these particular people at
all.

It makes sense to speak of trust (and of distrust) over this variety
of contexts. The attitudes called trust in each case are in central ways
similar to trust between friends or intimates in involving confident
expectations of benign action (competent and well motivated); an
overall sense that the other person or party is basically decent and

will act decently towards us; acceptance of risk and vulnerability; and dispositions to interpret the actions of the other in a positive way. Although the feelings accompanying trust vary considerably between intimate and less intimate contexts and depending on who the trusted party is, the basic attitudes and beliefs – dare I say the essence, or logical core of trust – remain the same.

We may also trust or fail to trust ourselves. For example, I may trust myself to give a lecture after minimal preparation but not to care for a dangerously ill child when I am tired.[2] Attitudes of trust and distrust can meaningfully be extended to institutions in which various social roles are, as it were, meshed together (the government, the postal service, the university, the United Nations) and to collectivities such as nation-states.[3] We may in some general sense trust the university and distrust the postal service; trust Britain and not trust Germany. Canada's foreign policy may indicate trust of the United Nations, less trust of Libya. We can speak in senses more or less extended of trusting seeing-eye dogs, donkeys on mountain paths, word-processing systems, "technology," or "science." But that is not the focus here.

HOW IS TRUST POSSIBLE?

Trust is possible because we are believing, feeling creatures who have a sense of ourselves and our own needs. We are, in addition, creatures who respond naturally to other creatures, primarily to other human beings, on whom we depend and who depend on us. We have a sense that other people are beings with whom we will be involved in close relationships, that they are our caretakers and potentially our sympathetic companions, and that they are free agents who could choose to harm us but usually will not.

In life we are fundamentally related to other human beings. We depend for our survival on a material world, but we depend equally on other people, with whom we live in a social world. The centre of human development is our relationships with other people, and the centre of these lies in encountering them as other people – as free and original selves independent of our own selves. These ideas are central in Martin Buber's philosophy. Buber stresses the significance of dialogue and open, receptive relationships between people. He argues that we enter this world destined for intimate relationships with other people:

It is not as if a child first saw an object and then entered into some relationship with that. Rather, the longing for relation is primary, the cupped hand into which the being that confronts us nestles; and the relation to that, which is a wordless anticipation of saying You, comes second.

... in the beginning is the relation.

And in all the seriousness of truth, listen: without It a human being cannot live. But whoever lives only with that is not human.[4]

What we live for is not It, but You. For all his emphasis on interpersonal relations, encounter, and dialogue, Buber says relatively little about issues of trust. But clearly trust is implicitly central to his outlook on the world, according to which what is most important happens in "the between" – between I and You. For honest and open dialogue to occur, You and I must trust each other to speak truthfully and listen genuinely.

The attitude of trust presupposes inductively grounded beliefs and confident expectations that go further than strict induction would warrant.[5] So it presupposes something we well know: we are creatures who reason inductively, and we have a tendency to extend our confidence beyond the evidence. If we know that someone has acted honestly on five occasions, we have a great tendency to infer that she will act honestly on a sixth; we go further to believe that she will act honestly on every occasion similar to the five we have known; many of us even have some inclination to believe that she will act honestly on every occasion, period. And we like to confirm beliefs we already hold, so we build more trust on the trust we have. A parallel phenomenon exists, sometimes counter-productively, for distrust, which also tends to build on itself. Trust is possible because we are inductive creatures who extend induction to provide ourselves with confident expectations about the future. Many of these expectations are about other people.

Trust presupposes that we make value judgments about our situation in the world; we have a sense of what would be good for us and what bad. We have a sense of what we need in the world, of how we could be vulnerable and hurt. Yet, even knowing or sensing our vulnerability, we are not always fearful. We are able to relax enough so that we do not continually struggle to defend and protect ourselves. We have some sense of other people. Who are they? What sorts of people are they? What are they likely to do? We are to a reasonable degree capable of understanding their actions, and we come to have beliefs about the likely motivations behind those actions and what kind of character or what degree of integrity is implied. In some cases our beliefs are based on discrete evidence, in others on a kind of holistic intuition or feeling about what sort of person the other is.

It may sound unattractive to speak of judging and assessing people, summing them up, thinking what they are likely to do, estimating how their attitudes and actions might be beneficial or detrimental to us. But to some degree we do this sort of thing whenever we reflect on whether or not to trust another person. And a sense of the other's character and fundamental intentions is implicit in any case of trust; we have, in some sense and by some means, come to believe or assume that the trusted other is fundamentally a good person who is unlikely to harm us.

Trust of other people is made possible by our inductively extended beliefs, our responses to others, our sense of ourselves, our position in the world, and our values. Trust is possible because we are not only knowing and believing creatures but valuing creatures who relate in a profound and profoundly natural way to others.

SOME BACKGROUND

The psychoanalyst Erik Erikson, in *Childhood and Society* (1950), emphasizes the crucial role in human development of what he called basic trust. Erikson believed that babies developing normally in normal circumstances do so because they have a certain elementary or primitive trust in their parents. Such trust derives from elementary functions such as feeding and from other aspects of care. It was regarded by Erikson as absolutely essential for normal psychological development:

The first demonstration of social trust in the baby is the ease of his feeding, the depth of his sleep, the relaxation of his bowels. ... The infant's first social achievement ... is his willingness to let the mother out of sight without undue anxiety or rage, because she has become an inner certainty as well as an outer predictability. Such consistency, continuity, and sameness of experience provide a rudimentary sense of ego identity which depends, I think, on the recognition that there is an inner population of remembered and anticipated sensations and images which are firmly correlated with the outer population of familiar and predictable things and people.[6]

Absence of basic trust can be seen in infantile schizophrenia, while its lack is also apparent in some severely disturbed adult personalities. The crucial factor in the development of trust based on infantile experience was, for Erikson, "the quality of the maternal relationship." Mothers who regularly and sensitively care for their children and communicate their own trustworthiness within a regular framework of cultural expectations convey to their children a sense of who they are, where they belong, and what they should become.

Erikson's concern was not with trust as such but with patterns of normal and abnormal human development. He did not really try to define trust but seems to have thought of it as a kind of confidence in regularities. An infant becomes familiar with his or her environment and gains confidence in such regularities; the caring parent (assumed in this account to be female) thus shows her trustworthiness. The idea that infants and small children trust their parents and must do so in order to develop is a recurring one. But there is little general exploration of trust as such to be found in Erikson's work.

During the 1950s and 1960s, in experimental psychology, considerable work on trust was done in laboratory situations in which subjects participate in variations on the two-person Prisoner's Dilemma games.[7] The term "trust" was given a simple behavioural interpretation in these studies. Trust was operationally defined as "making a co-operative choice in the game." If players who do not know that their co-player will choose co-operatively, nevertheless choose co-operatively themselves, they are deemed to have made a trusting choice. The players are not known to each other and do not communicate.

Work on trust, co-operation, and experimental Prisoner's Dilemma games was pioneered by Morton Deutsch. Deutsch regarded parties in a Prisoner's Dilemma situation as having to make a choice about whether to trust. Let us say Joe and Fred are prisoners awaiting trial. They cannot communicate with each other, but they are interdependent because what happens to each depends on what the other does. They are told that if both keep silent, each will get two years. But if either one confesses and his accomplice does not confess, the one who confesses will get only one year, and the one who does not confess will get four years. If they both confess, they will get three years. What should they do?

Fred does not know what Joe will do. Fred can reason as follows. Either Joe will confess or he will not. If Joe confesses, then Fred will get three years in jail if he confesses too, and four years if he does not. So if Joe confesses, Fred is better off to confess. But suppose that Joe does not confess. Then Fred will get one year in jail if he confesses and two years if he does not. So in this case too, Fred will be better off to confess. Either way, it seems, confessing seems to be the course of action that will give Fred the best outcome. Obviously Joe can reason exactly the same way. Reasoning separately and pursuing their rational self-interest, each allowing for possibilities of "defection" and "co-operation," they each calculate that they should confess. As interpreted in the Prisoner's Dilemma, "reason" seems to argue against "trust." Following "reason," Joe and Fred both confess. As a result, neither makes a trusting choice, and both get three years in jail. Had both kept quiet, "trusting," they would have had only two years.

The Prisoner's Dilemma shows how, reasoning from self- interest, we can end up working against our own self-interest. If Joe and Fred were less "rational" and each had assumed that he should calculate and work for their *joint* or *collective* interest instead of their *separate* interests, they would have saved themselves a year in jail. If they had believed, trusting, that the other would co-operate and they *should* reciprocate and be trustworthy, they would have had a better result. Thus either a sense of solidarity and collective interest or a sense of trust and accompanying moral obligation would prevent the dilemma from arising. Or, if they had been able to communicate, reason together, *and believe each other*, they could have avoided the dilemma together. The Prisoner's Dilemma has fascinated social theorists because it serves to indicate the self-defeating character of the single-minded and solitary pursuit of one's own self-interest.

Many laboratory games and experiments have been based on various versions of the Prisoner's Dilemma. Usually small rewards, dependent on the structure of choice, are offered to subjects. Subjects in these games are not able to communicate with each other. If a subject makes a "co-operative" choice (which would be not confessing in the example just given), he can be interpreted as trusting the other party to make a co-operative choice as well. The other choice, the choice to confess, may be interpreted as a distrustful choice. Deutsch noted that a trusting choice may be based upon despair, conformity, impulsivity, innocence, virtue, faith, masochism, or confidence; his concern was with trusting choices based upon confidence.

A major problem with the use of laboratory games involving the Prisoner's Dilemma as a way of studying trust is that the context is so artificial. Trust and distrust as ongoing attitudes scarcely have a chance to emerge. The subjects of these studies were making discrete choices in isolated and unrealistic situations. In addition to this simplification, the game situation misleadingly polarizes trust and distrust, encouraging us to forget that there are degrees of both. If Joe does not confess or otherwise makes a "co-operative choice," we are to assume that he "trusts" Fred. If Joe does confess or makes a "defecting choice," we are to assume that he "distrusts" Fred. There are no degrees; there is no mid-point.

So far as trust and distrust are concerned, the set-up is horrifyingly simplistic. In real situations we cannot infer a complex attitude like trust or distrust from a single choice. In real situations we have varying degrees of information about the other person; we have varying degrees of commitments to relationships, and we find ourselves more or less immersed in social roles and affected by social institutions. Fascinating as Prisoner's Dilemmas are, laboratory games with these dilemmas are not a promising way to study trust and distrust – not if we want to understand these attitudes as they function in daily life and out-of-the-lab society and politics.

In some Prisoner's Dilemma experiments there is only one subject. A set of responses from the "other" is programmed in advance, and these responses are to be regarded by the subject as the responses of another person who is also participating in the experiment. In such cases a kind of deception is built into experiments on trust. Psychological experimenters, who for the subject are "unknown others," deceive those subjects in order to test their trust in unknown others. The irony makes a sad commentary on moral sensitivities but is rather delicious all the same.[8]

Julian Rotter, a social psychologist, devised a scale to measure interpersonal trust. The Interpersonal Trust Scale (ITS), was used in the 1970s and 1980s by social psychologists interested in trust and distrust. Its purpose was to measure roughly the difference between persons low in trust and persons high in trust and it produced some interesting results – mainly for samples consisting of college students.[9] Rotter, who first published his scale in 1967, summarized in 1980 some of the work done using it. He concluded that subjects who were high in interpersonal trust tended to be more trustworthy, better liked, and happier than subjects measuring low in interpersonal trust.

Rotter was interested in a specific type of interpersonal trust: people's willingness or tendency to trust an unknown other person. His scale was not intended to measure people's trust in their spouses, lovers, or friends, or even in professionals or colleagues with whom they had experience: "It is the trust of a generalized other – a person or group with whom one has not had a great deal of personal experience – in which we are most interested." Rotter was interested in anonymous interpersonal trust: interpersonal because it concerns trust between two individuals, but anonymous because that trust is not based on any specific knowledge, feeling, or experience of the individual.

Rotter was interested in tendencies to trust other people – general attitudes to human nature as regards honest, reliable behaviour. He defined trust as an an expectancy held by an individual or a group that the word, promise, or verbal or written statement of another individual or group can be relied upon. Rotter defined trusting others as expecting them to keep their word – to do what they say they will do. Some of Rotter's test items deal with such things as whether the subject expects students to cheat on an exam. This item makes sense, given our ordinary understanding of trust and trustworthiness; trustworthy people will not cheat. But in this and many other inclusions Rotter significantly departed from his own definition. After all, people rarely make a *verbal commitment* not to cheat on examinations: we do not explicitly promise not to cheat when we take an exam. Rather, it is assumed that we know honesty is implied for the examination to be meaningful and that, as participants, we will conform to the rules.

Not living up to our word is an especially clear kind of untrustworthiness. Doing what we say we will do is a kind of minimum reliability, and thus trusting another person means, at the very least, feeling confident that he will not lie to us and will keep his explicit promises. Even so, Rotter's definition of trust was too narrow, and too narrow in an important way. We often trust others to do things even though they have not explicitly indicated that they will do them.

Consider the case of hiring a baby-sitter. If I hire a baby-sitter, I trust that person not to have a party in my home while I am absent, to contact me or a doctor or other responsible person if my child suddenly becomes ill, to listen for cries from the child, not to leave the child alone in the home, and so on. If I did not trust the baby-sitter in these ways, I would not hire her. But the baby-sitter does not promise all these things explicitly when she takes the job. If I trust her, I assume it goes without saying.

Trust involves many expectations that are not spelled out. In fact, one of the most important and interesting things about trust is its open-ended character. It is precisely this open-ended character that is missed if we define trust in terms of keeping verbal commitments. The misunderstanding is fundamental: a major reason we need trust is that in most cases we do not – and in some cases we could not – spell out everything a trusted person is supposed to do and not do.

B. Schlenker, B. Helm and J.T. Tedeschi sought to synthesize elements of Deutsch's and Rotter's accounts. The need for trust arises in a risky situation; what happens to us depends on what another person does. We have some information from that other person that bears on our willingness to go ahead as though he or she will act appropriately.[10] Schlenker and his co-authors allow that a communication between the trusted person and the one who trusts may be *implicit*, based on a behavioir or gesture or a sense of what the other is willing to do. The amendment introduces considerable vagueness, though. There are many ways in which various "behaviours" might or might not be taken to "communicate" intentions to do this or that.

If the baby-sitter takes a dirty coffee cup to the kitchen in the short interval before we leave for the evening, does this action communicate her intention to do up the messy supper dishes? An intention to take the job seriously? An intention to be polite? Or no particular intention at all? There is no clear answer.

K.S. Isaacs, E.A. Haggard, and J.M. Alexander wrote about trust from a psychoanalytic perspective.[11] These authors comment that the entire social world appears differently to those who are able to trust, as opposed to those who are characteristically distrustful. They sought to distinguish trust from both faith and gullibility. Faith is "an undoubting, unconditional belief in which data for proof or refutation are ignored." Trust is different from faith because it "connotes an affective attitude primarily directed outward, involving a sense of comfort, confidence and reliance that certain acts and behavior will or will not occur." Both trust and faith require undoubting belief. But where there is trust as opposed to faith, that undoubting belief is not the result of ignoring pertinent evidence. To the contrary: doubts have been raised in the past and resolved. Trust, for Isaacs, Haggard, and Alexander, is more grounded on evidence, more sensitive to evidence, and thus closer to reality than is faith.

Though faith and trust should be distinguished, this account overstates the difference and puts it in the wrong place. There is such a thing as unwarranted trust. We sometimes continue to trust in contexts where suspicion would be warranted by pertinent evidence. The mother still trusts her son to come home after school and do his homework, even though, after promising to do it, he has been unreliable on several occasions. Why does she trust him? Perhaps she thinks he is becoming more mature and will do better; perhaps she is deceiving herself; perhaps she thinks that as his mother she should believe him. Whatever the case, it is possible for her to trust him even though she has some evidence that he is not entirely trustworthy in this respect.

Neither do Isaacs, Haggard, and Alexander seem correct in their claim that faith involves ignoring the evidence. What is characteristic of faith is not so much ignoring the pertinent evidence but interpreting that evidence so that it is in accord with one's faith. The point was beautifully made by John Wisdom in his essay "Gods." Wisdom develops the analogy of a garden, where growth is viewed by one person as the work of a gardener, never seen, and by another as something that developed on its own:

Two people return to their long neglected garden and find among the weeds a few of the old plants surprisingly vigorous. One says to the other, "It must be that a gardener has been coming and doing something about these plants." Upon inquiry they find that no neighbour has ever seen anyone at work in their garden. The first man says to the other, "He must have worked while people slept." The other says, "No, someone would have heard him and besides, anybody who cared about the plants would have kept down those weeds." The first man says, "Look at the way these are arranged. There is purpose and a feeling for beauty here. I believe that someone comes, someone invisible to mortal eyes. I believe that the more carefully we look the more we shall find confirmation of this." They examine the garden ever so carefully and sometimes they come on new things suggesting that a gardener comes and something they come on things suggesting the contrary and even that a malicious person has been at work. Besides examining the garden carefully they also study what happens to gardens without attention. Each learns all the other learns about this and about the garden. Consequently, when after all this, one says, "I still believe a gardener comes" while the other says, "I don't," their different words now reflect no difference as to what they have found in the garden, no difference as to what they would find in the garden if they looked further, and no difference about how fast untended gardens fall into disorder. At this stage, in this context, the gardener hypothesis has ceased to be experimental.[12]

One person has faith that a gardener exists; the other does not. One person sees the garden as tended by someone and thinks there is an unseen gardener whose works are manifested to them. The other thinks there is no gardener. Their difference in faith is one of attitude. These two people do not disagree about observable facts, and discovering more facts would not change their attitudes. But that is not to say that they have ignored the facts; on the contrary, they have studied the garden closely.

Similarly, Wisdom argues, a person of religious faith has a different attitude to the world from that of the non-believer. He looks at the world differently and interprets events differently. But that does not mean that the person of faith holds a faith that is oblivious to the details of his world. He attends to details; it is just that he interprets them differently from the non-believer. The faithful believer's understanding of what the evidence implies may strike a non-believer as *ad hoc* and unconvincing, or even arbitrary. But that understanding need not be based on ignoring the evidence; it is more a matter of perspective on the evidence. Typically trust is more qualified and sensitive to evidence than is faith, but the contrast should not be overstated. Faith is sensitive to evidence in its own way. Faith and trust can be distinguished, but not on the grounds that faith ignores evidence whereas trust pays attention to it.

What about the relationship between trust and gullibility? Gullibility is a readiness to believe that which is wished for, a positive readiness to be deceived, an absence of reflectiveness and critical thinking. Is trust a form of gullibility? A gullible person is one who is easy to deceive because he or she does not take probabilities properly into account. "Did you know the word 'gullible' isn't in the dictionary?" Anne asks Sue. "Really?" Sue replies. "Why not?" "Gotcha," Anne laughs. In this exchange Sue is gullible because she accepts an implausible claim without taking the time to stop and think about it. She misses the tone of Anne's remark and assumes Anne is offering information, not telling a joke. Trust need not imply gullibility: people who trust are not all like Sue in this example. They can be perfectly sensitive to context and evidence and they may be thoughtful, reflective, and careful.

Barnett Pearce defines trust as an assumption that another person will not harm us.[13] Such an assumption, he says, is based on our perception of the other person as knowledgeable, competent, and well intentioned towards us. We assume that the trusted person's knowledge and motivation will avoid disastrously harmful outcomes. Pearce distinguishes trusting behaviours, which increase the vulnerability of the trusting person, from trust itself. Although he restricts his attention to trust between individuals, his account applies both to known persons like friends and family members and to strangers.

Pearce's account seems to apply quite plausibly to familiar cases such as that of the baby-sitter. If I trust a person to baby-sit, I assume that he or she is worthy of trust, which would mean assuming that he or she is knowledgeable, competent, and well intentioned in the various respects pertinent to responsibly and reliably carrying out this particular job. The baby-sitter has to know enough to take care of the child and deal with emergencies, and be competent to exercise that knowledge appropriately, and must also be well-intentioned towards me and my child. That means not being motivated to hurt the child, steal my possessions, and so on and so forth. In this account "and so on and so forth" is the most important factor. But contrary to Pearce, we do not trust others only to avoid disastrous outcomes. We do not hire a baby-sitter only to prevent such disasters as running into traffic or being abducted. Avoiding disastrous outcomes is most important, to be sure, but when we trust, we anticipate good, or at least moderately decent outcomes. The baby-sitter should put the child to bed early enough that he will be able to function at school the next day, prevent him from stuffing himself with junk food, and keep him contented and secure.

J.K. Rempel, J.G. Holmes and M.P. Zanna explore trust in close relationships because they are interested in dimensions of developing trust between intimates:

First, trust is seen to evolve out of past experience and prior interaction: thus it develops as the relationship matures. Second, dispositional attributions are made to the partner, such that he or she is regarded as reliable, dependable, and concerned with providing expected rewards. Third, ... trust involves a willingness to put oneself at risk, be it through intimate disclosure, reliance on another's promises, sacrificing present rewards for future gains, and so on. Finally, trust is defined by feelings of confidence and security in the caring responses of the partner and the strength of the relationship.[14]

Rempel, Holmes, and Zanna postulate three stages in the development of trust between friends or intimate partners. As people are getting to know each other, they develop a sense of what the other is likely to do; here it is the predictability of behaviour that is at issue. Then they shift from behaviour to characteristics and qualities, and begin to trust in the other person as a whole, not just in his or her specific actions. They gain a sense of what sort of person the other is and how dependable he or she is. Relationships must confront many new situations. Where there is a fully developed trust between partners, these authors believe it amounts to a complete trust that can be called faith. With full trust between partners, each has the sense that the other can be counted on to care for himself or herself and for the relationship, *no matter what happens*. Such complete trust (which we may suspect to be quite rare) requires "setting doubts aside, even though the evidence warranting such emotional risks can never be fully conclusive." At this stage the trusting partner is emotionally secure with the other person. While trust is relatively slow and difficult to construct, it is notoriously easy to destroy. That fundamental sense of emotional security is easily lost.

The use of "faith" in this account, to refer to the closest and most complete trust, points to the dispositional aspects of trust. How would we respond to evidence that someone we know intimately and deeply trust has lapsed in a significant way? If we deeply trust him and are convinced that he will always stand by, no matter what, we reject indications that he has done wrong or been unfaithful. We will not take these indications at face value; we will tend to discount or reinterpret them, in much the way that Wisdom's believer reconciled weeds with the existence of an invisible gardener, or a theist interprets the events of history to be compatible with his faith in God. Deep trust of an intimate partner or friend is like faith in that it greatly affects how we receive and interpret further evidence.

Philosopher H.J.N. Horsburgh was influenced by Gandhi's ideas on non-violent action, trust, and forgiveness and published several papers on these themes. In "The Ethics of Trust"[15] Horsburgh contrasts trust in the sense of perfectly general confidence in another with trust in a person as regards specific acts. He says that general trust is more common than specific trust since "doubts, once they have occurred in relation to one aspect of a person's conduct, are liable to arise in relation to every other aspect of that person's conduct." Horsburgh distinguishes between trust and reliance, and develops a concept of therapeutic trust—an act of placing one's trust in someone known to be untrustworthy, an act deliberately undertaken with the intent and hope of bringing out the best in him. To illustrate therapeutic trust, consider the teacher who loans thirty dollars to a somewhat unreliable young man in his community. Asked if he doesn't know there is some risk he will not get the money back, he replies, "I told him I needed it and was counting on him. Besides, if no one ever trusts him, how will he learn to be trustworthy?"

Horsburgh makes a number of interesting comments about distrust, and also distinguishes among various different kinds of trustworthiness and untrustworthiness. He claims that trust gives "moral space" to people and makes moral development possible. In the therapeutic sense, he argues, it is often our duty to trust others, even others whose past conduct might not strictly warrant it. Taking an attitude of "systematic and pervasive distrust" towards anyone, he argues, is morally wrong; this denies the other's status as a moral agent.

D.O. Thomas, another philosopher, emphasizes the contrast between two basic attitudes to trusting other people. As classic examples of the two, he chose Hobbes, who recommended generalized suspicion, and Jesus, as portrayed in the Biblical Sermon on the Mount, who recommended generalized trust.[16] Trust is, by definition, risky, and this is the point Hobbesians emphasize. We are all competing for scarce resources, and each person is the potential enemy of every other; Hobbes would advise caution and suspicion. But Hobbesian accounts tend to ignore the fact that not trusting also poses risks and imposes costs. According to Thomas, Hobbes overemphasized suspicion. Hobbes was right to think that my reasonable fear that another could threaten my personal security is a reason for not trusting him, but it is an error to exalt this reason into an overriding one in every context. To be sure, if I trust too readily, I may come to harm. But if I am too suspicious, I may cut myself off from other people, misunderstand my social world, and miss out on valuable opportunities. There are risks in distrust. Attempts to supplement reliance by threatened or imposed sanctions are likely to destroy the possibility of maintaining mutual respect. Trust and mutual confidence are essential to social institutions. The more violations there are, the more impoverished social life becomes.

Annette Baier, another philosopher, has published several influential papers about trust.[17] Seeking a general account, Baier says that trust may be conscious or unconscious, wanted or unwanted, directed at an unspecified group of others or at some particular other. "Trust can come with no beginnings, with gradual as well as sudden beginnings, and with various degrees of self-consciousness, voluntariness, and expressness." Both natural and artificial persons (clubs, groups, corporations, nations) can be involved in relations of trust, according to Baier.

A slight oddity in Baier's account is her belief that we trust others not to do or refrain from various actions (as all other accounts imply) but to care for various *things*. "Trust, I have claimed, is a reliance on others' competence and willingness to look after, rather than harm, things one cares about which are entrusted to their care." But this difference is smaller than it looks. Baier understands "things" to include such abstractions as one's own physical security, as the following example makes clear: "Suppose I look quickly around me before proceeding into the dark street or library stacks where my business takes me, judge the few people I discern there to be nondangerous, and so go ahead. We can say that my bodily safety, and perhaps my pocketbook, are the goods that I am allowing these people to be in a position to threaten ... So what do I trust strangers in such circumstances to do?"[17] Fundamentally, not to mug me, rape me, or kill me. I am trusting them not to steal my property, assault my person, or threaten my life while I am using the library. I am not, Baier adds, counting on them to save my life if it is suddenly threatened by mortar that begins to fall from the ceiling as I am perusing books in the stacks.

According to Baier, trust can be rational; so can distrust. Either trust or distrust can be appropriate, depending on relationships and circumstances. Baier suggests that "Trust is rational, then, in the absence of any reason to suspect in the trusted strong and operative motives which conflict with the demands of trustworthiness as the truster sees them." According to Baier, our presumption should be in favour of trust. Contrary to Hobbes who saw all others as basically threatening and would have us begin by distrusting others, Baier advises that we should begin by trusting others, and trust until there is some specific reason not to do so. We start with the hypothesis that another is trustworthy; then, if he does something indicating the opposite (making offensive remarks, lying, trying to manipulate or coerce, brandishing a weapon), we begin to be suspicious. Baier notes that relations of trust can sometimes be exploitative. By trusting others to perform in various ways, we can put pressure upon them to do more than we are entitled to expect – as would be the case if I were to go out of town and say pointedly to my neighbour that I'm counting on her to tend my rare and delicate orchids, which need twice daily watering. Baier's cautionary remark about the pressures of trust may be applied to the "therapeutic trust" described by Horsburgh. Many people feel a pressure to live up to the expectations of others, and that common human sentiment often makes therapeutic trust effective. But the very same human tendency to try to live up to expectations can make overly conscientious people vulnerable to exploitation. When others count on them, they feel they must live up to expectations; thus, when others expect too much, they are easily exploited.

Another recent philosophical discussion of trust is that of Lars Hertzberg in "On the Attitude of Trust." Hertzberg's account owes much to Wittgenstein's *On Certainty*, which describes basic beliefs that we cannot doubt and that serve as a kind of riverbed or foundation of our other beliefs and of life itself. Hertzberg regards trust as a fundamental attitude that is presumed by our very capacity to understand what reasons are. Hertzberg's entire account is directed towards describing how children trust their parents and teachers when they are learning language and basic facts and skills. Trust, for Hertzberg, is absolutely fundamental. It does not depend on reasons or evidence because it comes prior to them. On this account, trust must of necessity be unreflective and uncritical: we learn by trusting, and understanding reasons is one of the things we learn. Trust, Hertzberg claims, is more basic than reliance, since reliance entails exercising judgment concerning the person relied upon and is undertaken in the light of particular purposes:

In relying on someone I as it were look down at him from above. I exercise my command of the world. I remain the judge of his actions. In trusting someone I look up from below. I learn from the other what the world is about. I let him be the judge of my actions.

... In so far as I trust someone, there will be no limits, given in advance, of how far or in what respects I shall trust him. If I trust someone, I cannot at the same time reserve for myself the judgment concerning the purposes for which he is to be trusted. It is from him that I learn what he has to teach me. I go along ... When I trust someone it is him I trust; I do not trust certain things about him.[18]

According to Hertzberg, to trust a person is to take his or her conduct at face value, not even making the contrast between what is "outer" and "inner," not thinking for a moment that the person is other than what he appears to be. On this account, trust is total, and apparently it is by definition a good thing. To say that a relation between individuals is based on trust is, to that extent, to approve of it.

This account is plausible for the learning of young children, but it is not correct for many other contexts. Unlike Baier, Hertzberg does not allow for the possibility that trust could be ill founded and even wrong, that for some contexts and given some circumstances, distrust could be the appropriate attitude. The account is striking in its emphasis on basic trust. But again we have a narrow or partial account. Trust founded on evidence from experience, trust that is restricted to a role or context, trust that is partial, trust in groups or institutions, trust that has a potential for exploitation – all these turn out by Hertzberg's definition not to be trust at all.

Sociologists studying trust tend to see it as a pervasive feature of social life, one that is critical to the functioning of complex, highly modernized societies. Harold Garfinkel argues that people conceptualize events in everyday life on the presupposition that others see things as they do. A common-sense environment is one whose features are known in common by social actors.[19] At the basis of our common-sense world is a kind of trust in how things work and what people think. What an event means or what an object is we cannot determine for ourselves. Understanding, reactions, intentions, and routines must be shared. The kind of trust presumed in games (others will follow the rules and expect us to do so too) may be applied also to everyday situations.

Garfinkel's theory led him to set up several experiments in which students treated a situation in a non-standard way. In one a university student addressed a fellow shopper in a store as though she was a clerk. In another students attempted to behave as though they were boarders in their own family homes. There were strong adverse reactions. "Family members were stupefied and vigorously sought to make the strange actions intelligible, and to restore the situation to normal appearances. Reports were filled with accounts of astonishment, bewilderment, shock, anxiety, embarrassment, and anger as well as with charges by various family members that the student was mean, inconsiderate, selfish, nasty, and impolite." On hearing that the situation had been experimental, family members did not respond with enthusiasm. In fact, they were annoyed to the point of being angry. If there is anything we should be able to take for granted it is routine behaviour by members of our own families in our own homes. We do not live in our homes as potential subjects for social-science experiments, and we do not, in our daily lives, entertain and reflect on the hypothesis that family members may be acting unnaturally because they are participants in a sociological research project! As a result of the protests, Garfinkel stopped the experiments.

Garfinkel's interest was in common assumptions about events and responses to them, assumptions that structure our everyday social world and our responses to it. He used the notion of trust because of his interest in our confident expectations about what other people will do, and our mutual dependence. Such trust enables our social world to make sense.

Another sociological approach derives from the work of Erving Goffman. Goffman's theory of social roles was applied to the topic of trust by James Henslin, who wrote about trust and the cab driver.[20] Henslin's work was based on his doctoral dissertation on cabdriving, which he completed while working as a cab driver in St Louis, Missouri, in the 1960s. Following Goffman, Henslin believed that trust is one of the most fundamental elements of any social interaction. Without trust the social interactions we are familiar with would not exist, and the world would be a completely different place. Henslin restricted his account to an attempt to explain what trust means for a cab driver, focusing primarily on the question of what circumstances, and for what reasons, a driver will accept a person as his passenger.

To explore this question, Henslin worked out a definition of trust based on Goffman's *Presentation of Self in Everyday Life*. Goffman there portrays social life as the interactions of people who occupy and are playing out various social roles. In a nearly literal sense we play parts for others, who are our audience. In effect, we wear masks in order to present ourselves to others. As social actors we have a kind of "front," which has three standard parts: the setting or background, our appearance (especially aspects that indicate social status), and our manner or style (haughty, meek, assertive, shy, or gentle.) As social actors we offer a self-definition to an audience – those to whom we present ourselves. If the audience is willing to interact with us on the basis of this definition (or a substitute acceptable to it and us), we and our audience are in a situation of trust. On this account trust is more a sociological phenomenon than a psychological one. It is tied to agents who define themselves as players in social roles: baby-sitter, cab driver, passenger in a cab, dentist, teacher, landlord, daughter, mother, bank teller, and so on.

Henslin applies these ideas to the situation of the cab driver and his prospective passenger. A passenger is someone who wants to go to a destination in the cab and is willing and able to pay the fare to do so; he is going to ride in the cab without harming the cab driver by robbing, assaulting, molesting, or abducting him. (As prospective passengers, many of us have no doubt wondered whether we could trust the driver; Henslin's discussion shows the other side of the dilemma.) Using cues of appearance, location of call, stated destination, tone of voice, and so on, the driver and his radio contacts reach a conclusion about whether an unknown individual who puts himself forward as a passenger should be accepted as such. Trust is paramount in this context. The cab driver will be vulnerable to his passenger; they will be alone in a vehicle, and he or she could be robbed, attacked, or sexually approached. The passenger is almost certain to be a stranger. The driver has to trust the passenger in these respects. The driver will be vulnerable, and he or she has to make a decision whether to accept a passenger on the basis of limited information.

A cab driver will accept a passenger if that person apparently wants to go to a destination or obtain a service that the driver can provide, seems willing to pay a reasonable amount for it, and does not seem to pose a risk to the driver. If a person tries to present himself as a passenger but seems to be the sort who might be planning a robbery or a sexual advance, the driver will not trust that person and will not take him in the cab.

This account, applying Goffman's theory, seems appropriate and plausible for the situation of cab-driving. Its validity, however, depends in the end on Goffman's theory, and there is something stilted and untrue about Goffman's view that social life is wholly composed of people acting out various roles. Have we no stable personality and identity apart from constantly shifting and adapting series of roles? Do we not express that personality, that self, even when we are acting in roles? Roles intersect and can conflict. We express ourselves in them, but we also amend them to suit ourselves. I can stand in various roles: wife, mother, daughter, sister, philosopher, writer, teacher, activist, organizer, mediator ... These are different roles; they imply different responsibilities and actions. And yet I have a personality and personal style; I have ways of speaking, responding, and acting that are characteristic of me and that I express in all these roles, and values that I apply to all. I am a person with character and personality, and that comes through; I do not *only* play these parts.

Nor can these doubts about Goffman's view of social life be discounted when we come to the topic of trust. One thing that makes us trust people is what we perceive as their genuineness or authenticity, our sense that they are *not* just filling a role. In *Being and Nothingness* Sartre describes a waiter in a café who behaves as if he were *only* a waiter; Sartre argues that the man is in bad faith, deceiving himself because he is acting so as to imply that his authentic human character is overwhelmed by the role. (Or that he has no such character at all; if he has indeed lost it, that would be a greater tragedy and self-betrayal.) One reason we may suspect that a person is not genuine is a sense that there is no one behind the role. We seem more trustworthy to others when we depart from a social role in authentic and original ways, especially if such departures involve doing more, or doing better, than the role itself requires.

J.D. Lewis and A. Weigert usefully distinguish among cognitive, emotional, and behavioural components of trust.[21] Cognitively, they claim, trust is based on a chosen "leap" from considered evidence to beliefs beyond what that evidence would warrant. Emotionally, there is a kind of bond between those who trust each other. Behaviourally, trust permits us to take risky actions in the expectation that other people will act "competently and dutifully." All three aspects – cognitive, emotional, and behavioural – are required for trust to be a social reality. Without cognitive content we would have not trust but blind faith or fixed hope. Without emotion we would have not trust but calculated risk-taking. Without a behavioural component, trust would be inoperative.

Lewis and Weigert's account seems to make trust a chosen attitude, one that is to some degree warranted, based by definition on some relevant experience with the person or institution trusted. The emphasis on cognitive, emotional, and behavioural dimensions is useful and important. Characteristically, trust is cognitive, having to do with evidence, interpretation, belief, and confidence. Characteristically, it is also emotional: we feel secure with, often close to, those we trust. And characteristically, trust has behavioural implications: we are more willing to co-operate and to rely on others when we trust. Lewis and Weigert's definition may be criticized as too narrow because the notion of "cognitive choice" omits unconscious trust, basic trust in Erikson's sense, and blind trust. On their account it will be true by definition that trust is based on good evidence.

In "On Modern Confidence" (1982), Ann-Mari Sellerberg, a Swedish sociologist, describes a number of interviews to explain how fundamental trust or confidence is in the operations of society. Sellerberg describes trust, or confidence, as it would exist in simple village life and contrasts that with the more impersonal situation of modern urban-dwellers. She ties modern trust more to people's sense of how institutions operate than to their attitudes towards unknown individuals.

In village life in Sweden people trusted those they knew – neighbours, relatives, and a few figures of authority – but there were few bonds that would establish any basis for trust beyond this limited circle. Farmers from rural Sweden, interviewed by Sellerberg, described their pleasure in buying from dealers they knew personally and who knew them, even if the goods were not better or cheaper than what they could buy elsewhere. In urban life, however, confidence is only rarely based on personal knowledge. So far as retail sales are concerned, people in Sweden do feel confident, but they base their attitude on consumer legislation, declarations about content on packages, and a self-service system of merchandising that gives the impression nothing is hidden:

> The new consumer legislation, systems of comparisons, the visibility of goods as well as the general controls of customers—constitute the "building stones" of today's confidence relations. These serve – usually without our thinking of it – as a basis for trust and consequently lead to a very important quality in modern trade transaction: The parties start out from what they experience as an initial state of confidence. "I trust the things that they sell," said a man. "I don't think that they're allowed to sell any poor stuff." "They're under controls," said a woman.[22]

Instead of trusting individuals, these people trust institutions, expressing confidence in the operations of law and bureaucracy. Where a person feels especially vulnerable, she may try to obtain extra confidence by personalizing a relationship: women often chat to hairdressers, for example, about personal problems and family life as a way of imitating an intimate relationship that would make their enforced physical proximity more normal. Basically, however, modern confidence or trust is depersonalized. "The retailer may now place it in technological devices, particular credit cards, etc. In various trust devices we have to trust," Sellerberg concludes.

Sociologist and philosopher Niklas Luhmann offers a systematic account of trust in *Trust and Power*, originally published in German in 1974.[23] Luhmann sees trust as an attitude oriented towards the future. By trusting we are able to reduce the complexity of the world because we do not have to take every possibility into account; trusting, we assume that an indefinitely large range of harmful and dangerous things will not happen. Under normal circumstances we do not take into account the possibility that there is an underground lake corroding the road, that a piece of our mail will contain a bomb, or that the milkman is scheming to use members of our family in a political plot to assassinate the prime minister. Not having to consider such possibilities does simplify life! Trust emerges as our way of dealing with the complexity that enters the world because other human beings act in ways we cannot (usually) predict; they are free agents who may do things we do not expect them to do. Trust is based on a blend of knowledge and ignorance; we know something about other people, but we do not know just what they will do next. Trusting, we generalize from our limited experience, extending it to what we assume will be similar cases. Such generalization is made possible by the operation of social systems and systems of representation, which are selective; we do not attend to everything. In families, Luhmann says, we learn not only trust but how to learn trust – how to generalize from a range of experience involving other selves who are free agents.

Because the basis for trust is often slender, trust tends to be precarious. Often, when we cannot comprehend something, we have to trust others, and we know that we are vulnerable. In such cases we tend to take very seriously even marginally relevant evidence that the "mediating agent" is not reliable. Consider, for example, our attitudes to political representatives. We often find ourselves in the position of having to believe political figures who seek to inform us about such matters as interest rates, unemployment, and foreign policy. For many of us such complex matters are barely comprehensible; even those who could comprehend are often preoccupied with other things and have no time to collect current information. To believe political leaders, we have to rely on their word. How can we reasonably rely on their word? We must trust that they are sufficiently competent to know what is going on and sufficiently honest to tell us the truth about it. Notoriously, political leaders are often not competent and honest, and equally notoriously, people often do not believe that they are competent and honest. But often we are dependent on their word. (How large is the deficit? Was there information indicating that a riot was about to occur?) When such representatives lie to us, make ignorant remarks, indulge in sexual affairs, or seem in other ways to be irresponsible, we easily lose what trust we might have had. Even though personal peccadilloes and verbal *faux pas* may have nothing to do with the subject at hand, we are vulnerably dependent on these people, and we will take seriously any evidence that they are careless, immoral, dishonest, or incompetent.

In complex societies we need to trust many other people. The modern world is not the traditional small village, and we are unable to know most of these people personally: "It is all too obvious that the social order does not stand and fall by the few people one knows and trusts. There must be other ways of building up trust which do not depend on the personal element. But what are they?"[24] Luhmann's answer comes in three surprising parts: money, truth, and legitimate political power. What these have in common is their role in reducing the complexities of a life in which innumerable free human agents are interdependent. There is an inevitable reflexivity in the phenomena. These devices, which for Luhmann form the *basis* of social trust, also *require* trust. There is a circle here. Money, for instance, solves problems of trust, but we would not use money had we no trust in other people and in the relevant financial institutions. We can use money to address certain problems of trust, but then the very use of money presupposes that certain other problems of trust have been solved. Truly, there are webs of trust.

In Western industrialized countries people typically have confidence in accepting and using money because of a kind of "system trust." Using money, we have confidence in its continuing exchange value, which means, in effect, that we trust implicitly financial and governmental institutions and other people who use the same currency. We exchange dollars instead of working out a basis for trust in particular individuals (bartering carrots for singing lessons, for instance) with whom we are involved in countless unrelated transactions. Political and social problems can make a currency unstable and, in extreme cases, affect the use of money. On a recent trip to Russia my family and I experienced a mild version of this instability, which may serve as an illustration. The ruble, officially now a convertible currency, was subject to some devaluation because of inflation. Because of this, vouchers for our train tickets on the Trans-Siberian Railway, paid for in Canadian dollars, were not exchanged by Intourist personnel until the last possible moment. Sometimes this was only an hour before the departure of our train. We never missed a train, but we nevertheless found the practice inconvenient and slightly nerve-wracking. The Intourist personnel were reasoning that, with the ruble diminishing in value, they could hope to obtain more rubles for the tickets by waiting until the last moment. Their lack of confidence in the ability of the ruble to hold its value directly affected their behaviour and our ease of travel. The somewhat unstable nature of Russian political and economic life affected international confidence in Russia, which in turn affected the value of the ruble; that affected the behavior of Russian staff, whose confidence was lowered due to the relatively low international confidence. Their behaviour in turn affected our confidence about being able to board the train on time.

In our normal use of money, outside inflationary contexts, people assume that the money will retain its value and that differences of a few days or hours are not financially significant: one hundred dollars today will be worth one hundred dollars tomorrow. In a reasonably stable society we can assume that a system is functioning to make the currency reliable. With money, our trust is placed in the system and not in individual people. It is on this basis that Luhmann argues personal trust yields to system trust. What is at issue in most currency transactions is not the individual trustworthiness of one agent but rather the stability of the society in which the currency is based. When a currency such as the ruble is decreasing in value, it does so because influential people somewhere have less confidence in the system.

As for truth, to deal with others we must have a common basis of beliefs. This means that people have to establish common meanings; trust is possible only if we are able to reach agreement about what is going on in the world. For example, Allan can trust Juan to look after his cottage only in so far as he and Juan share beliefs about where the cottage is and how it should be looked after. To do this, we depend and rely on the way other people process information:

Behind every experience of objects there are possible statements and ... behind every statement there lie processes by which information has been worked on and worked out by people – not some immutable *Truth of Being*.

... Does one trust the chemist or his assistant or the doctor, or is it medicine, science, or technology?[27]

Luhmann's answer is: all of the above. Of course the trust needed to come to a consensus on the truth is diffuse: we do not need to be personally acquainted with all the people who have worked out this knowledge.

As for political power, the methods for establishing its legitimacy are unclear. Voting presupposes some degree of trust. Minimally, we must be confident that the candidates are reasonably decent and the votes will be counted fairly. It is to no avail to imagine that a social contract was established at some time in the actual or hypothetical past. Luhmann suggests that confidence in political legitimacy arises incrementally, emerging from many small actions and decisions. The political process is made trustworthy because it is reached after going through many small stages and is open to new information at each stage.

Luhmann argues that in the modern world it is system trust, not personal trust, that is paramount. Personal trust cedes to a kind of trust in the ability of systems to maintain conditions of performance. Like the Swedish shoppers interviewed by Sellerberg, we implicitly trust large organized systems that regulate things or process information. The aims of these systems are not the aims of the people who work within them. Social trust is an intricate, tangled web. We must trust ourselves, trust that others trust us, and trust that others will trust third parties in about the same ways that we do. It may even be said that we must trust our own trust; when, on reflection, we realize that we are trusting in all these ways, we must be willing to judge that our trust is all right, on the whole, that it has worked for us in the past and will continue to do so in the future. Usually, all this is implicit; we do not reflect on it and are not even aware of it. People tend to be more willing to trust if they are self-confident and secure enough to cope with disappointments and adapt to changing circumstances. Luhmann does not deny the existence of interpersonal trust or denigrate its importance. Such trust is fundamental in the family and with colleagues and friends, and it provides a necessary basis for social trust. But in the modern world it will never be enough. To live in a complex society without going mad, we must have trust in systems too.

2 Is It a Jungle Out There?

An acquaintance who works with street teens once said to me, "They live in a completely different world." She did not mean only that street teens live downtown and not in the suburbs, sleep under bridges and not in beds, eat in soup kitchens instead of restaurants. She meant that street teens experience a social reality radically different from the reality of those who have lived most of life in a relatively sheltered and stable middle-class environment. They have a different view of other people, of social authority, of human nature, of political and social institutions. As my acquaintance understood it, this difference resulted from experiences at home and school, experiences with adults who were at best negligent, at worst abusive and hostile. Children were not cared for at home, fared poorly at school, then ran from home to the street. The street teens she knew were hostile and despairing, and expected others to be the same.

A fundamental difference was in the area of trust: these teens lacked trust in family, teachers, peers, police, even those who sought to help them – and apparently for good reason, given the circumstances from which many of them emerged.

Which people and institutions we trust and which we do not fundamentally affect our outlook on the world. Our trust in another individual is based on our sense of what sort of person he or she is. If we trust someone we know, we regard that person as liable to conform to moral norms, as a person of good character. In short, we regard that person as one who is trustworthy, and we are willing to rely on him or her. In this case we are acquainted with the other person and have knowledge based on personal experience of what that person does and says. We interpet and evaluate the other person's actions. Is the other honest, open, sympathetic, reliable? Or is he or she, by contrast, manipulative, deceptive, uncaring, or hostile? When we trust other people, we expect them to act decently towards us, and we are inclined to interpret what they say and do according to those expectations. Trusting another person, we are inclined to understand what she says and does in positive terms. For instance, we are unlikely to see minor instances of unreliability such as lateness or a missed appointment as indications that the other person does not care or is breaking a promise.

Trust exists not only between people who know each other – intimates, lovers, friends, and colleagues – but also as an attitude towards people with whom we have only a slight personal acquaintance or even none at all. We trust doctors, dentists, school principals, and storekeepers, whom we encounter as individuals and rely and depend on but do not know well. In a more remote sense, we generally trust meat packers, car mechanics, airport maintenance personnel, and drivers on the road. Although these forms of social trust are so essential to modern life that social theorists have referred to trust as "social glue," we tend not to notice social trust unless it begins to break down.

Social trust and interpersonal trust are different in significant ways. Interpersonal trust is based on experience, sometimes deep and intimate experience, with another individual. In some cases of social trust we may have limited experience with the other persons involved; in others we have none at all. Our actions, expectations, and feelings differ because the context is different. Though we trust a storekeeper or car mechanic in various ways, we are unlikely to confide to him our deepest fears or look to him for advice about personal problems. But despite these differences in experience and emotional tone, it is neither an accident nor a logical mistake that the word "trust" should be used across personal and broadly social contexts. In all these contexts, when we trust we confidently expect reliable behaviour that will not harm us; we have expectations that go beyond what evidence would strictly warrant; we interpret what is said and done according to these expectations; we are vulnerable; and we accept our vulnerability.

Many relationships are based on social roles: we have dealings with the doctor, the dentist, the lawyer, the teacher, the accountant, and so on. In seeking the help of a doctor, we must trust her to be medically competent and motivated to improve our health, to be non-exploitative (honest, not just trying to make money) and concerned for our well-being. Yet often relationships between doctor and patient are scarcely personal at all, and patients who trust their doctors typically know little about their personal lives or social roles outside the office and the hospital. Similar comments can be made about other professionals; initially, people often trust them due to their sense of what their social roles involve and how people are socially authorized to fill those roles.

Although trust based primarily on social role is different in emotional tone from personal trust between family members, lovers, or close friends, its logic and structure are essentially similar. Trust entails positive expectations about what the other is likely to do. These expectations are based on a sense of the other's motivation and capacities, a willingness to allow ourselves to be vulnerable, and a disposition to interpret what he or she says and does in a positive way.

In modern life people are interdependent to an extraordinary extent. Implicit in many cases of such interdependence is a kind of trust in others who are strangers to us. In his recent book *Living Morally* Laurence Thomas defines a sense of *basic trust*.[1] For Thomas basic trust is our confidence that others will treat us in accordance with the basic precepts of morality. Basic trust, or basic social trust, is an expectation that others whom we do not know are not deliberately setting out to harm us – by lying, wounding, or killing. With basic trust we can assume that strangers we ask for directions or simple information ("Do you have the time?") are likely to reply to us truthfully, that people we pass on the street are not set on maiming and murder. Without such basic trust, Thomas says, life would be "unbearable." In daily life in complex urban societies we trust others whom we do not know. We trust them in the sense that we expect them to act within some basic moral limits. In going about daily life, we are in various ways vulnerable to many thousands of people we do not know. Mundane activities such as sending children to school, driving, eating in restaurants, using subways, and shopping involve such vulnerability – whether we realize it or not.

Thomas distinguishes between familiar strangers and complete strangers. Familiar strangers are people who seem familiar despite lack of acquaintance because we have observed them on various occasions – for example, the news anchors on television networks, the school crossing-guard who is always on the corner at noon, the letter carrier. For millions of Canadians the late Barbara Frum was a familiar stranger. We felt as though we knew her because we had so often followed her interviews on radio and television. We knew her style of questioning, her intonations, her smile, her fashion sense – and when she died, many felt a personal loss. This was a very familiar stranger. Of familiar strangers we have some knowledge based on repeated observation even though we are not personally acquainted with them. But in modern societies there are countless people on whom we depend and rely who are yet complete strangers to us. We are not acquainted with them; we have not observed them previously, and we know virtually nothing about them. Yet we may be vulnerable to them and depend on them in countless ways.

If even a tiny percentage of the complete strangers with whom we distantly interact while driving, teaching, using a subway, or eating in a restaurant were "out to get us" – or were believed to be so – life would be intolerable. Our attitude towards complete strangers is fundamental to our well-being and general sense of the world in which we function. Street teens, for instance, live in a cruel world. From bleak experience they have constructed a bleak picture of the world, and partly for this reason, they live in a bleak world.

Given that complete strangers are *complete* strangers, our only basis for expectations about them is some vague and general sense of what "most people" are like, a kind of picture we have of human nature in general. When we encounter such strangers, we may rely on cues of "self-presentation" – social role, in conjunction with dress, voice, deportment, and demeanour.

For many of us, our own dispositions to behave in a moral way will be affected by our expectations about how others are likely to behave. To the extent that we believe that other people will abide by moral and legal norms, we are more likely to do so ourselves; to the extent that we believe that most other people are unlikely to conform to such norms, we are less likely to do so. In this sense social trust underlies social morality and the rule of law. We have counter-factual expectations about other people – beliefs about how they would act if certain non-actual circumstances were to come about. What would people do if there were a police strike in our community? If a major department store left its doors unlocked overnight? If a child were lost and help were needed for a public search? Beliefs about how people would respond in such hypothetical circumstances may be positive or negative: we may expect the best or the worst. And to some degree the beliefs we have are likely to be self-reinforcing. Those who are expected to conform to moral norms are more likely to do so than those who are not. We can affect each other's social virtue by our expectations and attitudes towards each other.

Attitudes of trust do not apply only to individuals. They can be extended as well to institutions in which various social roles are meshed (the government, tax authorities, the police, the military, the social welfare system). What does it mean to trust an institution, such as the national taxation service? It means that we have fundamentally positive beliefs and expectations about our interactions with it. To the extent that we trust a government taxation service – Revenue Canada, for instance – we feel confident that its officials are, on the whole, honestly and reliably doing their jobs. We believe that they are accurate in their calculations, that they do not set out to audit people because they want to harass them, that they do not try to charge a higher tax for political reasons, and so on and so forth. We are vulnerable and at risk (financially and, to some extent, personally) when dealing with such an institution. Thousands of individuals work within it. To the extent that we trust the institution, we assume that its procedures and rules, management, and hiring and firing practices function to keep most of those individuals functioning within appropriate limits so that Revenue Canada has an honest, reliable, and competent staff. Should we fail to trust an institution, we do not have this sort of confidence. As this book goes to press, the Somalia Inquiry has gone on in Ottawa for many months, and many Canadians have lost considerable confidence in the military due to the horrendous Somalia affair, in which racist Canadian soldiers from the Airborne Regiment on a UN peacekeeping mission tortured and killed a Somali teenager. Apparently, officers were not in control of troops, and higher-up military officials kept back documents, lied, and otherwise sought to cover up the horrors.

At all the levels and in all the contexts in which trust exists, distrust is also a possibility. Distrust exists when there is a lack of confidence in the other, a concern that he or she may act so as to harm us, that he or she does not care about our welfare, intends to act harmfully, will not abide by basic moral norms, or is hostile toward us. When we distrust, we are fearful and suspicious about what the other might do. Like trust, distrust implies interpretive dispositions. When we distrust, we regard with suspicion behaviour that might otherwise have struck us as benign or helpful. We may interpret apparently innocent behaviour as malevolent, motivated by some sinister underlying intent. A colleague whom we distrust, or an intimate whom we cease to trust and begin to distrust, we regard as potentially threatening. We may well be vulnerable to the actions of such a person and have little confidence that he will act well, and in a case of distrust or suspicion, that vulnerability makes us insecure and uncomfortable. We may have little choice but to continue a relationship with someone we distrust, or we may have little option save to co-operate with or rely on a distrusted person. This circumstance is an uncomfortable one that we would change if we could.[2]

Although there are contexts in which distrust is warranted and useful, prolonged distrust poses real and troubling problems. Sometimes when we do not trust another person, we can simply avoid all interaction and interdependence. But this simple strategy is often not possible; often we must encounter that other person, perhaps even work with him, under circumstances of ongoing and deepening suspicion.

Radical problems emerge when distrust becomes systematic and widespread, an underlying motif in an entire outlook on the world – as it was, apparently, for the street teens. Writing from a psychoanalytic perspective, K.S. Isaacs, E.A. Haggard, and J.M. Alexander note pervasive relevance of distrust or trust as basic elements in our outlook on the world: "The fact of trusting or not trusting determines by itself large aspects of the subjective world of the individual. Expectancies, anticipations, and hope are influenced by it. Perceptions and conceptions of self and others, and the interpersonal possibilities are vastly different for the trusting and the non-trusting. Thus the trusting and the non-trusting live in different worlds."[3] This comment fits the street teens. Those who are inclined to be trusting will see people and situations differently from those whose tendency is to be suspicious of others. They will structure their social world differently and will for these reasons encounter different opportunities and relationships. Whether we trust or distrust greatly affects the picture we have of social reality.

In reflecting on trust, distrust, and the construction of social reality, it is the dispositional aspects of trust and distrust that are most significant. When we trust another person, group, or institution, we have a positive picture, and we tend to preserve and strengthen that positive picture. We have a sense that these people are of good character and integrity and are likely to function reliably, complying with basic moral norms. Given such beliefs, we go on to predict what people will do, to act on these expectations, and to interpret responses accordingly. The distrusted person, by contrast, is one we regard anxiously, as a potential threat; and we interpret and remember his actions accordingly.

There is considerable evidence to support the idea that attitudes of trust and distrust affect the nature and quality of our social reality. A 1972 management study by Dale Zand indicates that a group in which the leader was trusted was able to operate with openness and creativity to address problems. In a comparable group in which the leader was mistrusted, members operated so as to minimize risk to themselves and resisted what they regarded as managerial attempts at control. Zand concludes that groups in which there is "high trust" can solve problems more effectively than low-trust groups.[4]

In his recent book *Trust: The Social Virtues and the Creation of Prosperity* Francis Fukuyama argues that the level of social trust in a society is a highly significant factor in its economic organization and performance. If cultural and historical patterns are such that people are unaccustomed to trusting strangers, businesses tend to stay within families. The inability to take on professional managers from outside the family or make close alliances with firms run by "outsiders" can be a significant handicap in contexts where expansion would serve business interests.

Fukuyama describes at length the "lean manufacturing" system pioneered by Toyota in Japan. (Japan, Fukuyama claims, is a "high trust" society.) In lean manufacturing, every worker has a cord at his work-station. If he detects a problem, he can pull the cord, and the entire assembly-line will grind to a halt. Because all workers are responsible for spotting problems, all need to have an overview, knowledge of the manufacturing procedure as a whole. If a worker is incompetent or malevolent, he could stop the entire assembly-line for no good reason. Workers have to perform as a team, and have a broad collective responsibility to solve problems. This system, which is very economical and leads to high-quality products, depends on high trust between workers and between workers and management.[5]

Trust builds on itself. Mark Snyder offers a synthetic account of a number of psychological studies indicating ways in which our beliefs about social reality affect that reality. If we assume that others are aggressive and competitive, we are likely to approach them in a suspicious and combative way, and the interactions resulting from such attitudes are likely to call forth behaviour that will confirm our hypothesis. For example, if we think people are going to be competitive and act on that assumption, we nearly always find that they are competitive. We often do not appreciate the extent to which social beliefs affect the behaviour of other people, but their role is nevertheless very real. Impressions, labels, and beliefs tend to generate anticipations, and these in turn produce their own "confirmation" or "validation." Snyder cites sixteen articles confirming the thesis that beliefs and expectations about other people have a self-fulfilling character. We have expectations about another person, and we test our hypotheses mostly by seeking confirmation for them. Logically, we should check out hypotheses by seeking both confirming and disconfirming evidence, but psychological experiments indicate a "confirmation bias"; we tend to look only for confirming evidence.[6] One who suspects or believes that another person is jealous of her tends to interpret what that person does as indicative of jealousy. If she did

not suspect jealousy, she would interpret her actions in another way
– as indicating, perhaps, insecurity.

Groups and whole nations can be affected by self-perpetuating
attitudes. There is evidence, for instance, of distrust of Russian competence and honesty even among Russians. One woman with considerable experience in Russia and a number of Russian friends
reports a conversation that perfectly illustrates the tendency. One of
her Russian friends was looking for a new job. She told him about a
Canadian initiative beginning in Moscow, adding that the organizers
wanted to turn it over, to be run by Russians themselves, within three
years. "That does it," he said. "It's sure to be a failure." He assumed
that Russians could not run a viable and honest business; he had little trust in his countrymen and – perhaps as a corollary – little in himself.

Evidence suggests that expectations and beliefs affect not only
future interactions with others but even our recollection and interpretation of past actions. An example may be found in the marriage
that ends in a bitter divorce. A person may have difficulty accepting
that he ever had moments of joy and happiness with the other.
Courtship, a wedding, births of children, and other moments that
were experienced as shared and joyful are forgotten or reinterpreted
so that the ex-partner, now regarded as one who never really cared,
is discredited for the past as well as for the present and future.

Among social beliefs Snyder includes beliefs about the self, and
cites evidence that they too tend to have a self-fulfilling character:
hypotheses about the self, he says, have considerable inertia. Extrapolating from Snyder's account, we can conclude that a person who
has self-esteem and self-respect will tend to act and see her actions so
as to preserve her positive sense of self. One who has a negative sense
of self will tend in the other direction. Thus both self-trust and the
lack of it will be self-perpetuating.

Snyder's work is about social beliefs in general. He never mentions
trust or distrust as such. But since trust and distrust are based on
beliefs about people (their motivation, competence, character, and
tendencies to action), Snyder's conclusions have clear implications
for trust and distrust. Social beliefs tend to confirm themselves, and
work to create a social reality that confirms them. Thus trust in others will tend to produce trustworthy others, as distrust in others will
tend to produce untrustworthy others. Relationships of trust and distrust will tend to persist and reinforce themselves. Those who trust
will tend to have their trust confirmed and will persist in trust. Those
who distrust will tend to have their distrust confirmed and will persist in distrusting. Extrapolating from the empirical evidence cited by

Snyder, we can expect spiral effects – for trust in others and, as well, for trust in ourselves. Such effects may be anticipated at other levels – personal, social, institutional, and political – and will be intricate in nature.

Rosy Spirals: Trust Perpetuating Itself

(a) Pierre trusts Susan, so he expects the best and acts towards her with warmth, openness, friendliness, and confidence. Sensing Pierre's openness and friendliness, Susan responds in a positive way. Pierre's idea that Susan is a trustworthy person is confirmed, so he continues to act towards her in this way, and she continues to respond in kind, confirming his beliefs.

(b) Angela tends, in general, to be a trusting person. She tends to regard people as benign, co-operative and unthreatening – unless she has quite definite evidence to the contrary. Her "default state" is one of trust, from which she can be moved by specific evidence of unreliability or dishonesty on the part of the other. Having a tendency to approach other people in a trusting, open, and positive manner, Angela usually gets a response in kind. Thus her hypothesis that human nature is basically benign is confirmed.

(c) John trusts himself in the sense that he regards himself as a person of integrity, sound values, and reasonable abilities. He has confidence in his ability to cope appropriately with situations that may arise, and he is reasonable hopeful about his future. John approaches others in a confident and hopeful way, appearing to them a person of competence and integrity. Others tend to assume that he is a person of competence and integrity and treat him accordingly, thus validating his self-trust.

Blue Spirals: Distrust Perpetuating Itself

(d) Juanita does not like the gloomy look of the new faculty member and finds his style and tone when he speaks out in meetings obscure and rhetorical. He strikes her as manipulative, even sinister in some way. Her impression is not improved when she hears that he is editing a journal in an area she regards as trendy but non-substantial. She is quite suspicious of him. When she meets him casually, she is not especially friendly and talks to him only briefly and of superficial things. He responds coolly to her. They have not had any meaningful conversations, although they have met on many occasions. Juanita's ideas of this man are confirmed: he is not open, not friendly. He seems to be hiding something.

(e) Bob is bright but has no education past high school. He had a number of different small businesses, none of which were very successful. Bob knows that many people less intelligent than he enjoy a better economic and social standing than he has been able to achieve for his family. He resents this, is bitter about his life and cynical about the abilities and achievements of other people. Bob looks on strangers and acquaintances with suspicion, jealousy, resentment, and a degree of fear. His default state is one of distrust. Other people have to prove themselves to him. He finds it surprising if people are open and friendly. Bob conveys a kind of bitterness, cynicism, and hostility to others. Most people, finding that he seems a little angry and hostile, do not treat him with warmth and openness. So his ideas about other people are confirmed by his experience.

(f) As a small child Sereen was sexually abused by her grandfather. Only six years old at the time, she felt "dirty and wrong." She grew up with a sense of herself as a vulnerable, flawed person meriting little respect and having little control over her actions and responses. Wanting acceptance and intimacy, she had sexual encounters with many men, but her lack of self-respect and confidence made her vulnerable to exploitation and unable to stand up for herself when it occurred. Men treated her badly, further undermining her self-respect and self-confidence. She continued to convey a sense of weakness and easy exploitability, and went on to further flawed relationships that confirmed her sense that she was a weak person unable to gain the love of better human beings.

Cases a and d above involve trust or distrust in a particular other person; b and e involve tendencies to be more or less trusting towards other people generally; c and f begin with self-trust or self-distrust. All such attitudes are likely to be self-buttressing – as is indicated both by common life and by social-scientific research.[7] The tendency to be more trusting than not is especially relevant to one's attitudes to strangers and those known only slightly. We allude to this in ordinary speech when we speak of people as being, in their character or personality, "trusting" or "suspicious." Such general tendencies to trust or distrust express beliefs or assumptions about human nature in general.

From a more philosophical point of view, the idea that observations are theory-laden can be applied here. We have beliefs about particular other people, about other people in general, and about ourselves, and we rely on those social beliefs in living our lives. We observe and interpret actions, remember, hypothesize, respond, predict, understand choices and possibilities, make decisions and act –

all according to those social beliefs. A trusting and trustworthy person will understand himself and others in a positive way, will tend to experience a more benevolent world, will find trustworthy and caring friends and meaningful intimate relationships, and will thereby have an optimistic sense of the world and his future within it. One who is suspicious, cynical, distrustful will have a negative sense of self and others, and so will construct and encounter a different world. Similarly, people who see their own history and capacities in a positive light, who have trust or faith in themselves, are more likely to build a well-functioning and caring society than those who look disparagingly upon themselves. Street teens live in a different world partly because their distrustful and hostile attitudes have led them to construct a different picture of the world.

TRUST AND "REAL PARADISE"

In a recent paper about the importance of trust for the quality of life, Alex Michalos points out that to some extent we construct the social world. Michalos argues that we can and should do this in a more benign and positive way than we do. Such a construction, he argues, would require a higher level of trust than we have at present. We would be better off if we could manage to be more trusting.[8] Michalos does not mean that we construct the world in the fullest and most literal meanings of "construct" and "world." There is, he acknowledges, a physical world out there, relatively independent of human beliefs and perceptions, one that contains material things with objectively measurable properties. But we fill in many gaps in our picture of the world, and in social relationships there is a considerable extent to which faith in a fact can work to create that fact. To the extent that we construct our social world, we could presumably improve it by adopting a positive, optimistic, confident, and trusting attitude towards other people and ourselves.[9]

Michalos imagines four different social worlds:

1. Real Paradise. In this world people are both trustworthy and trusted.
2. Fool's Hell. In this world people are trustworthy, but they are not trusted.
3. Fool's Paradise. In this world people are not trustworthy but are trusted.
4. Real Hell. In this world people are neither trustworthy nor trusted.

If we had to choose one of these worlds as our own, we would choose Real Paradise. There people are trustworthy; they merit others' trust, and others trust them. The resulting openness, intimacy, lack of crime and immorality, confidence, security, optimism, altruism, and good-will would make Real Paradise utopia indeed. Because generalized trust is a necessary condition of Real Paradise, which is decidedly the best of the four possibilities, should we try to be more trusting? This is what Michalos argues.

Michalos is inclined to think that most people are more suspicious and distrustful than they need be. He cites a number of interesting empirical studies to this effect. Several suggest – somewhat paradoxically – that *most* people judge themselves to be more generous, altruistic, and trustworthy than *most* other people. (The situation is ironic: for most of these people to be right, they would have to be wrong!) For example, a 1985 study of business executives showed that 98 per cent reported that they themselves deemed the padding of an expense account to be unacceptable behaviour in any circumstances. However, only 54 per cent thought that the "average executive" would regard such behaviour as unacceptable. Similarly, 51 per cent said they thought it was not right to pay a fee to get a business contract, but only 21 per cent thought that other executives would take this stance. A study at the University of Guelph, asking students whether they would stop to help an old man and woman experiencing car trouble on a country road, found that 88 per cent said they themselves would stop to help. But of these, only 62 per cent thought that others would stop to help.

Such results suggest that people do not want to believe that others are more trustworthy, honest, and altruistic than they are themselves. And the results are strange. If most people are right about their own reactions, most people are wrong about others' reactions. Michalos brings out the peculiarity nicely, saying, "If most people would have granted that most people were like themselves, they would have found most people nicer than they imagined themselves to be."[10] The people interviewed in these studies were inclined to regard themselves as somewhat more morally upright and trustworthy than others.

Indeed, there is other evidence to support such a conclusion. We tend to have a "partisan bias" towards ourselves or our side and interpret evidence more favourably and sympathetically when it bears on our own case.[11]

Such socio-psychological evidence forms an important part of Michalos's argument that we should all be more trusting than we are, and thereby construct for ourselves a more optimistic and beneficent social reality. We have a positive picture of ourselves; we should extend that to others. Michalos argues in addition that this advice is reasonable because it is a necessary step towards Real Paradise, the most desirable social world. Since trust and trustworthiness are both based on respect for others, principles of non-harm and altruism, Michalos argues that moving to greater trust as a step towards Real Paradise is morally warranted.

We may add to this argument evidence for the prudential benefits of greater trust. There is empirical evidence that people who are more trusting benefit in life. Michalos cites studies by the social psychologist Julian Rotter, who claims that those who are more trusting tend to be more attractive, popular, and successful than those who are less trusting. Rotter, whose results emerge mostly from studies of university and college students in North America, reported that people who were more trusting tended to be happier, more attractive to the opposite sex, more desirable as friends, and more trustworthy than those who were "low trusters." Other researchers have found evidence that attitudes of suspicion and hostility are aspects of "Type A" behaviour correlated with heart disease. Russell Hardin has also argued that people who tend to trust readily have an advantage in life. Their greater willingness to communicate and collaborate with others opens many opportunities. People who, for whatever reasons of background, are not willing or able to trust others except on the basis of extensive positive experience, are handicapped by comparison.[12]

The argument Michalos presents is highly intriguing but raises important questions. A major problem is that the four social worlds of Real Paradise, Fool's Paradise, Fool's Hell, and Real Hell do not exhaust the relevant possibilities. Two significant alternatives are:

5. Epistemic Paradise: In this world people are trusted or distrusted to an extent exactly commensurate with their evidenced trustworthiness or lack thereof. Those who have given perfectly consistent evidence that they are trustworthy are trusted completely by everyone. Those who have shown themselves to be completely untrustworthy are distrusted completely by everyone. Those who have been trustworthy only in some contexts are trusted by others in just those sorts of context, and so on and so forth. In this world, when we have no evidence about a person's trustworthiness because we do not know him or her, we are exactly neutral in our attitude. We neither trust nor distrust.

6. The Wise but Hopeful Paradise: In this world people are trusted to an extent that slightly exceeds their evidenced trustworthiness,

and distrusted to an extent slightly less than would be logically warranted by what they have done. People base their trust and distrust on their relevant knowledge of other people's actions and character. However, they understand the self-reinforcing effect of trust and distrust. Regarding trust as, on the whole, a more desirable attitude than distrust, they seek to give others the benefit of the doubt to a small extent, in the hope that this will lead to more positive interactions. Towards those they do not know they maintain an attitude of slight trust unless and until they acquire some evidence of unreliability. Real Paradise is clearly the winner against Fool's Paradise, Fool's Hell, and Real Hell. But to defend Real Paradise against Epistemic Paradise or Wise but Hopeful Paradise would not be so easy. These are not hell; they seek to allocate trust according to trustworthiness. While not as paradisical as Real Paradise, they have a definite reality advantage and afford some protection, because untrustworthy people are distrusted.

RISK AND VULNERABILITY

The evidence Michalos cites, wherein "most people" appear to trust "most people" less than they should shows that *if* most people are right about their own actions and attitudes, then they are wrong about the attitudes and actions of others. But perhaps people are not right about their own actions. Perhaps they are wrong about themselves and right about others. Or perhaps they both overestimate themselves and underestimate others.[13] Asked on a survey whether one would stop for stranded seniors experiencing car trouble, I would probably say yes, either to protect my standing with an interviewer or in the sincere belief that this is what I would do, were the circumstance to arise. Yet all the same, I might not help in an actual case; were the circumstance to arise, I might feel pressed for time and tempted to go on, be frightened by the context or the appearance of the stranded people, or rationalize that someone else would soon come along to help them. Michalos is aware of this sort of problem and discusses it, but in the end he cannot rebut the possibility that people overestimate their own trustworthiness. He admits that harsh judgments might result from egocentric biases or intentional distortion.[14]

Without strong empirical evidence that we underestimate the trustworthiness of others, Michalos's argument for greater trust as a step towards Real Paradise is open to the criticism that it urges us to risk too much. We should "trust more" and construct a better world, Michalos contends. The problem is that this advice is insufficiently sensitive to the obvious fact that we are vulnerable when we trust. Someone who trusts a stranger, offering him a ride in her car, may be raped and murdered as a result. There are people who are grossly untrustworthy – who commit serious crimes, are deceptive, manipulative, and exploitative, are uncaring, unkind, lacking in sympathy and generosity.

NEGATIVE SOCIETIES

The studies on which Julian Rotter based his claim that more trusting people are generally happier, more attractive, and more trustworthy than the less trusting were done with North American college and university students. Rotter notes this feature as a limitation, remarking that most psychological studies of trust, including his own, were primarily of white, relatively affluent middle-class people in North America. The benefits of trust alleged for this group cannot with great confidence be applied to people in other sorts of societies. Over a billion people live under a repressive regime in China; millions more live under other forms of totalitarianism in such countries as Syria and Iraq, where government spies are feared to be everywhere. Hundreds of thousands have been tortured. Even within North American society, those who are members of marginalized groups or who live as homeless people or street teens might not experience the correlation between having a trusting personality and being happy and well adjusted described by Rotter and endorsed by Michalos. Although Michalos cites Rotter's results favourably and in detail, he neglects to note the limitations in the samples on which those studies were based. By contrast, Russell Hardin observes that trust is learned, and people who grow up in hard circumstances learn not to trust. This is the right lesson in some circumstances. The capacity to trust is a by-product of experiences over which the individual may have had singularly little control. Trusting as a universal attitude might pay off, but only if the world is benign and the level of trustworthiness quite high.

The failure to relativize the benefits of trust to life circumstances is significant. Those who lead a safe, middle-class lifestyle in a relatively affluent and ordered society might benefit by "trusting more." But for a homeless person or peasant near starvation, such an approach could risk life itself. People whose social experience features harshness, poverty, discrimination, abuse, brutality, even torture and surveillance, are likely to gain an experience of the world that produces increased wariness, fear, and a sense of vulnerability and supports a negative picture of social and political life. For many such people life teaches bitter lessons. Complete and familiar strangers may seem threatening; home itself may be a place of bitter competition for food and other scarce resources. It does not seem plausible to discount such interpretations as biased, cynical, or paranoid. In such contexts the advice to "construct a better world" by trusting more seems inappropriate at best, dangerous at worst.[15]

WILLING TO TRUST

Michalos advises us to trust more than we do. This advice presumes that trusting more is something within our power, something we can do. Yet trust is based on beliefs and feelings that, though sometimes alterable after critical reflection and deliberation, cannot be created or abolished at will. If someone has lied on several significant occasions and has broken important promises, we will in all likelihood have come to believe, on the basis of relevant evidence, that she is unreliable, potentially manipulative, and untrustworthy. We will not be likely to believe that she is telling the truth on a significant future occasion, especially not if that occasion is similar to the past situation of deception and betrayal. Still less are broad attitudes towards strangers or "most people" likely to be changed by decisions and acts of the will. We can of course choose to *act* in a trusting way, but it is not plausible to think that we can simply choose to trust, or choose to trust more.[16]

These shortcomings in the Michalos argument are connected: all involve the relationship between experience or evidence and trust and distrust. Trust and distrust are not attitudes that can be put on or taken off like jackets. To be sure, they are in part constructed; they are based on encounters and experience that we help to structure and create; they affect our interpretations, hypotheses, and feelings. Yet there is a reality level too. What we expect of the world and other people also depends on what really happens. If relatives simply disappear, if people are starved, beaten, and tortured, if their friends and colleagues have turned out to be spies for a brutal regime, those are realities of social experience.

To say that people may overestimate their own altruism or ethical behaviour is to say that they may trust themselves too much, having more confidence than they should in their own moral virtue. The additional social worlds of Epistemic Paradise and Wise but Hopeful Paradise incorporate a relationship between trust and trustworthiness. Both involve a connection between trusting and having evidence to support that trust. Some people who are less trusting may have good reasons, based on their experience of the world, for being so. The issue of trusting at will raises the same problem about trust and evidence in another context. We cannot simply discount our experience of others, achieve greater trust in others by acts of the will, and thereby construct for ourselves a more beneficent world.

In his recent treatment of the significance of "high trust" and "low trust" attitudes for economic performance, Francis Fukuyama regards patterns of trust and distrust in societies as characteristics that emerge over a considerable period of time. They result, he thinks, from religious and cultural traditions and styles of governance. Fukuyama maintains that Chinese societies are "low trust"; he seeks to explain the phenomenon by the Confucian emphasis on loyalty to the family. Fukuyama also regards France as a "low trust" society. In France, he argues, there is an extreme centralization of power. In addition, work is highly dependent on hierarchy and rules. These characteristics of French organization have not encouraged "spontaneous sociability."

Fukuyama's hypotheses are debatable. But they do seem to point in reasonable directions: towards deep and pervasive characteristics of society as causes of characteristic social attitudes.[17] If there are trust attitudes that broadly characterize whole societies, then these are likely to emerge from cultural styles and the broad conditions of material and social life. So caused, they are not likely to be amended because we have been convinced by an argument that we should "trust more."

TRUST AND TRUSTWORTHINESS

As for "high trust" and "low trust," one has to be careful about this sort of talk. Speaking about "trusting more" or "trusting less," or even about who is "trusting" and who is "mistrustful" or "suspicious," can be misleading because it is insufficiently specific. Such talk encourages us to neglect the contexts, evidence, and aspects of degree that apply to trust and distrust. Such distinctions are important even in cases involving only two individuals – a fact that points to the tremendous glossing of detail that must necessarily result when we attempt to reflect, as Fukuyama does, on the difference between high-trust and low-trust societies.

We may trust a person completely in certain respects, scarcely at all in others, and have no view as to his trustworthiness in another area, all because of our own past experience. I completely trust my dentist in his function as a dentist regarding such matters as cavities, root canals, and health of gums: over many years he has done relatively painless and completely reliable work on me and my children. When

he offers cosmetic advice, recommending the replacing of dis-
coloured fillings with new ones, I do not assume that he is lying or
trying to deceive me, but I slightly discount the advice and think
hard about my time, my comfort, and my wallet before taking it. I do
not hesitate because I think he is lying to me or trying to make more
money by encouraging me to go through unnecessary procedures.
Rather, I believe that dentists as a profession have a standard for the
good-looking mouth that is unnecessarily perfectionist. Now, switch
the context again. Suppose that my dentist offers his services as a
tour leader for a soccer team of young boys, including my own son.
In this new context, I will feel less confident of his trustworthiness
than I am when he is filling my teeth. My experience has little to do
with this new situation. Nevertheless, I would be ready to trust him
because I would apply my experience of him in a professional context to the context of tour leader. My experience indicates that he is a
person of integrity, an honest, reliable, and caring person. But the
context of soccer-coaching is so different from the one in which I have
real knowledge of this man that I would know there is a gap, a leap
to be taken.[18] There is nothing I know that rules out his having a sexual interest in young boys. I feel quite confident that he does not, but
I have no experience relevant to this matter. Hence, trust makes a
leap.

Whether we are dealing with attitudes to the self (self-confidence,
self-esteem, self-trust) or with attitudes to other people, trust, distrust, and related beliefs cannot be detached from relevant experience
and evidence. Understanding the self-buttressing effect of trust, the
importance of trust in attitudes towards ourselves and others, and
the centrality of trust in supporting an optimistic and positive conception of the world, it is tempting to think that we could improve
our social world by trusting more and to recommend "more trust," as
Michalos does. In some contexts this recommendation makes sense.
We can become too cynical and suspicious; in so being we may harm
ourselves and limit our possibilities. But whether more trust is desirable depends on the context and on what we know. And if it is desirable to trust more, the question of how to bring it about remains
open. It is not psychologically possible simply to *decide* or *choose*, or
to take on an attitude of "high" as opposed to "low trust." Even if it
is true, as Michalos argues, that "most people" do not trust "most
people" enough, the advice to "trust more" so as to construct a more
beneficent world cannot solve the problem. This is not a choice we
can make, and furthermore the advice is too decontextualized to be
sensible.

Yet there is something attractive and important about the argument Michalos offers. An adaptation of his advice suggests itself when we recall that his Real Paradise had two aspects: trust and trustworthiness. Trusting more as a step towards Real Paradise is not desirable or feasible. However, the objections raised do not apply to the aspect of trustworthiness. Being *trustworthy* is also a necessary step towards living in a world in which people are trusted and are trustworthy. Being trustworthy is a matter of having integrity and concern for others, living up to their legitimate moral expectations, and reliably carrying out tasks and duties. Being trustworthy is something that can be generally and less controversially recommended. We are asked to be reliable and caring, and to comply with moral norms.[19] We do not have to will to believe new things, to adopt new attitudes; we have only to act in more trustworthy ways. Acting as trustworthy persons is something we can do. And from all that has been said, we may expect the effects on our own and others' attitudes to be significant. A trustworthy person gives others the knowledge that she is trustworthy and that (some) people can, without risk, be trusted and relied upon. By character and actions, he or she supports a positive picture of human nature to which others will respond in a positive way. In so doing, the trustworthy person strengthens his own self-esteem and self-trust as a basis for continued trustworthy action.

There is evidence that we tend to have a picture of human nature that is tied to our understanding of ourselves. We are unwilling to see others as more virtuous and conscientious than we are ourselves. In the introduction to his *Leviathan*, Thomas Hobbes admitted as much: "whosoever looketh into himself, and considereth what he doth, when he does *think, opine, reason, hope, feare*, etc., and upon what grounds; he shall thereby read and know, what are the thoughts, and Passions of all other men, upon the like occasions. I say the similitude of Passions, which are the same in all men ... not the similitude of the *objects* of Passions ... He that is to govern a whole Nation, must read in himself, not this, or that particular man; but Man-kind."[20] Hobbes "read" mankind in himself. In trying to estimate what motivated other people, he looked inside himself to ask what he would do in similar circumstances, and why. Hobbes recommended looking at others, looking in oneself, and comparing circumstances to make appropriate amendments.

A good man is likely to trust too much, a bad one to trust too little, Hobbes commented. Apparently it was from looking inside himself that Hobbes was led to his view of humankind as fundamentally lusting for glory and power, continually threatened in life pursuits by other human beings. The implications about his own personality seem obvious, and unattractive. Should such traits discredit a man as an observer of human nature and society? For thousands of readers and thinkers through the centuries they have not. Hobbes lived and wrote in the seventeenth century, but many moderns have found in his theories echoes of themselves and have constructed their picture of human nature accordingly.

Hobbes's advice that we read others in ourselves points to a common tendency: we tend to ask ourselves what would motivate us, what we ourselves would do in a similar situation. Then, reasoning from our own case, we proceed to infer either that other people are similar and would do much the same or that others are less virtuous and capable than we and would behave less well.

A person who is greedy, selfish, dishonest, and out for himself is unlikely to regard others – especially unknown others – as altruistic, straightforward, honest, and reliable. The pop-psychology maxim that "before we can love other people we have to love ourselves" seems to apply to trust. If we do not see ourselves in a good light, we are unlikely to see others so; if we do not trust ourselves, we are unlikely to trust others. By acting in a trustworthy fashion ourselves, we support an image of ourselves as trustworthy and thus support in ourselves a tendency to be more trusting of others. In contexts where attitudes towards complete strangers are in question and must be based on general assumptions about human nature, we will have built in ourselves, by virtue of our own actions and sense of ourselves, a more positive sense of other people and of human nature in general. In contexts where we have interacted with people, where our attitudes are based on experience and evidence, we will have contributed to better interactions and more positive relationships. From our own actions, attitudes, and self-knowledge, we will have created small bits of evidence to support optimistic hypotheses about human nature.

In her moving and perceptive article "Secular Faith" Annette Baier points out that conforming to moral principles requires a belief that enough other people will do so for our actions to make sense. Such a conviction amounts to secular faith in the law-abiding character of a reasonable proportion of our fellow citizens. Religious believers may escape the need for this kind of faith because they have another kind of faith: God and the promise of Heaven function to guarantee the meaningfulness of our moral order. For those without faith in God, the moral order requires faith in humankind.

Suppose that a trustworthy and conscientious person decides not to cheat on his income tax although he has evidence that plenty of other people are cheating and he could probably get away with it. Is his conformity futile? Is it entirely one-sided, unilateral? That may appear to be the case, but Baier argues that the appearance is misleading.

On Baier's account, apparently futile unilateral and possibly self-sacrificing action is neither futile nor unilateral. It is not futile because it keeps alive the possibility of qualified members for a just society. And it is not unilateral because the one just person has a "cloud of witnesses," all those others whose similar acts in other times kept alive the same hope. Individuals who, unsupported by their contemporaries, act for the sake of justice do not necessarily hasten the coming of a just society, but they do rule out one ground on which it might be feared impossible – that people are incapable of acting justly. In this very modest way the just man's actions confirm his faith, demonstrate that *one* condition of the existence of a just society can be met, that human psychology can be a psychology for people who are autonomous and willing to discipline their actions to conform with principles of justice. Thus every action in conformity to a just but threatened institution, or in protest against an unjust but supported one, furthers the cause, keeps the faith.[21] The sweeping advice to "trust more" is open to objections, but the advice to "be more trustworthy" is supportable and has profound implications.

Understanding the role of trustworthiness, trust, and distrust in constructing reality is of practical as well as theoretical importance. We should be aware that our attitudes and beliefs about other people tend to be self-fulfilling and self-buttressing, and we should make a special effort to be open to counter-evidence to such beliefs. In cases where we are slightly suspicious or even positively distrustful of others, we should try to act so as to elicit a positive response. We should be especially careful of hasty and negative imputations of motivation and intent, and of negative interpretations of character and actions. When we are inclined to make negative assumptions about strangers, we should check ourselves and ask why. An enlightened application of critical-thinking strategies to social beliefs, especially those implying attitudes of distrust, will yield beneficial results. Interestingly, however, a general tendency to trust other people turns out to be a prerequisite of critical thinking itself.

3 Needing Each Other for Knowledge

Human beings are social beings who have become social beings because we develop and live in the company of others. Living and functioning within a society, we implicitly trust many others, many of whom are total strangers. One of the clearest and most important areas in which social trust exists is that of knowledge and belief. If we did not trust in the word of other people, we would not have beliefs beyond our own immediate experience. In fact, we would not have a language. Knowledge based on what other people tell us presupposes trusting other people. Accepting evidence from others is reasonable only to the extent that we regard them as reliable, competent, and sincere. And this is to say it is reasonable only to the extent that we trust them.

DEPENDING ON WHAT OTHERS TELL US

Suppose we read in a newspaper that there has been a serious accident involving a school bus and a train just outside a nearby small town, that two children were killed and three others seriously injured. We may simply accept such a report as providing information about events beyond our own immediate experience. If so, we accept something told us by another – the reporter – taking his word for it that these things did happen. If we were feeling more sceptical, we might check out the truth of these claims for ourselves. Seeking to avoid hearsay, we might travel to the town, find the spot of the alleged accident and see the train, bus, and dead and injured passengers. Using such means we could, indeed, avoid dependence on the reporter alone. But we would still depend on others for information.

To travel to the spot, we would have to rely on maps and road signs. These devices are provided by social institutions; they tell us where roads are going, where towns are, and which town is which. Upon arriving, we would ask people the location and nature of the accident, thus relying on them – as well as on our own observations. If we saw a smashed bus beside a damaged train, we would still need to know that these were the vehicles involved in the accident, and we could discover this only by asking other people. Finding a smashed bus and train near the town, finding three injured children who say they were hurt in the recent accident, attending funerals for two others being mourned by their parents and townspeople as casualties of the accident – all this could provide compelling evidence to support the newspaper reports. But there remains an important sense in which we would not have checked matters *by ourselves*. We would have depended upon information and reports from many other people.

The necessity of believing what others tell us has been emphasized by C.A.J. Coady. Coady imagines visiting a foreign city such as Amsterdam. When he arrives at his hotel, he fills in a form indicating his name, age, date of birth, passport number, and citizenship. The hotel clerk accepts all this as true because Coady says it is true. Other people will accept it as true because the clerk will tell them Coady said it was true. When he wakes up in the hotel the next morning, Coady may phone the hotel clerk to find out what time it is. When the clerk tells him, he will believe it. Suppose he is early for breakfast. He may read a history book full of claims that neither he nor the author can support either by direct personal observation or from memory, or by deduction from observations or memory. The book might, for instance, describe the long-ago deeds of Napoleon Bonaparte, all performed in places that neither Coady nor the author has ever visited. The reality of these places is accepted on the word of others:

I reflect that on arriving at a strange airport a day or so earlier I had only the aircrew's word that this was Amsterdam, although since then there has been much else in the way of testimony to support their claim. Venturing forth from my hotel I consult a map and commit myself once more to a trust in my fellow human beings, just as I do moments later when I buy a copy of *The Times* and read about a military coup in Spain, an election campaign in Britain, an assassination in France, and a new development in medical science.[1]

Testimony, then, is centrally important in supporting our beliefs. In everyday life we rely extensively on what other people tell us, whether we are explicitly aware of this or not.

The hotel clerk simply *accepts* identity and passport information from the stranger arriving in Amsterdam. A sceptic might insist that people have been known to lie about their identity and to travel around on false passports; the clerk was perhaps careless in accepting Coady's credentials too readily. In telling this story, Coady perhaps trades on the reader's trust in him as a respectable professor and author – so depicted on the dust-jacket of his book – who would never do such a thing. But such quibbles are beside the point. Coady does not tell this story as part of an argument that believing what others tell us provides us with *infallible* knowledge. Rather, he is illustrating how natural and fundamental it is, in everyday life, simply to accept what others tell us.

We deviate from this normal practice only if we find good reason to do so. And when we do check up on one person, we nearly always have to rely on other people in order to do it. Suppose, for instance, that the Amsterdam hotel clerk has been warned by police that a sturdy middle-aged man with an Australian accent (Coady is Australian) and passport is wanted in connection with diamond smuggling. He might then question Coady about his papers, or call the police to check out the suspicious character. Such checking would be possible only because the clerk is willing to trust the police and officials in Australia – he could not assess the validity of these documents by himself.

People depend on each other for knowledge and evidence, a fact that is even more obvious when we consider specialized knowledge. One philosopher who has vividly described this dependence is John Hardwig. Hardwig argues that he believes many things for which he does not possess evidence. He cites such beliefs as that smoking cigarettes causes lung cancer, that the car stalls because the carburetor needs to be rebuilt, that slums cause emotional disorders, and that his irregular heartbeat is premature ventricular contraction: "The list of things I believe, though I have *no evidence for the truth of them*, is, if not infinite, virtually endless.

And I am finite. Though I can readily imagine what I would have to do to obtain the evidence that would support any one of my beliefs, I cannot imagine being able to do this for *all* of my beliefs., I believe too much; there is too much relevant evidence (much of it available only after extensive, specialized training); intellect is too small and life too short."[2]

Hardwig remarks that he has *no evidence* for many of his beliefs. By this he means that he does not have a certain kind of direct evidence: he has not been in the scientific laboratories to witness personally the experiments that give evidence for these claims. Still, Hardwig does have evidence of a sort. That evidence comes from *other people* who (he assumes) are qualified to vouch for what they say and whom he believes.

Consider the matter of smoking and lung cancer. If his case is typical, Hardwig's belief that smoking causes lung cancer is based on his exposure to media reports that researchers have evidence that smoking causes lung cancer. Some such reports give a simplified summary of data so that readers may reflect independently on the research. A person could gain some understanding of the evidence experts have gathered by reading these reports. So some non-specialists could have decent vicarious evidence for the belief that smoking causes lung cancer.

On most topics, similarly, most people are non-experts who depend on experts for many of their beliefs. We can check some claims and reports made by other people, but only by relying on the claims and reports of still other people. In fact, dependence on the testimony of others is unavoidable even for specialists. Expertise is based on training and theoretical study, and both are based on the experience and knowledge accumulated by others. Active research in the quest of new conclusions is based on the results and theories of other people. Questions and hypotheses emerge from work done by other scholars, thus presuming in a general way scholarly or scientific integrity and competence.

Steven Shapin provides another telling example. He considers the factual proposition that "DNA contains cytosine," saying that this is something many scientifically educated readers would know because they have been taught it. Some people, however, would know this proposition on the basis of "direct experience," and that group would include him; he once verified it "for himself":

When I worked in a genetics laboratory many years ago, I extracted DNA from mammalian cells and then subjected it to chemical analysis. It may therefore be said that I enjoy firsthand, and properly founded, knowledge of the identity of DNA. Here was what I did: I was given some pieces of rat liver which I then minced and froze in liquid nitrogen; I ground the frozen tissue and suspended it in digestion buffer; I incubated the sample at 50 degrees C for 16 hours in a tightly capped tube; I then extracted the sample with a solution of 25:24:1 phenol/chloroform/isoamyl alcohol and centrifuged it for 10 minutes at 1700 x g in a swinging bucket rotor. Transferring the top (aqueous) layer to a new tube, I added ½ volume of 7.5 M ammonium acetate and 2 volumes of 100% ethanol. A stringy precipitate then formed in the tube, which was recovered by centrifugation at 1700 x g for 2 minutes. I rinsed the pellet with 70% ethanol, decanted the ethanol, and air-dried the pellet. I went on to hydrolyze the sample and to perform a chemical test confirming the presence of the nucleotide cytosine. This was DNA; I had it in my hand; and I had verified the facts of its composition.[3]

However, to do this Shapin still needed other people's knowledge – for instance, he knew, because he had been taught, that a certain outcome of a chemical test stood for the presence of cytosine, and that the dried precipitate that he held in his hand was DNA. The possibility of scepticism about some aspect or stage is always there, Shapin comments. But when we are sceptical about one aspect, we work through that particular bit of scepticism only by taking for granted some other relevant knowledge. To verify that DNA contains cytosine, Shapin had to take on trust the identity of the animal tissue supplied, the speed of the centrifuge, the reliability of thermometric readings, the qualitative and quantitative make-up of various solvents, and the rules of arithmetic. He could have distrusted some of these things, but to verify any one aspect he had to take other propositions on trust.

Although details of our dependence on socially established knowledge vary, dependence as such is inevitable. Animal scientists use reports of animal behaviour in the wild; their studies assume that field researchers will accurately report what they have seen. Anthropologists similarly depend on field research, which in turn presumes that subjects interviewed will honestly recount their experience. Psychologists often recount events in laboratories, requiring accurate testimony about events in the lab and honesty on the part of the subjects whose responses constitute the basic data.[4] Historical research includes appraisal of testimony from the past and reliance on other historians who have sifted through data.

Hardwig provides a compelling example from modern physics. An article recording "charm events" and measuring the lifespan of charmed particles had ninety-nine co-authors. The experiment was one of a series that had cost a total of some 10 million dollars and employed equipment that required about fifty man-years to construct. Approximately fifty physicists had worked some further fifty man-years to collect the data: "When the data were in, the experimenters divided into five geographic groups to analyze the data, a process that involved looking at 2.5 million pictures, making measurements on 300,000 interesting events, and running the results through computers to isolate and measure 47 charm events. The West

Coast group that analyzed about a third of the data included forty physicists and technicians who spent about sixty man-years on its analysis." According to the physicist who described this work, no one person could have done it. Many of the co-authors would not even understand some parts of the paper. Though extreme, the case vividly illustrates the need to rely on others' observations, interpretations, calculations, and conclusions. No one literally works out results for himself; all must trust that each team-member is doing his part competently and conscientiously.

WHAT IS TESTIMONY?

In the broadest sense, testimony is "what other people tell us" – often in response to questions:

– What time is it?
– Where is Baker Street?
– Did Napoleon die on Elba?
– How many Bushmen are still living in South Africa?

When someone replies to such a question, he *tells* another the answer, offering his *testimony*. By stating the answer as though he knows it and intends to inform the other, he vouches for its truth. In the broad sense of testimony there is little restriction on just what may be told. People may reply with reports about what they have perceived or felt, or with learned information.

The word "testimony" suggests a context of witnesses, people *testifying* to what they have experienced and can remember – as when someone says he saw two men attack the victim. Testimony in this sense of witnessing is also central in evangelical religious traditions, where adherents *testify* to religious experiences or the benefits of religious belief. In these contexts testimony applies only to matters where a person has direct experience of the events he is telling about. But there is also a broader sense in which testimony is *what people tell us*, a sense not tied to witnessing, personal observation, or experience. In this broader sense we offer testimony when we tell each other what words mean, what is grammatically correct and incorrect, what we have read, or seen on television, or heard from friends, what we deem to be true or probable, or what our impressions are.

A question arises and a speaker makes a statement, vouching for the truth of some claim about it.[5] Assuming that the speaker is in a position to know, the listener takes his statement as true. The speaker has vouched for it. What he says, or his "say-so," transmits that knowledge to another:

- Where is Baker Street?
- Just three blocks south of Gardner.
- Thanks.

- Is *Thelma and Louise* a good movie?
- I didn't think so. There's an awful lot of violence in it.
- Really? Well maybe I won't bother to see it.

Knowledge and beliefs are transmitted from person to person because we tell each other what we think and know – and we believe each other. In these interactions we usually assume without reflection that we can acquire knowledge from each other: that's why we ask questions. We ask for simple information, and when we get an answer, we assume we know. It would not work unless the person asking the question was willing to trust the other to give him the answer.

In a formal legal framework the concept of testimony is carefully restricted and defined. A person must be qualified and competent to vouch for a claim, in the case of eyewitness testimony because he was a suitably located and presumably competent observer, or in the case of expert testimony because he is given status as an expert. Here the distinction between hearsay and first-hand observation is of the utmost importance. Obviously there are important differences between testimony in daily life and the more restricted formal testimony of the courtroom. And there are many other distinctions between various sorts of testimony. Testifying on the basis of expertise is different from testifying on the basis of experience. We can distinguish institutional testimony (as in maps, road signs, birth and wedding certificates) from personal testimony. Oral testimony can be contrasted with written testimony, contemporary testimony with testimony from the past, and so on. The distinctions between these various sorts of testimony are interesting and, for many purposes, important. But their existence should not blind us to the common elements in all the cases where other people tell us things. We rely and depend on each other for information and ideas, and communicate beliefs and knowledge to each other.

TRUST AND BELIEVING PEOPLE

When someone tells us something and we accept the claim on his say-so, trust is involved.[6] We presume the other person intends to tell us the truth and is sufficiently competent to do so. We take his assertion at "face value." All this is simply to say that to believe another person is to trust him or her.

Suppose that we want to buy a new car and like Toyotas, and a neighbour, who knows this, says "There are bargains on Toyotas at Crown Motors." We would quite naturally take the neighbour at her word. If all goes well, we would thereby come to know that there are bargains on Toyotas at Crown Motors. In the absence of reasons to the contrary, we presume that someone who presents herself in the role of a helpful neighbour is just that and is genuinely attempting to provide information. We assume she really is asserting something, is sincere in asserting it, and is in a position to know what she is talking about. Taking another's word for something requires trust because it requires that we take the other person's speech at face value and presumes her sincerity and competence to vouch for what she says.

We are able to believe *propositions* (that Toyotas are a bargain at Crown Motors, for instance) because we believe, or have believed many people who have taught us and told us things. In fact, believing people is a prerequisite of all other forms of belief. For logicians it has seemed most natural and clear to think of the objects of belief as propositions or statements. But we could not have propositional beliefs without the linguistic and logical skills and background knowledge we acquire from parents, teachers, and the general social milieu. Believing persons is more fundamental than believing propositions.

Young children characteristically believe their parents and teachers; they uncritically follow their language use and customs, uncritically accept from them what they are told. Were they not to do so, they could not learn. In everyday life, especially on mundane matters, we often simply believe people. We are told something, believe the person who tells us, and come to know something new. What could be more natural? We train each other, teach each other, transmit knowledge to each other. If we did not, we would have no language, no way of life, and no culture. To believe a person is more than merely believing that what she says is true. It means having confidence or trust in that person, accepting what she says because we believe or assume that she is competent and honest.

People tell us things we do not already know, and we accept these things because we believe those people. We quite naturally accept that those whom we believe to be reliable sources are in a position to vouch for what they say. Wittgenstein put it this way:

As children we learn facts; e.g., that every human being has a brain, and we take them on trust. I believe that there is an island, Australia, of such-and-such a shape, and so on and so on; I believe that I had great-grandparents, that the people who gave themselves out as my parents really were my parents, etc. This belief may never have been expressed; even the thought that it was so, never thought. The child learns by believing the adult. Doubt comes *after* belief.[7]

Different kinds of cases are involved here. That we have brains and great-grandparents are facts we could deduce from biology, once we knew that. By contrast whether those who said they were our parents really are, or were, is a matter of appearance and reality in family life. Were we to doubt such a matter, deep issues about family relations would certainly be implied. Wittgenstein's point is that there are all kinds of things that, as children, we simply accept because we have been taught them. These fundamental beliefs provide our overall sense of the world. Without them, even doubt would be impossible.

Believing people is not reducible to believing propositions. And the missing element is trust. To believe someone is to trust that person to tell the truth, to regard him or her as someone who is in a position to know, who does know, and who is sincerely communicating knowledge.

Shapin makes the same point, saying that we cannot have knowledge of things without using our knowledge of people. This relationship of dependence exists in general, and in addition it holds for specific cases: what we come to know about particular sorts of things is shaped by our knowledge of particular sorts of people.[8] To say that believing people is basic in the development of knowledge is not to say that we should believe everyone and everything. Obviously, we should not believe everybody, and probably there is no one person whom we should believe in all circumstances. People are in many ways and for many reasons quite unreliable. Distinguishing who and what should be believed is a lifelong task. But the point remains that knowledge based on testimony is absolutely fundamental. We have believed some people and have to go on believing some people in order to develop, live, and survive.

SOCIAL ELEMENTS IN BASIC KNOWLEDGE

Accepting what others tell us is indispensable in human development and in the construction of a picture of the world. To learn language and thinking skills, children copy and believe adults – first parents and caretakers, then teachers. Our sense of place and time in the world is also based on the word of others: we know of times and places outside our own experience because we believe other people who tell us about them. Whether from friends, teachers, books, newspapers, television, or film, it is through the experience and testimony of other human beings that we know of ancient Greece, the Middle Ages, the Napoleonic wars, India, Patagonia, and a vast numbers of other times, places, and events.

But reliance on testimony is even more basic than this. Ultimately it is presumed in the distinction between what is real and what is imaginary. The distinction between material reality and private impression, between public knowledge and purely subjective belief, presumes some acceptance of the testimony of other people. What is perceptible by only one observer is imaginary. To be real, an object must be capable (in principle at least) of being perceived by more than one observer. If we seem to see a large orange rectangle, we seek corroboration from others; if no one else can see it, we deem it an illusion or hallucination. What is *perceived* is something in external public space, not an entity that exists solely in one person's mind. If the orange rectangle is a door, others can see and touch it, and we will seek to find out whether this is so by asking other people. There is no point in asking them if we are not generally prepared to believe them when they respond. The public status of objects in external space thus presupposes the reliability of testimony. Wittgenstein again: "I look at an object and say "That is a tree," or "I know that that's a tree" ... But if all the others contradicted me, and said it never had been a tree, and if all the other evidences spoke against me – what *good* would it do me to stick to my "I know"?"[9] For a person to insist that he knows he saw a tree when everyone else says otherwise is quite useless. He can go on saying "I know, yes I *know* I saw a tree," but that will not convince anyone. Trees must exist in public space, which means they have to be perceivable by other people. The very concept of material reality – of the existence of things like trees – makes an implicit reference to testimony, to our acceptance of other people as accurate perceivers who can and will tell us honestly what they have seen.[10]

The same point can be made for claims of memory. What we really remember (as distinct from merely seeming to remember) must be events that actually occurred. To make this distinction, we rely on other people. I seem to remember a personal altercation with a high-school teacher, in which the teacher burst into tears. I am not sure whether this really happened or whether I made it up. The only way to check my impressions is to seek others and try to discover whether anyone remembers the altercation. If no one does, I cannot know whether it happened: perhaps, perhaps not.

As this case suggests, even knowledge of ourselves involves the testimony of others. (Was I really the sort of teenager who provoked a teacher until she wept?) We are not sole authorities on ourselves, our actions, and our attitudes. Our judgments about what we perceive and remember, who we are, and what we are doing are open to correction by others. Consider, for instance, a man who thinks he loves his son and daughter equally. His daughter begins to accuse him of favouring the son, citing various examples of his past behaviour towards them. He at first rejects her ideas, but, becoming less secure about his attitudes, he asks his wife, son, and parents for their impressions. They might agree with the daughter, adding various examples of his past behaviour. If this happens, he should probably change his mind, for he is not the only observer and interpreter of his own actions and feelings. Responsible beliefs about ourselves have to take into account what other people say about us. Other people are not authorities – but what they say counts.

Many ordinary beliefs are based in part on results of investigations by various researchers and experts, and these too presume acceptance of what we have been told. Genes, electrons, viruses, the immune system, the ozone layer – even oxygen and the revolution of the earth around the sun – are ideas we understand only because we have been taught or have read about knowledge accumulated by others, in some cases generations of scientists or scholars building upon each other's work. Our constructed view of the world depends on many other people, and we can discover what these other people have experienced and what they judge to be the case only because we generally believe their testimony. In daily life and even in research we accept countless claims on the testimony or authority of other people.

This trust in other people is so basic, in fact, that it is a condition of our having any experience at all. We need trust to observe and remember events in the world and to maintain knowledge of ourselves. Such trust can be argued to be *a priori* because there is a sense in which it is logically prior to experience itself. It is prior because it is a *condition* of experience: without trust in others, without assuming that they are competent observers of the world from whom we can learn, we could not even have experience. Human beings may think individually as well as in dialogue, but we seek to confirm our thoughts, our words and reasonings about the world, together with other people. To do so we must listen to each other and, when appropriate, believe each other. To be able to do so, we must learn from each other. Knowledge comes from speech and sharing.

Niklas Luhmann argues that trust is a device for reducing the inevitable complexity in life. When we trust, we disregard a whole range of possibilities. Luhmann sees intersubjective agreement in the definition of *truth* as one of the main devices for simplifying the world. Rather than taking into account every actual and possible account of objects, people, and events, we posit and define a "truth" that everyone can agree on. We place our trust in that intersubjective account, thereby presuming honesty, competence, and reliability on the part of the people and social institutions who define it. Truth presumes trust.[11]

A person who seeks to ignore intersubjective beliefs and standards will stand isolated from the life of others and the knowledge and practices of the community. Acknowledging and accepting intersubjective truth means relying on the processing of information done by other people. Some will be strangers to us, yet we have to rely on them when we stand within public systems of knowledge and belief. Systems and institutions provide knowledge and authority; people collaborate and must trust each other to define truth. The statements we take to be true have been "worked on and worked out" by people who use a common language and methodology. Luhmann argues that it is this collaborative practice, not some metaphysical absolute, that gives us truth. To define truth together, we have to have confidence in each other.

JUSTIFYING OUR RELIANCE ON TESTIMONY

How can we justify our extensive reliance on other people for knowledge? There are two levels of questions about justification. First, there is the general question of what justifies us in *any* reliance on other people's testimony. What, if anything, makes it appropriate ever simply to accept what other people tell us as true, as a basis for our own knowledge or for reliable beliefs? Why should any testimonial claims be accepted? Second, there are more specific questions about the distinction between reliable and unreliable testimony. Granted that we are justified in accepting some testimonial claims, what distinguishes justifiable from unjustifiable reliance on testimony? What about conflicting testimonial claims? Testimony from people who seem to be biased? Testimony that conflicts with things we already believe? Written testimony from centuries past, of unknown authorship? These particular questions about distinguishing justifiable from unjustifiable reliance on testimony are fascinating and important. But the general question of what justifies our reliance on testimony is more fundamental. If there were no justifiable general reliance on testimony, then questions about particular cases could not arise.

In effect, the answer to this general question has been given. There is no real alternative to trusting other people for the truth. We are justified in believing other people at least some of the time because, without this trust and acceptance, we could not develop as human beings or experience reality. Intellectual autonomy must be understood as a matter of judiciously combining our own experience and knowledge with careful reflection on the testimony of others.

We might think that reliance on testimony could be justified by an appeal to our successful reliance on it in the past – by inductive logic. Consider: "I have been told many things and I have checked out many of these things for myself. In most cases I find that what I have been told is true; there is a general correlation between what other people tell me and the truth. Thus I have inductive reasons for believing other people, based on what I have discovered by my processes of investigation in the past." But this kind of argument will not work. In logical terms, it begs the question. The problem is that even a single person's experience presupposes reliance on testimony, and thus one cannot through experience validate the general reliability of testimony. As previous examples have shown, one cannot check out some testimonial claims without relying on others. One's acceptance of testimony is too basic in life to be validated by induction.

If we move from the individual case and try to speak of "our" being able to establish by inductive investigation that testimonial claims are reliable, the problem is not resolved because the question is still begged. To speak of *human* observation and experience is to presuppose that the observations and experiences of individual human beings are pooled, that there is a product or result based on a consensus of accumulated reports. But this cannot *justify* relying on testimony because it again *presupposes* relying on testimony. If one says, for example, that human experience teaches that sexual lust is a poor basis for enduring love, one is saying that most people who have the relevant experience have found lust to be a poor basis for enduring love. A perfectly sensible remark, this, but it presumes that people have been able to share their feelings and beliefs about the matter, which in turn presumes that they have generally accepted each other's testimony. Inductive appeals to human experience in an attempt to justify our reliance on testimony beg the question because they must assume what they attempt to demonstrate. Acceptance of testimony is simply too basic to be justified by induction.

In a complex critique of inductive attempts to justify our reliance on testimony, Coady shows that a major problem with such attempts is that they assume the possibility of our having language, perception, and memory even in the event that people's claims should turn out to be largely incorrect. If testimonial claims are to be checked against other claims about the world, these two sorts of claims must be logically independent of each other and separable into two sets. It must be one issue *what people say* and a quite distinct issue *what is true*. But the crucial problem for this approach is that these issues are intertwined, not separate. It is impossible that we should have a language including such words as "orange," "rectangle," "chair," or "sad" in which people usually told either lies or falsehoods when they used those words. In such a circumstance the words would not be used in a sufficiently reliable way to have any established meaning, which is to say that they would not be words of the language. To a considerable extent, intersubjective agreement *constitutes* the correctness of these judgments. To distinguish between what we accurately observe or remember and what we only seem to observe or remember, we fall back on what others tell us, which means that we must be willing, at least in standard circumstances, to believe them when they tell us what they have observed or experienced. There is no way of distinguishing one set of claims that are "things told us by other people" from another set that are "things true of the external world now and in the past" and investigating the extent of overlap between the two sets. The claims cannot be put into two sets in the first place.

Another line of justification for accepting testimonial claims is based on our social practices of asking and telling. These practices presume that we can acquire knowledge from others, whom we believe when they respond to our questions. Because knowledge is communicable, we have social practices of *asking questions* and *telling answers*. Asking, people request knowledge, which can be communicated to them because they believe other people who answer their questions. Thus propositions come to be known because people are believed.[12]

– What time is it?
– Three o'clock.
– Oh good. I've got just enough time to get to the bank before the children come home from school.

If we ask another what time it is, we in effect regard the other as a source of knowledge. She tells us the time; we believe her; we then know the time. Thus the mundane activities of asking and telling presuppose that others are reliable sources of knowledge – that they can be trusted to tell us the truth. If we assume that mundane asking and telling are essential to a functioning society, then trusting others for the truth can be argued also to be essential on these grounds. Mundane asking and telling are taken for granted in Western societies. They permit the sharing of knowledge and beliefs, presuming that we can generally trust others to respond honestly and accurately to our mundane questions. A generalized trust in the word of others is in this sense a presumption of our way of life. In Western cultures we ask routine questions and expect and receive straight answers. We find doing so to be normal and convenient; we take for granted the fact that we can rely on other people in this way – to give us routine information when we need it and ask for it. In doing so, we trust each other to tell the truth.

A quite different argument for general trust in the word of others is based on our attitudes to ourselves as generally reliable observers and interpreters of the world. As individuals we generally presume that we can sense and feel and tell what we have experienced, that we can recall and interpret what we have undergone and communicate it in a moderately accurate way to others. We have to do this to function at all. Some self-trust is needed for stable thought. Trusting ourselves, we regard our experiences, beliefs, and judgments as having some intrinsic merit. In conversation and discussion with others we expect to be listened to and to have some influence on others. But discussion is a reciprocal matter. If we expect others to listen to us, we must expect also to listen to them. When we tell others what we have experienced and believe, we do so in the general expectation that they will believe us. If we did not have this expectation, there would be little point in talking. We regard ourselves as credible and reliable observers and actors in the world. To anticipate such credibility for ourselves and be unwilling to extend it to others would be unreasonable. Human beings have essentially the same capacities for perception, memory, speech, interpretation, and judgment. No one can reasonably assume that she and she alone is equipped to witness and interpret the world. There is no general truth, available to everyone, to the effect that "I am credible and others are not, because I am more truthful, accurate, and reliable than other people."

To assume basic credibility for oneself and deny it to others would be strictly impossible during early stages of language learning and cognitive development and unreasonable at later stages of life, indicating an unjustifiable bias towards oneself. We all know that our personal judgment is fallible and may sometimes be unreliable: we easily make mistakes when we are emotionally upset, tired, distracted, and so on. But normally we regard ourselves as reasonably sensible, accurate, and reliable, and we expect to be so regarded by others. For reasons of consistency, then, we should grant that basic credibility to other people.

H.H. Price puts the argument in ethical terms: "Am I treating my neighbor as an end in himself, in the way I wish him to treat me, if I very carefully examine his credentials before believing anything he says to me? Surely every person, just because he is a person, has at least a *prima facie* case to be believed when he makes a statement."[13]

In the absence of any special reason to the contrary, when another person tells us something, we should trust her enough to accept it, just as we would normally have confidence in our own observations and judgments. Taking another at her word is the automatic, normal thing to do – the default mechanism, we might say – and we deviate from this approach only in so far as we find a specific reason to do so. Speaking of the gentlemanly culture that enabled English scientists to trust each other's testimony about unusual events they had witnessed in their laboratories, Shapin refers to a kind of Golden Rule of testimony. If one was too demanding and sceptical of others, they could act the same way in return, questioning one's own testimony. It was obvious that critical questions had to be tempered by good manners.[14]

One might be inclined, as many philosophers have been, to suspect that beliefs founded upon testimony are especially unreliable. But this suspicion cannot be warranted because ultimately it assumes a false contrast. In an ultimate sense there is no genuine contrast to be drawn between beliefs founded upon testimony and other beliefs: every belief depends on testimony at some point.

STAGES AND LEVELS OF TRUST

As children and primary learners we typically must accept what we are told and follow along so that we become trained in social conventions and norms. At the earliest stages of learning we have what might be called an *innocent trust* in those who are guiding us. At this stage the question of their being mistaken, misguided, or malicious does not arise. We simply follow along, assuming so thoroughly that everything is all right that we never consider doubts; we could not even articulate doubt. This stage of innocent trust is one of pure naïve acceptance: we allow ourselves to be guided by all-knowing mentors, typically parents. Simple acceptance is, in effect, what Wittgenstein describes in *On Certainty*, where he emphasizes repeatedly how doubt, belief, and knowledge all presume a foundation of taking things for granted. In primitive and simple cases, when we acquire competence in language and learn basic facts and elementary skills, we simply accept what we are told – unreflectively, unjudgmentally: "I want to say: our learning has the form "that is a violet", "that is a table". Admittedly, the child might hear the word "violet" for the first time in the sentence "perhaps that is a violet", but then he could ask "what is a violet?" ... A doubt that doubted everything would not be a doubt."[15] If we had to doubt that our hands were hands, we would be too paralysed to doubt at all. At the earliest stage of human development and language learning there is no viable alternative to trusting and following other people. We believe people and, if things go well, we come to do and know what they do and know because they have taught us. We trust others innocently and implicitly; we stand in an attitude of uncritical dependence. There are contexts where this is perfectly appropriate because it is the only thing to do and because it is necessary in order to go on.

At later stages of life, trust in the word of the other is still the norm. But now our trust is no longer the innocent trust of the child. Trust and acceptance constitute a kind of default system, operative unless there is reason to pause and reflect. We will accept what another says unless there is some particular reason not to, as in a case when the claim made strikes us as implausible or the other person seems careless, confused, biased, or dishonest. If we believe that there are no buses on Sunday and someone says there are buses on Sunday, we will stop and think about the matter, not just believe him. There is reason for doubt: we thought we knew something different. If we are told that the price reduction on stereos ends today, by a salesman who will personally profit from our believing him, we should stop and think. Again, there is reason to doubt: this person has, after all, a vested interest in one's coming to believe that it really is the last day to get a bargain. There are countless cues that may alert us. The other person may seem biased, tired, pushy, overly emotional, dishonest, incoherent, unintelligent, manipulative; any of these factors provides reason not simply to believe him. When we have reason to suspect insincerity or inaccuracy, we may reject the claim or reserve judgment. Given a pertinent cue, some reason to question, we do not unhesitatingly believe.

Normal mature trust in the word of others is no longer the innocent trust of the child. As mature persons we will unhesitatingly believe others much of the time, not because we cannot countenance their error or bias, not because we are incapable of doubt, but because we have no special reason for scepticism. If, after pause and reflection, we nevertheless come to accept a claim made by another, our acceptance is still based on a kind of trust. We still acquire the belief from another person, and we remain to some extent dependent on what he says. But our trust in such a case is reflective, qualified, and carefully considered.

Thus we can distinguish three stages or degrees of trust in the word of others: innocent trust, implicit (default) trust, and reflective trust. Innocent trust is the simple acceptance of the child or novice. Implicit trust is the automatic trust granted when there is no indication that anything might be wrong, by a mature thinker capable of doubt and scepticism. Reflective trust is the residual belief in another person granted after consideration of his reliability. In innocent trust and implicit trust, knowledge or belief is transferred from another person to ourselves because we simply believe her, accepting what she says and trusting her for the truth. In reflective trust we consider carefully just how trustworthy the other person is. We use our own background knowledge and critical skills to evaluate what she says: we are fully aware that she could be wrong or could seek to mislead us. If we decide that she is honest and competent, then her telling us something gives us reason to believe it.

With reflective trust there are three strands for consideration: first, the saying, or "speech act"; second, competence; and third, sincerity. As to the matter of speech acts, when people talk or write, they are not always trying to tell others things in the sense of making assertions to communicate information. They may be joking, teasing, play-acting, babbling, or simply venting their feelings. In such cases they are not making assertions, and the issue of whether to believe them does not arise. The issue of competence varies, depending on what is claimed and how important it is to be accurate. If a person is called as an eyewitness to testify in court, the issue of competence is basically that of perceptual ability, memory, and an absence of confusion. We generally assume that people are capable of seeing, hearing, and remembering, but in some contexts these things cannot be taken for granted and have to be established. Contexts where expertise is more technical and specialized, such as economics and medicine, raise more complex questions of competence. To be a competent expert requires human sensitivity, common sense, the ability to make accurate observations, and flexibility of mind – in addition to theoretical training, recognition by peers, and experience.

In reflective evaluation of testimony the issue of trust is most clearly apparent when we come to the matter of sincerity and truthfulness. A person's word will be useless if he is untruthful. Only if he believes what he says can his assertions be a reliable guide to reality. Trust in the speaker's honesty or sincerity is the confident expectation he will not attempt to deceive, that he is saying what he really thinks, attempting to inform and not to mislead or manipulate.

Given that we judge a speaker to be competent and sincere and to be making an assertion, we will believe him or her unless we have countervailing reasons not to believe. In such cases we do not trust without question, but in the end we still trust. Without trust we would not believe the person; we would not judge that his or her belief gives *us* reason to believe. In such a case our trust is qualified and reflective. It is not unhesitatingly assumed. But it is still trust. Another person's belief becomes part of our reason to believe.

From another person we gain vicarious access to the world; we can acquire beliefs or knowledge based on experience we do not have ourselves. Reflective trust is likely to be qualified, partial, and context-dependent. By no means is it uncritical. But it is still trust.

EXPERTS AND COUNTER-EXPERTS

To acquire knowledge from experts, we must believe what they say, and to do this we must trust them. It is not enough to assume the theoretical competence of an expert: we must trust him or her to be a person of integrity, with good judgment. The trustworthy expert must have enough self-consciousness to be aware of the limits of her expertise and must resist the temptation to make confident pronouncements about matters on which she does not have secure knowledge. She must be honest and uncorrupted, unwilling to manipulate parties made vulnerable by their relative ignorance. A trustworthy expert cannot be "bought"; she serves the interests of knowledge itself, or the public good, and not a particular corporate or political cause. Notoriously, many so-called experts are not trustworthy in these ways.

For experts' claims to provide knowledge they must be consistent with each other. Psychiatrists are, in a sense, experts, and testify as such in courts of law. Yet there is considerable scepticism and mistrust about their findings and their testimony. Not only are such experts often paid by one or another party to a legal dispute: their testimony is usually favourable to the side paying them, so that even the pretence of disinterestedness is dropped. And such experts frequently disagree; even the most trusting listener could not possibly believe all of them because there are simply too many inconsistencies. The task of sorting out inconsistencies and deciding whom, if anyone, to believe, falls on the audience – in a court context, primarily on the judge and jury.

Nor are such situations of disagreement restricted to courts. The problem of determining whom to believe when supposed experts disagree confronts us in many contexts, from everyday matters such as nutrition and health to policy issues and theoretical research. To legitimately acquire knowledge from an expert, we need knowledge and careful reflection. We must know when an issue is one that requires expert knowledge, where that expertise should be sought, whether experts in that area agree with each other, and which experts are reputable and honest.

But ideal circumstances, in which all relevant experts agree and all are reputable, honest, and without vested interest, are rare. Experts are often not disinterested, and they frequently disagree with each other. Furthermore, for some issues it is not clear what the relevant area of expertise is. Suppose, for instance, that a political leader in the 1970s had wanted to know what would deter Iran from attacking Iraq. Should he consult a military person? A civilian strategic analyst? A regional expert about Iran and Iraq? A historian specializing in Iranian history? A political psychologist? He might try to consult experts from various disciplines and try to synthesize their responses. If he were lucky, the responses would be consistent and point in one policy direction, but there is no guarantee of that.

Clearly, thinking for oneself and resorting to experts are not incompatible. Often, resorting to experts requires considerable thought and analysis. Intellectual autonomy in such cases means being sensitive to the sort of question we are asking, the kinds of expertise that might be relevant to it, the possibility of disagreement among relevant experts, and the status, integrity, and competence of the experts we appeal to. Trusting experts in this sense is not a matter of blind trust and passive acceptance. It requires careful thought.

Hardwig, who has so vividly described our dependence on the knowledge of experts and has also emphasized the role of trust in this dependence, warns that if we were unable to trust experts, we would be unable to use the most carefully accumulated knowledge our culture has to offer. Suppose, for instance, we concluded after study that strategic analysts cannot provide a source of reliable knowledge on military policy and strategy. If this were the case, we would then find ourselves with no reliable source of knowledge on those topics. These are people our society has designated experts on such matters; if they do not have this knowledge, then (apparently) no one does. Sometimes expertise goes awry. If we cannot trust society's designated experts, we are left without reliable sources of answers to our questions.

There are significant cases where we should not trust society's identified experts and their answers. The consequence, obviously, is scepticism. Knowledge requires trust; without trust, there is no knowledge. We must admit to not knowing and do without reliable knowledge. In the longer term, for important questions, alternative expertise will have to be developed.

While the need to depend on experts cannot be denied, nor can misuses of expertise in contemporary culture. Knowledge yields power, which can all too easily be abused. By deferring too readily to experts, we can unwittingly lend ourselves to co-optation. And yet it is not possible to investigate thoroughly every matter on which we need to hold reasonable beliefs. If we become sceptical about some particular area – say, psychiatry or strategic studies – we can try to form our own views in that area and accumulate theories and facts from a wide variety of sources. But life is finite; this approach is workable only for a small range of cases. Furthermore, in our individual efforts to know we are not relieved of dependence on other people, at least some of whom will have been trained in institutions and contexts that in some sense "serve the interests of power."

The dilemma is perplexing, if not intractable. One approach is to ask why, and in what respects, we have deemed untrustworthy those who have been given the status of experts. Is it because they function sometimes to serve vested interests? Because they have a bad track record and have been wrong on significant matters in the past? Because they have unwittingly described a biased sample – as in cases where only men have been studied in tests of drugs and other medical research, and the results of those studies then rather cavalierly applied to women? Because they disagree so significantly among themselves? Because they never disagree, even in the face of value dilemmas and considerable complexity? Or because their very assumptions are open to question?

The most radical distrust of an area of expertise comes when we reject its constituent assumptions and role. We may have good reasons for doing this, even without being experts ourselves. American strategic studies during the Cold War period clearly existed to serve the interests of the military establishment and defence of the West against the Soviet Union. They were based on an adversarial conception of the relationship between the United States and the Soviet Union, an abstract and non-historical modelling of the Soviet "opponent" and a calculus of consequences in which nuclear use and nuclear war were assumed to be viable policy options. Some critics identified the assumptions of strategic science as implausible and concluded that the strategists were too strongly identified with state interests even to merit stature as intellectuals.[16] One response was to seek alternative disciplines, looking to history or psychology for the relevant expertise. Another, perhaps more suitable in this case, was to establish an alternative discipline ("peace studies," "conflict resolution") based on alternative assumptions and serving different interests.

To say that we must inevitably in some way or other depend on other people for our knowledge and beliefs is not to say that experts and existing disciplines are immune from criticism. Obviously – notoriously – they are not. To say that we must in general trust the testimony of others and that we must, for specialized knowledge, trust experts is not to say that we must believe every testimonial claim, or trust all experts.

A SOCIETY WITHOUT TRUST?

In a moving book entitled *The Mountain People* anthropologist Colin Turnbull describes the brutalized and tragic existence of an African tribe, the Ik. Many questions arise concerning this tribe. Of special significance for the issue of testimony is the fact that the Ik as Turnbull describes them had virtually no moral scruples about lying and deception. Does Turnbull's testimony about the Ik provide a counter-example to the claim that human beings living together have to trust each other to tell the truth?

The Ik had been a hunter-gatherer people living in a mountain area. When much of their territory was made into a national park, they were moved some distance from it and fell into a condition of despair and semi-starvation. In their original location the Ik had a workable culture and shared religious and ethical beliefs. They co-operated in hunting and sharing food. To overhunt was considered a major crime, a sin against the divine command. Women gathered vegetables, which were a major source of nourishment for the group. The Ik had lived in small social groups that typically included several biological families. They identified strongly with their mountain homeland, seeing their mountains and their tribe as inextricably bound together.

Turnbull comments that most hunter-gatherer peoples have cultures with simple formal structures but featuring a high degree of co-operativeness. They are typically kind, generous, considerate, affectionate, honest, hospitable, and charitable; they need these qualities in order to survive. And African peoples generally are renowned for their affection and strong family bonds. Expecting to find such qualities among the Ik, Turnbull was intensely disappointed. They lived in an alienated and isolated condition where each person was solely out for his own good. There was virtually no co-operation, nurturance, or care for the young, the old, or the sickly. There was apparently little or no trust between members of the group. In their despair and deprivation, the Ik were neither hunters nor farmers. The people lived in loose groups exhibiting almost no social cohesion, and they were unfriendly, uncharitable, inhospitable, and generally "as mean as any people can be."

Turnbull came to understand this phase of Ik culture as one in which people were categorically and brutally individualistic, placing individual survival above all other values to a truly astonishing degree. Children were turned out by their parents at the age of three. Even at younger ages they were not loved or appreciated by their parents, and were cared for only grudgingly. In one case an Ik mother saw her infant carried off by a leopard. She appeared amused and delighted to be rid of the burdensome child, and later joined happily in a feast where the leopard (presumably with her baby inside him) was consumed. Old people were not cared for by their children. The suffering of the aged, even in cases where they literally collapsed from hunger, was a source of amusement to others. Old people were supposed to look after themselves.

Among the Ik the good of the self was paramount, and it was understood in very primitive terms. There was one common value: food. In the discourse of the Ik at this time, a good person was one with a full stomach. There was no room for such niceties as family bonds, friendly sentiment, or love. People were too close to starvation, and competition was too extreme. Food was typically consumed alone. If one obtained something to eat, he would try to hide it and take it far away from the others so as to avoid any need to share.

Turnbull lived among the Ik for many months. He learned some of their language, beginning with a basic vocabulary of four hundred words and elements of grammar he had established with the help of two Icien mission boys, Peter and Thomas.

The tragic tale of the Ik is important and provocative in many ways. Of special interest here is the apparent absence of norms of truthfulness in Icien society. The Ik had a reputation among neighbouring peoples for being troublesome, elusive, tricky, and dishonest. They positively delighted in not telling the truth. Deception about directions, names, locations of settlements, the safety of mountain paths, and key events such as deaths was practically routine. The Ik seemed to take deception and lying as normal, and found it amusing when others were naïve enough to believe them. Some of the lies described in Turnbull's book were motivated by self-interest – ultimately by pursuit of more food for oneself – but others seem to have been motivated by malice or mischief or to have sprung purely from habit.

When he arrived near the site of his study, Turnbull had read and heard that the name of the Ik tribe was the Teuso. Eventually Peter and Thomas told him otherwise:

After a week they confided in me that Teuso was not their proper tribal name at all ... Their real name was Ik (pronounced as Eek), and the language was

Icietot (Eechietoht). I had begun to suspect that Teuso was not their real name, but to my direct questions they had always answered that it was, until they decided to say the opposite. I found out that most Ik share this habit. It is a kind of a game, to see how effectively you can lie and fool someone. Then when you have proven your ability you have the additional fun of telling your victim. Many a time I was to hear them say, "You don't really believe what we told you, do you?"[17]

Here Turnbull acknowledges that eventually – even in this group – people tell each other the truth, and one does come to know. But the frequent evasions, lies, tricks, and cruel jokes along the way make the process exasperating and inefficient.

On another occasion Atum, who had been Turnbull's confidant and guide, told repeatedly of his wife's illness, obtaining food and medicine from Turnbull as a result. Turnbull eventually discovered that at this point Atum's wife had already been dead for several weeks. Atum had been selling the medicine. Such deceptions can happen in any culture, but what was striking in the case of the Ik was that they were regarded as nothing to be ashamed of. Atum did not seem to think this deception should have any effect on his subsequent relationship with Turnbull. Lying was common, useful, just as easy as telling the truth, and a good source of amusement if people were foolish and gullible enough to believe.

Clearly, among the Ik, a person would not simply ask a straight question and expect a straight answer. Truthfulness and honesty were not respected, and trust among the Ik seems to have been minimal or non-existent – even in contexts of mundane questioning and answering. The question then arises: does the existence of such a group provide evidence that human beings need not depend on each other's testimony? Does it show that truthfulness and basic confidence in the word of others are not necessary elements of a functioning human society?

On reflection, the answer seems to be no. The story of the Ik does not show that societies and human beings can function without testimony. For one thing, the Ik as Turnbull knew them had emerged from a stronger and more cohesive culture where there were traditions, ethical norms, and effective co-operation, where people lived in families, had friends, and tended their children and old people. What Turnbull saw was not a full-fledged culture or even a functioning society. It was the tattered remnants of what had been a culture and society. In addition, even among the Ik as Turnbull knew them there was enough truth-telling left for minimal functioning. Peter and Thomas, who lied repeatedly and enjoyed doing it, nevertheless taught Turnbull four hundred words and the basic grammar of their language. So Turnbull was able to learn this from them. And he used this core of the language quite effectively with other Ik.

To teach these elements of their language, Peter and Thomas must have been honest and competent at least with regard to simple vocabulary and usage, and Turnbull had to trust them to be so. Those with whom Turnbull used the language must have been straightforward in their usage at least some of the time. In effect, they called a bag of sugar a bag of sugar, and a hut a hut. Apparently the neglected Ik children also somehow learned their language and some basic activities, presumably from their rather uncaring parents and from each other.

Deceptions described by Turnbull include some in which he found out the truth after near-fatal encounters with reality, as when he nearly plummeted fifteen hundred feet down a cliff, off a dangerous path he had been tricked into taking. But some deceptions were revealed when people eventually told him the truth, or "confided in him." At some point, and somehow, these people who had been bent on joking, tricking, and deceiving him became *believable*; Turnbull was then able to learn from them. Often lies were corrected with reference to later testimony. Just what made people believable at these moments when they were congratulating themselves on having been deceptive before, Turnbull does not say. Perhaps it was that what they were then saying was plausible in its own right; perhaps it was the existence of corroborating testimony and evidence.

Many of the dimensions of knowledge and belief for which people in Western industrialized societies need to trust in the word of others do not seem to have existed among the Ik. As Turnbull describes them, the Ik did not have radio, television, books, newspapers, or courts of law. They had relatively few interactions with strangers; they did not attend classes or lectures by people they had never met. They had no tradition of scientific or historical expertise. There were some old people who could remember aspects of the older Icien culture, with legends, places, and customs that had a played a key role in their former way of life. These people might have played an expert role, as elders often do, had others sought and valued their knowledge. But from what Turnbull says, it appears such knowledge was seldom in demand. The elders were not respected story-tellers and purveyors of custom and tradition but laughable sickly objects soon to die a humiliating and unregretted death.

Though important in many ways, the tragic story of the Ik does not provide an example of a viable society in which people had no need to trust in the word of others. The surviving Ik scarcely formed a society at all, far less a viable one. Turnbull believed the Ik were beyond saving as a society. People found it hard to believe his descriptions of the tribe, for they had not directly encountered their way of life. "One had to live among them day in and day out watching them defecating on each other's doorsteps and taking food out of each other's mouths, and vomiting so as to finish what belonged to the starving, to begin to know what had happened to them," he writes. As described by Turnbull, the Ik scarcely had a society. Yet even they did not entirely escape the need to believe each other.

4 Trust, Professions, and Roles

Many people are uneasy about dependence on experts and professionals. Sensing professional power, intimidated by specialized knowledge, people feel vulnerable. Sexual abuse of women patients by doctors; malpractice suits; deceitfulness and fraud on the part of lawyers; corruption or vested interest on the part of scientists and professors; child molestation by teachers and clergy – all are ongoing stories in the press, making many people uncomfortable with the status and power of professionals. Those who cannot avoid relying on professionals often resent that dependence, complaining that the status and power of professionals exceeds what their competence and morality would warrant. Many ask whether professionals can be trusted to fulfil the crucial roles society has assigned to them. If possible, prospective clients should learn to investigate professional expertise and behaviour for themselves. In turn, professionals complain that clients are unwilling to trust them. As they see it, media publicity about unrepresentative cases has rendered the public unnecessarily suspicious.

ROLES AND PROFESSIONAL ROLES

In a theatrical production, a role is a part one plays. If a woman plays the role of Ophelia in *Hamlet*, she takes on the persona of a young and innocent woman, troubled, in love. She plays her character in a particular style, acting a part. She says her lines, expresses certain emotions, performs certain actions. The role imposes definite expectations, imposing limits but providing a range of opportunities.

A social role too brings with it particular expectations, limitations, and possibilities. Roles serve functions within a society. When we think of social roles, we tend often to think of occupations: the roles of doctor, lawyer, dentist, teacher, mechanic, bus driver, waiter, professor, cook, civil servant, or politician. When a person acts in the role of a dentist, for example, he presents himself as suitably competent and appropriately motivated. His demeanour and office decor will be designed to communicate that effect, to project an image through speech, dress, title, and mannerisms. He is expected to have specialized knowledge and technical competence, a professional demeanour, and a concern for dental health and appearance. Role-playing in this sense is a fact of social life. To know someone as a dentist is something short of knowing him as a person. Seated in the dentist's chair, we may encounter him many times, even converse in a limited and uncomfortable way, yet have only a limited sense of his style and personality outside this role. He is playing a role: being the dentist.

Although professional roles may seem scripted and restricted, variations in personal style and attitude mean that different people fill them in different ways. Professional roles make high demands in terms of competence, energy, and commitment to others. But no more than any other role should they fully consume the energy of the person filling them. To know someone as a teacher, waiter, or mechanic is something quite different from knowing her as a neighbour, parent, friend, or citizen. In modern societies people fill many occupations and social roles: parent, neighbour, citizen, and friend; dentist, doctor, engineer, teacher, nurse, journalist, mechanic, waiter. Most people fill several roles at once.

A person in a particular social or occupational role is not quite the person as such. Although people in roles are not necessarily inauthentic, neither are they always able to act according to their own autonomous judgment or individual wishes. Social and occupational roles carry with them expectations and demands, ranging from the general and open-ended expectations of "friend" to the specific requirements of judge or counsellor. Roles imply various rights and duties. A dentist, for instance, has the right to prescribe antibiotic medication for infections in the mouth – something teachers, engineers, and parents cannot do – and the duty not to overcharge his patients or give them misleading information about their dental health.

Professional roles are occupational roles with special characteristics. In modern parlance, professional status presumes that occupational skills are based on the possession of well-grounded theoretical knowledge that has practical implications of central social importance. In addition to law and medicine, science, pharmacy, dentistry, and engineering clearly qualify as professions according to standard contemporary accounts.

A professional occupation is grounded on systematized knowledge that has a strong theoretical basis and a specialized character accessible only to those who have the ability and discipline to acquire it. Professional knowledge is typically not possessed by people outside the profession. A professional is one who "professes" the ability and intention to help others, promising in effect to help those who need it. Because professional knowledge has significant social applications, it gives its possessor special power. The professional can do socially significant and necessary things that others cannot do. Lay people need a professional's knowledge and standing in order to accomplish various things, sometimes even in order to survive, and they depend on the professional to communicate that knowledge accurately and honestly and to use it appropriately on their behalf.

Bernard Barber cites three features essential to being a professional. These are the possession of *powerful knowledge*; considerable *autonomy* in regulation; and a high level of *responsibility* to serve the interests of clients and the general public.[1] This responsibility, often called "fiduciary," is most obviously related to the theme of trust. If certain people are provided with powerful and socially useful knowledge that few others have, and given broad powers to regulate themselves, then they must not use their special position to serve their own interests. If they do so, the interests of other individuals and of society are jeopardized, and under such circumstances it would be hard to justify providing the social resources necessary to train and maintain these professionals.

Over the long run the interests of a profession lie in good service to its clients and the public. Experts and expert knowledge are sustained because society needs and respects them. Those who have acquired such knowledge must define their social function and role as one of serving society and its members. A doctor has powerful knowledge and singular technical skills; he is expected to use these to keep people healthy and (where possible) cure them of diseases – not to line his pockets, enjoy illusions of power, boost his self-esteem, or find sexual playmates. People in professions are entrusted by society with special knowledge that gives them special power, which, like any other power, implies some potential for abuse. Because professionals and experts have special knowledge and status needed by others, people have to trust them to use their knowledge and power properly, in the interests of their clients or the public at large.

Professional status is a matter of degree. The most powerful professions, which Barber deems to be medicine and law, are grounded on theoretical knowledge that has clear applications in the natural and social worlds. Barber regards such occupations as nursing, teaching, journalism, and social work as semi-professional. In these areas the qualifications of practitioners are somewhat variable, knowledge is less general and systematic, and central theories and claims more subject to dispute.

Professionals have considerable autonomy. They tend, by and large, to set credentials for admission into the profession and to be self-regulating. Doctors, for instance, gain their qualifications from medical schools staffed by other doctors, and doctors by and large regulate themselves. To a considerable extent the same has been true of lawyers, judges, scientists, engineers, and professors. Self-regulation is changing in character, with growing recognition of the role of lay persons and outside specialists in regulatory institutions. Reasons for these shifts include the need to avoid the pursuit of vested interests; the tendency of professionals to rally together against outside critics; abuses of power; and a growing suspicion that specialized professionals may have a narrow perspective. Autonomy in regulation has been a natural by-product of the specialized knowledge professionals possess. The assumption used to be that lay people, lacking this specialized knowledge and the experience that knowledge makes possible, were not equipped to participate in regulating bodies. But this traditional assumption is coming into question.

Professionals are highly placed persons within societies dependent on specialized knowledge. Typically, they have high socio-economic status.[2] Their standing awards them respect from the public at large, and special rights and duties. A professional has a duty to be responsive to people seeking information or assistance and to assume responsibility for serving them. If a lawyer accepts someone as her client, she has a duty to seek to protect the legal interests of that person; if a doctor accepts someone as her patient, she thereby also acquires the duty to seek to protect and improve that person's health. Scientists have a role-based obligation to search for empirical or theoretical truths using rigorous methods, and to communicate their knowledge accurately to others in their profession. Professionals also accept responsibility for maintaining their profession. Professors, for instance, assume the responsibility of maintaining standards in professional journals, for which they evaluate and edit submissions – an often laborious task for which they are not paid.

In a number of occupations with only slight theoretical knowledge, the claim to be "professional" is put forward with great seriousness.

Realtors, funeral directors, upholstery cleaners, and insurance sales-men, for example, often claim to be professional. They claim special-ized knowledge. And to some extent they even possess it, though the knowledge is not especially deep or profound. But however sincere, such claims of professionality are fairly transparent attempts to enhance the social standing of an occupation and its members. The label "professional" carries status, implying a high socio-economic position, systematic knowledge, and personal power. Many occupa-tional groups would like to claim these benefits. But to say that vir-tually any occupation is professional is to rob the term of any clear and useful meaning. "When everybody's somebody, nobody's any-body," and if every occupation is deemed professional, the claim to be professional will cease to be significant.

THE NEED TO TRUST PROFESSIONALS

A professional has specialized knowledge that equips him or her with special abilities and powers to act. This knowledge is pertinent to other people who do not possess it but nevertheless may need it – sometimes desperately. There are many circumstances in which lay people cannot act safely, or cannot act at all, without the help of a pro-fessional. If a person has a heart attack, she depends on doctors to tell her what to do to regain good health – whether she needs more exer-cise, less exercise, a special diet, medication, bypass surgery, or some combination of these. And she depends on doctors again to make the right prescriptions, or to perform surgery competently. Similarly, people depend on lawyers – often in circumstances of heartbreak or emergency, such as death or divorce. Lawyers advise their clients how to remain within the law and protect themselves against risks of suit or prosecution. We depend on engineers to design safe roads, bridges, nuclear reactors, factories, and buildings; on computer sci-entists to design reliable machines competent to perform vastly com-plex and important tasks rapidly. In such contexts, serious issues of personal and public safety are involved.

Given our needs and wants, we who do not have specialized knowledge and training in these areas typically have no option but to rely on others. We want something done and we have neither the knowledge nor the power to do it ourselves, so we must depend on someone else to do it for us. We must assume that the professionally qualified person has the competence to do what is needed and the integrity and motivation to act on behalf of the client. We are vulner-able; we submit to another's judgment and technique; we know there is a risk; and yet we go ahead. In short, we trust.

In submitting her projects, interests, and needs to a professional in this way, a person is vulnerable. Her interests, sometimes her very life, hang in the balance, and she has to depend on another to act on her behalf. Yet she does not have the specialized knowledge she needs to judge whether the other person knows what he is doing. The client clearly has to trust the professional, both to be a competent practitioner and to be a conscientious human being. She must regard the professional as a properly qualified practitioner operating within a profession that is knowledgeable and well-regulated. To feel secure, the client must trust both the profession itself and the individual practitioner who is one member of it. At both levels, competence and integrity are factors of equal importance.

Consider, for instance, the matter of going to a dentist. When we do so, we are vulnerable. Most of us even feel vulnerable. We have to presume that dentistry is a knowledgeable, honest, and well-regulated profession and that the particular individual we have selected to be our dentist is a trustworthy member of it. We trust that he has the professional qualities of theoretical knowledge, appropriate credentials, and technical skill and is a person of moral integrity.

Lack of confidence in any of these areas would make going to the dentist downright frightening. And there would be more than pain and discomfort to worry about. If we thought that the profession as a whole was based on quackery or corruptly regulated, we would approach a dentist only in the most dire emergency, or perhaps not at all. The trust we have in a given profession affects our attitudes to its practitioners, but only within limits. If we believed that our dentist was personally corrupt or incompetent, confidence in the profession in general would not outweigh lack of confidence in him as an individual. After all, it is he, not the profession as a whole, who is going to probe and drill in our mouth.

We need professionals and are vulnerable to their power; hence we need to trust them. Often we do. The relatively high status of some professions, such as medicine, dentistry, the judiciary, and science gives many people an initial disposition to trust their members. Typically, such professionals present themselves as trustworthy people: they have clean, attractive offices, with well-spoken, genteel, and apparently competent staff; they display relevant credentials, dress in an upper-middle-class manner, speak in even, reasonable tones, and generally give the impression of being socially responsible, concerned for clients and prospective clients, sensitive to social interests, and possessed of knowledge and integrity. Even in periods when there has been extensive media publicity about dishonesty or outright abuse, professional standing still tends to carry a certain initial credit. Most of us still take it for granted that we can generally trust most doctors, judges, scientists, professors, and lawyers – even those who are total strangers – because they have been duly certified. We assume that such professions have reasonable norms that will be respected by practitioners. The professionals' social standing, credentials, and self-presentation establish a presumption that this is the case. Credibility based on professional role typically is established before there is any direct contact between professional and client. Without this initial trust, prospective clients would not approach professionals in the first place.

When the professional meets the client, he must act so as not to upset these expectations. At this point the personal style, character, ability, and self-presentation of the professional as an individual become significant. To be reliable, the professional needs appropriate knowledge and skills, sensitivity to the client, competence, a capacity for organization, and a personal style and demeanour that connote these qualities to clients.

In addition to finding a given professional reliable in the role, a client needs a sense of the professional as a trustworthy person. Even in specialized professional roles, moral qualities are essential for trustworthiness. In their absence, technical expertise and theoretical knowledge can be more disturbing than reassuring. A dentist who is highly skilled technically but wants to do an unnecessary root canal solely because he needs the extra income would be a fearsome being. Clearly the possession of credentials and trappings, and the ability to present oneself as a qualified, reliable, and consistent person capably filling a social role, do not guarantee trustworthiness. There is such a thing as a successful hoax, and the fact that people are often unwilling to confront those in high-status positions and roles directly makes it relatively easy for good actors to simulate professional status.[3] To trust the professional, we must believe that his self-presentation as a qualified expert is genuine. And this is just the beginning. The client, who is seeking compassion, care, and empathy, must judge the professional to be someone who can provide these. In one sense trust in the professional is assumed: people generally have overall confidence in the workings of the relevant institutions. In another sense, on the personal level, that trust must be earned.

In a recent essay on trusting professionals a writer refers to "the phenomenon of nakedness" in speaking of the vulnerability of the client. A patient or client must open her affairs to the professional, to whom she stands revealed and vulnerable. In the case of doctors, nakedness may be literal. The patient has a problem and must expose her body to the doctor in order to submit herself for treatment.

People facing criminal charges must reveal their deeds and circumstances to their lawyers if they want an effective defence. Those
seeking counselling from psychiatrists or therapists must reveal intimate aspects of their personal histories, sexual relationships, and
deep emotions to have a chance to be helped. In all these cases confi-
dentiality is tremendously important: the client must trust the professional not to divulge personal information to others. The professional should reveal such information only under extreme circumstances – as in a case where the client reveals that someone else's life
is in danger. If a man tells his psychiatrist about a dream in which he
undressed the mayor, he does not want the dream turning up in
tomorrow's newspaper or becoming a conversation piece at a dinner
party. If a middle-aged woman reveals her flabby abdomen to a doctor, she does not want to think that he will refer to her as a "fat cow"
when joking with his colleagues the next day. The "nakedness" that
is so often needed in relations with professionals requires confiden-
tiality and more: the sense that the professional is a reliable, competent person who will use professional expertise in our own interest
because he *cares*.

The circumstances in which one resorts to a professional tend to be
abnormal. Many are situations of crisis. A person is suddenly ill;
seeks a legal separation or divorce; is called into court as a witness;
needs scientific expertise on which to ground a legal case; has a child
who attempts suicide; is called upon to be executor of a disturbingly
untidy estate. In such cases we do not find ourselves in normal circumstances where the mundane assumptions of ordinary life can
unthinkingly be granted. The implicit trust we may place in a professional on the basis of qualifications and self-presentation is easily
disturbed. Should the professional express shock ("My God, I've
never heard of a case like this before"), seem callous and insensitive
("Go check on the terminal patient in room 32"), sexually arrogant
("Your breasts are too small"), or willing to exploit our problems for
his own interest ("This is an amazing skin condition; I'm going to
write a paper about it; hey, Fred, look at this!"), whatever initial trust
the client felt may vanish.[4]

DOING WITHOUT TRUST?

In an essay on trust and the professions Edmund Pellagrino argues
that any successful working relation between doctor and patient
must be founded on some degree of trust. A patient should, ideally,
trust medicine as a social institution embodying knowledge of health
and disease and a concern for the social good, and the individual

doctor as a qualified and caring practitioner within that profession. If trust fails in either quarter, relations are going to be uneasy and perilous for both doctor and patient.

Due to the impersonal, highly technological, and somewhat frantic character of medicine in modern North America, some commentators on medical practice avoid acknowledging any need for trust. With many specialists, huge hospitals, and patients who have considerable personal mobility, the friendly family doctor of years past is more the exception than the rule. Believing that a trusting personal relationship between doctor and patient is a thing of the past, some commentators on modern medicine have proposed strategies to avoid the need for trust between doctor and patient. These include living wills, ethics committees, contracts between doctors and patients, monitoring boards and agencies to scrutinize doctors' competence and procedures, the use of ombudsmen and other committees as intermediaries, and a strong emphasis on patient autonomy and informed consent.

While such approaches are largely unobjectionable and may serve important purposes, it is unrealistic to think that they eliminate the need for trust between doctors and patients. Living wills and contracts, for instance, cannot be worded so as to cover every detail or eventuality. Someone – in all likelihood a doctor – will have to interpret their import in particular cases. Also, we can feel protected by a contract only in so far as we are confident that the other party will live up to it. Far from avoiding the the need to trust doctors, the living will and other such contracts can work appropriately only if doctors are prepared to abide by them and to use good judgment in interpreting them.

Informed consent is similar. It is not an alternative to trust; based on information, it presupposes trust. Doctors have specialized knowledge about health, disease, and treatments, and patients do not. If patients are to make informed judgments so as to consent to various treatments and procedures, they have to acquire some of that knowledge, and they will acquire it from doctors. Pellagrino concludes that "trust cannot be eliminated from human relationships, least of all relationships with professionals." Relations between doctors and patients are typically characterized by urgency, intimacy, unavoidability, unpredictability, and extraordinary vulnerability. We may be able to reduce that vulnerability, but we are not going to eliminate it.

Trust between doctors and patients is typically neither complete nor easy, but it is needed if medical treatment is to go smoothly. To illustrate just why trust is so necessary in this professional context,

Pellagrino envisages the practice of medicine under an "ethos of distrust." If we were to conduct medicine assuming distrust between doctors and patients as the norm, we would assume that doctors are not committed either to the care of individual patients or to public health. Doctors, on this view, would practice medicine solely for their own good; they make a good living doing it and (perhaps) find it interesting. There would be no expectation that doctors and other medical staff should feel honest compassion for their patients and clients, or repress the impulse to pursue their own self-interest. Under an ethos of distrust, medical professionals would be careful not to make mistakes and maim or kill patients – but only because they sought to avoid loss of business, lawsuits, or inconvenient complaints. They would tend to limit themselves to the precise letter of various agreements and never "go that extra mile." Pellagrino argues that the resulting distrustful environment would discourage professional or personal virtue, leaving professionals and clients downhearted and suspicious. It would work against the disclosure of information and offer little assurance against deception and manipulation. The picture is not attractive. We cannot escape the need for trust between doctor and patient, and we deceive ourselves if we think we can do better without it.

In any relationship elements of distrust may develop. In relations between professionals and clients, where knowledge and power are unequal, vulnerability is great, and the situation is often one of crisis, there will likely be moments of doubt and distrust. These have to be acknowledged and confronted. But this is not to recommend a general ethos of distrust. Such an ethos implies that we can do without trust, and this is just not true. Trust is indispensable. Pretending that we can get along without it will not change that fact, and is likely to undermine the conditions in which it can be sustained.

Clearly, trust in doctors or other professionals is not going to be either global or absolute. On the contrary, it will typically be context-relative and partial. We should be able to trust professionals to act competently in realms where they have expertise, and not to use their expertise to exploit our vulnerability in their own interests. We should be able to trust them for accurate information providing for sensible decisions according to our own values. We want to trust them to carry out procedures in which they are skilled and which we cannot carry out ourselves. Without such trust doctor-patient relations would be fearful. For professions the alternative to an ethic of trust is "a minimalistic and legalistic ethic which is no ethic at all but merely a relationship of mutual self-defence."[5] With such an ethic professionals and clients will pursue their own interests while labouring under the false belief that they can protect themselves from all harm by rules, contracts, and personal control of every potential risk. This belief is a dangerous illusion.

An interesting example of an institution permeated by a baneful ethos of distrust is that of a western Canadian law school. A law-school context involves the intersection of two occupational roles, one commonly regarded as professional (lawyer), the other usually deemed semi-professional (teacher). Teaching is a nurturing role intended to foster the learning and growth of students, who in this case are expected to become professionals. The nurturing aspects of teaching are rendered somewhat problematic by the extremely competitive nature of the legal profession. Law is widely understood in adversarial terms. A good lawyer is sharp and quick and can fight and win battles in court. Although there are instances when lawyers work together on cases or engage in non-adversarial conflict resolution, the prevailing model of legal practice remains an adversarial one. Students attracted to law tend to arrive with or quickly acquire a "sharp" attitude and to pursue their own interests competitively at every turn. They want to get what they can from professors in the way of knowledge that will earn, tips about behaviour with clients and in court, and – most of all – grades.

Sensing aggressive competitiveness in many students and being thus disposed themselves, law professors may come to regard students as potential adversaries who will cut every corner and take every advantage. They may come to see themselves as needing protection from students, a stance contrary to that required in order to develop and nurture student competence and talent. Interactions between professors and students may take on an unhealthy dynamic wherein both display aggressive and hostile behaviour, all the while feeling miserably insecure. If law students possess advanced degrees in other subjects, professors may easily feel intimidated. Too insecure to allow students to use their knowledge as a common resource for the class, they may try to restrict the content of discussions and assignments, responding to insecurity by imposing rigid control in the classroom.

From the perspective of a law professor who is trying to get through the day without looking stupid, making a mistake, or giving a grade that results in an appeal, the sharp and competitive law student may seem a threatening being. "Watch it, they're out to get you," part-time instructors were advised at a meeting at one law school. Students might ask critical questions, revealing a professor's lack of knowledge or inability to be quick on his feet; they might connive to get higher grades than they deserved and make the professor look too soft. Thus professors sought to limit the content of debate so that they could be the experts, teaching students "how to draw the right conclusions" within "the right range" and avoiding areas of law where there is uncertainty.

To avoid cases in which students might launch awkward and time-consuming appeals about grades, course requirements at this law school were set out in tremendous detail, attempting to specify rules for every eventuality, stipulating even how grades calculated to decimal values would be rounded up or down. New professors and visiting instructors were advised to be "absolutely precise" and control students carefully. One might defend such an approach on the grounds that the adversarial and competitive nature of the legal profession demands it. But there is a vicious circle here. Students struggle against professors, whom they expect to be tough, narrow, and unhelpful. Professors struggle against students, whom they expect to be competitive, aggressive, and obnoxious. Each group makes the other worse. Once in effect, the ethos of distrust seems to be self-perpetuating, generating a need for itself.

As in medicine, people cannot really manage without trust in the teaching of law. Trusting the professor's *judgment* on many matters such as grading and curriculum is essential. Who else is going to set course material, compose lectures and exams, choose texts, and work through cases with the students? Because the role of professor, in law and elsewhere, demands good judgment, students, administrators, and the public at large must presume that professors can be trusted to make reasonable and responsible use of their professional knowledge and experience of students. A professed ethos of distrust is not really a viable basis for operating in a profession. An associate of the troubled Western Canadian law school said that the prevailing assumption was that "no one can be trusted to exercise judgment or discretion."

Hearing about this depressing atmosphere, we might ask whether faculty in this context at least trusted the support staff, on whom they depended for many routine matters such as delivery of messages, making appointments, scheduling meetings, and word-processing of letters, assignments, examinations, and research materials. The answer, apparently, is that in this case law faculty used staff services without much trust. Nor did support staff trust the faculty. Hierarchical lines between faculty, support staff, and students were rigid, with people at each level tending to treat those beneath them miserably. Support staff, viewed almost as servants by the professors, were seldom treated as social equals. Resenting the patronizing and domineering attitude of faculty, they tended to "work to rule" and take out their troubles on students, to whom they were often rude and unhelpful. In short, the ethos of distrust provided no atmosphere for openness, collegiality, critical thinking, creativity, or even just plain learning.

Such an atmosphere is not only inefficient and counter-productive; it is downright unpleasant. To think that people can do without trust in professional relationships is to misunderstand the need for judgment and decent human relationships in the transmission and application of professional knowledge. It is falsely to separate matters of character and morality from the human relationships that are at the center of professionality, and to ignore the practical implications of distrust between people who have to interact over a prolonged period of time. An ethos of distrust is counter-productive in professional institutions and relationships. It makes people and their projects worse than they could be.

Surprisingly, the claim that trust is essential in professional relationships has been denied by a recent writer on professional ethics. Robert Veatch argues that the very notion of trusting professionals is incoherent. Veatch maintains that professionals should *not* be trusted – not due to their fallibility, vested interests, or dishonesty but because the very assumption that professionals can, even in theory, be trusted is based on mistaken beliefs about client interests and professional knowledge.[6]

First, Veatch claims, it is impossible for professionals to know the *interests* of their clients. Increasingly, clients and professionals are virtual strangers. Their acquaintance is short. The professional with specialized knowledge is likely to have value commitments specific to his occupation. The interests of the client extend over many areas, not just those (health, finances, legal status, education, or whatever) that the professional knows and values. A doctor, for instance, knows about health, not other dimensions of life, so he cannot know his patient's interests when these include financial and educational matters. Since he does not even know what many of the patient's interests are, the notion that he is devoted to those interests makes little sense. It rests on a pre-condition that is not satisfied.

Second, the client is mistaken if she thinks she can trust the professional to give her advice that is *purely informative* and that she can then use to make her own decisions. There are no value-free facts, and thus no neutral information. If a doctor recommends chemotherapy to prolong the life of a cancer patient, or a lawyer recommends taking an ex-spouse to court to retrieve maintenance payments, these recommendations are not based on straight facts. Implicitly, they presuppose judgments about other values – most obviously those of time, money, and quality of life. When a professional selects possible strategies and procedures and explains them to his client, what he does always incorporates values as well as facts. He cannot give the client neutral information on which to base choices because, in these sorts of contexts, neutral information does not exist.

Third, Veatch argues, these difficulties about client interests and professional knowledge cannot be resolved by appealing to some idea of professional *virtues*. To think that each profession has attached to it some specific list of virtues is a mistake. If there were specific duties attached to each profession and the "virtuous" professional had to carry them out, those duties would have to be derived from a universal ethic. But, Veatch insists, no such universal ethic is available. There is no generic "law" and no generic lawyer to model virtues every other lawyer should emulate. There are feminist lawyers, libertarian lawyers, Buddhist lawyers, and so on, and there is no single set of rules specifying what a virtuous lawyer should do. The same argument will hold for other professions. Trust flounders not just because professionals may occasionally be corrupt or self-interested but rather because there are many different conceptions of professional virtue. A feminist doctor and a Catholic doctor may both have virtues – but they will be different ones.

However convincing all this may sound, Veatch seems to me to overstate his case. Though the professional will not know the *whole* of a client's interests, there are many reliable presumptions as to what is *against* a person's interests – being sexually seduced by someone exploiting his professional power, suffering unnecessary pain, dying a premature or avoidable death, giving birth to a stillborn baby, having friends and family injured or die, losing her home, being subject to prolonged anxiety, and so on. In trusting a professional, we expect him not work to against our basic interests *as defined by such presumptions*. And there are notorious abuses that demonstrate that even this minimal commitment to client interests, defined in the most uncontroversial terms, cannot always be taken for granted. To have a doctor who seriously understands that it is against the interests of his female patients to be assaulted or seduced and is going to act accordingly is something worthwhile. No amount of intellectualizing about the failure of professionals to know the subtleties of clients' interests can contradict this fundamental point.

As to Veatch's second point, the intermingling of fact and value in professional information and advice, a simple response is that many values that are implied in professional information will be shared by client and professional (enhancing health and wealth, minimizing pain, prolonging life, preserving quality of life, saving money, preserving family relationships) and can be taken for granted. If not, the professional can try conscientiously to make the client aware that these values are being assumed. In this respect Veatch's account seems to miss the forest for the trees. So far as the communication of information goes, clients are concerned that professionals "know what they are talking about" (that is, are not positively misinformed, according to canons of up-to-date knowledge in the profession) and are not deliberately deceiving their patients. Such basic competence and non-deceptiveness are not always present, as is illustrated by cases of error or abuse. A doctor forgets to take his patient's blood pressure, though it was dangerously high at her previous appointment. A lawyer does insufficient research and loses a key file. A therapist seduces his patient, telling her the relationship will help with her cure. Subtle philosophical considerations about the distinction between fact and value are interesting and may have practical importance in some cases. But they do not undermine the need to trust professionals to be up-to-date, non-deceptive, and non-exploitative when they are assisting or treating their clients. If we did not generally trust professionals in these respects, we would not consult them.

As for Veatch's claim that no profession comes ready-made with an uncontroversial list of attached virtues, this is true in a way. A Buddhist lawyer is likely to have different techniques, goals, and style from a libertarian lawyer, just as a Catholic doctor will not have the values of a feminist doctor. Yet anyone who is a lawyer must, as an aspect of her professional role, accept the function and responsibility of representing clients in legal conflicts and contexts and seeking to serve the interests of her clients in whatever way they deem appropriate. It is no doubt true, as Veatch argues, that there are no complete or universally accepted rules offering *complete* guidance on how to be a good doctor or lawyer, professor, scientist, engineer, or dentist. But far from showing that the notion of trusting a professional is incoherent, this variation only provides another indication of why trust in the individual professional is necessary. We need to rely on the *understanding* and *values* of this person. General knowledge and general rules cannot precisely and completely prescribe what to do in particular cases or indicate to a person how he or she is to perform as a conscientious and competent professional. The professional will have to exercise judgment in applying knowledge to cases, and the client has to trust the professional as a person because he is dependent on that judgment.

In concluding his essay, Veatch says that in so far as there is trust between professional and client it should be based on the presumption of *commitment* to the client. The professional should admit to the client that he cannot know client interests and cannot simply present to her value-free facts. The professional should openly acknowledge his or her background beliefs (libertarian, Catholic, feminist, or whatever). The client will then be better able to evaluate the professional's information because she will have a reasonably good sense of where it is "coming from." Oddly enough, at this point Veatch seems to allow just what his earlier arguments deny. To say that the professional may be presumed to have a commitment to the client is to say that he is not using the client's situation to pursue his, the professional's, own interests. The professional is seeking to serve the client. But that is just to say that so far as his motivation is concerned, the professional merits the client's trust. Often when clients worry about whether they trust professionals, it is just this commitment to client interests that concerns them. If he is competent and committed to the client, the professional deserves to be trusted.

So Veatch does not demonstrate that the very idea of clients trusting professionals is incoherent. In effect, he proposes an alternative understanding of how the professional may make a commitment to the client, may help the client while openly acknowledging her own limitations, and merit the client's trust.

WHY WE MAY DISTRUST PROFESSIONALS

In 1983 Benjamin Barber speculated about why trust in professionals was diminishing. He cited three factors: more power and professional knowledge; a public more competent and educated, capable of evaluating professional competence; and increasingly egalitarian values. In other words, professionals were gaining increasing power and knowledge while their clients, under the influence of egalitarian ideals and with increasing education and competence, wanted more autonomy in decision-making. In addition, Barber noted, the self-regulation that characterized most professions seemed to be working imperfectly. The French statesman Clemenceau once said that war is too important to be left to the generals. Similarly, Barber argued, medicine is too important to be left to the doctors, and law and science too important to be left to lawyers and scientists. The succeeding decade saw moves to include lay persons and other professionals as members of professional regulatory boards and agencies.

Barber's speculations about the sources of distrust in professionals may have been accurate for the 1970s, which was the object of his attention. Sadly, there are more extreme factors underlying present tendencies to distrust professionals. Sexual exploitation, greed, gross dishonesty, and callous disregard for client interests have been aspects of flawed relations between some doctors, lawyers, professors, clergy, psychiatrists, and their clients. In the course of managing a trust fund, one prominent lawyer in Calgary stole money from his own mother. Scientists offer conflicting testimony in court, apparently serving the interests of the highest bidder. Professors indulge their personal preferences and esoteric research interests when hiring colleagues to tenured positions to be funded by taxpayers for decades to come. And universities need to appoint grievance and sexual-harassment officers to protect students from faculty, and faculty from each other. Doctors are widely charged with arrogance, wanting to "play God," being impersonal, careless, callous, or over-specialized. These charges, often widely publicized, tarnish the image of the profession as a whole.

A recent film, *The Doctor*, offers a critical portrayal that expresses popular disenchantment with doctors. Jack McFee is a wealthy and powerful surgeon with a high-tech, high-pressure, impersonal, and callous way of relating to patients. His slogan for the practice of medicine is "get in, cut it out, get out." He and other doctors joke around during surgery and are insensitive to patients, whom they treat as hunks of meat. They function in a high-tech hospital where concern for patients is more the exception than the rule and bureaucracy is unrelenting. When Jake discovers that he has throat cancer and has to undergo radiation treatments and surgery, he discovers how medicine feels from a patient's point of view.

As portrayed in the early stages of this film, doctors are grossly untrustworthy. They are entirely willing to deceive patients. McFee does this himself almost as a matter of habit. While awaiting radiation treatment and discussing recovery prospects with June, a beautiful young woman with a terminal brain tumour, he cheerily tells her about a patient with the same illness who survived to become a grandfather. As June surmises almost immediately, this survivor is entirely fictional. Doctors are also depicted as untrustworthy in the way in which they cover up for each other's mistakes, even to the extent of lying in the course of a malpractice suit. They pursue technical competence, good statistics, and their own career advancement at the cost of honesty, integrity, and decent human relationships, and work within a bureaucratic structure that is insensitive to patient needs.

In the opening scenes of the film a group of bantering surgeons is shown operating on a man who has attempted suicide by jumping off the tenth flour of a building. They play raucous music in the operating room and joke around, treating the patient as an object of contempt. Jack McFee later brushes off the patient's appeal for sympathy, joking that if he wants to torture himself, he should try golf. Before his personal encounter with cancer McFee is the epitome of the technically adept but humanly incompetent surgeon. He tell his residence students not to care about patients. If they become emotionally involved, they will not be able to maintain the cool necessary to do technically tough things.

When McFee himself becomes ill, he is subjected to heartless bureaucracy, entailing multiple forms, waits, and delays of fundamental information; abrupt, unemotional, and uncaring treatment from a tough-minded woman doctor; mistakes in procedure (he is given an enema because the man who shares his room has a bowel problem); and general callousness. As a result he develops considerable sympathy for his patients and a gentler manner. He refuses to stand up for his partner in a malpractice suit and goes out of his way to help a troubled ex-patient who is fumbling for a key in the hospital parkade. He insists that his residents dress in humiliating hospital gowns and spend a few days as patients undergoing "routine" tests, to see how it feels. In coping with his illness, Jack is helped to some extent by his wife and other doctors but mostly by June, who has accepted her inevitable death.

The film reflects common complaints about North American medicine. Though severe in its depiction, it is optimistic when it comes to solutions. Jack McFee undergoes a personal transformation, but there is no hint of how more general changes in the attitudes of doctors and the callousness of hospital bureaucracy might come to pass. The solution is entirely individualistic; the system remains unaltered.

Doctors complain that patients are too quick to criticize and are overly litigious. But studies indicate that this is not the case. In one survey the National Association of Insurance Commissioners calculated that nearly 40 per cent of some 72,000 closed claims were cases of true negligence. Even in many cases where doctors themselves agreed that there had been negligence or incompetence, affected clients had not sued. Another study, of the Los Angeles area, estimated that only one-sixth of warranted cases were taken to court. Among eight thousand physicians, 0.6 per cent yielded 10 per cent of malpractice claims and 30 per cent of payments. The problem of incompetence and malpractice lay with a small set of visible physicians who were grossly untrustworthy.[7]

The pursuit of research goals without proper regard for the human subjects of research can also earn doctors a bad name, as in the case of the notorious Tuskegee study in which black men with syphilis went untreated so that a drug could be tested. There is often a conflict between the goal of technically competent performance in a high-tech culture and that of better human relations. Both technical competence and caring motivation are essential. But doctors may be caught in a dilemma if the pursuit of the first undermines the feasibility of the second.

Because medicine is so often a matter of life and death, its successes and failures are high profile. But medicine is not the only profession with trust problems. The legal profession certainly has its image problems, which lie partly in its being seen to serve mostly the interests of the affluent and the powerful, who can afford expensive lawyers. But problems go deeper. Some prominent lawyers have been found to abuse clients' deposits and trust funds and have been guilty of actual embezzlement. Some are suspected of hiding relevant information or lying on behalf of their clients, even in court. Lawyers are widely seen as too adversarial and competitive, of being committed to a win-lose approach that makes things worse for their clients in contexts such as divorce, and of increasing their own earnings and prolonging contests in ways harmful to the overall interests of their clients.

In addition, people suspect lawyers of colluding too much with their clients and of being willing to keep secret information crucial to public welfare, even in cases where their clients are involved in criminal activities. Lawyers must refrain not only from abusing their position to pursue their own self-interest but from deviating too far from public morality in pursuing the interests of their clients. As Sissela Bok has argued, morally basic constraints against violence, promise-breaking, deception, and excessive secrecy must be operative in any cohesive society. If lawyers and other professionals hold themselves above these fundamental moral principles, they do so at considerable cost to their own profession and the public at large.

Scientists are the creators and disseminators of the most highly generalized and powerful knowledge in our culture. They train students, moulding their ideas, values, and ideologies. They write textbooks for students at universities and referee textbooks for schools. And they help to maintain and advance knowledge for business and the practising professions. Through their research, teaching, writing, and public advisory roles scientists have a powerful effect on technology, culture, and public welfare. Scientists are paradigm examples of "experts," professionals whose knowledge and power affect everyone. It is important for the general public, which funds science and places its confidence in science in so many areas, to be convinced that scientists as a group have a general commitment to the public welfare.

In many ways it would appear that scientists still enjoy the public trust. We do not often hear of scientists breaking promises or sexually abusing students and research assistants. Although stories of fraud in science occasionally surface and receive media attention, science is nevertheless still regarded as the pinnacle of accurate and reliable knowledge. Research scientists and science professors – far more than philosophy professors, classicists, or literary critics – are regarded as experts *par excellence*. Yet there are problems. Scientists in different areas of specialization often disagree with one other when they approach the same practical problem. Within a specialty authorities may disagree and yet be willing to testify dogmatically in court or on behalf of commercial products to conclusions disputed by some of their colleagues. Such episodes tend to undermine public confidence in science.

The prevailing story about scientific research is that it is reliable because scientists are committed to a quest for truth and, in addition, check up on each other. When a scientific paper is submitted for publication it is carefully reviewed by peers. Ideally, scientific results from laboratories are checked by replication. However, these practices are insufficient to eliminate fraud, which some one-quarter to one-third of scientists believe they have witnessed at some time in their career.[8] It is difficult to establish oneself in a scientific career, and having publications helps a great deal. Scientific data may be esoteric and available to only a few people; reasoning is complex and may require highly specialized expertise. Funding to replicate experiments is often unavailable. Even professional referees for scientific journals may lack the depth of knowledge necessary to scrutinize a highly specialized submission thoroughly. The prevailing theory that traditional practices of peer review and laboratory replication mean scientists keep each other honest does not seem to be borne out by the facts.

There have been notorious cases of fraud in biomedical research; a recent account cites John Darsee, Robert Slutsky, John Long, Vijay Soman, William Summerlin, Mark Spector, Stephen Breuning, and Thereza Imanish-Kari. John Hardwig, who has written extensively about the need for scientists to trust colleagues, suggests that deterrents against fraud should be strengthened and supports the growing call for an ethics of scientific research. Because vast amounts of data are needed for some research and distinct areas of complex knowledge must be integrated in order to establish results, scientists are often completely dependent on each others' findings. Testimony is every bit as important in science as it is in everyday life. If there is significant undetected fraud in scientific publications, the flawed results seep through the system of science to make other results unreliable.

Cases of fraud that become public only highlight the fact that scientists have trusted and will continue to need to trust each other. Honesty, thoroughness, and conscientiousness are of central importance in the practice of science. Here as elsewhere, abuse and fraud do not show that trust is irrelevant or unnecessary, only that we must establish good grounds for it.

There is no way of conducting modern science without trust, so we must better deter and detect fraud and try to support an ethos of integrity. As Hardwig clearly explains:

Often, then, a scientific community has no alternative to trust, including trust in the character of its members. The modern pursuit of scientific knowledge is increasingly and unavoidably a very cooperative enterprise. Cooperation, not intellectual self-reliance, is the key virtue in any scientific community. But epistemic cooperation is possible only on the basis of reliance on the testimony of others: scientific propositions often must be accepted on the basis of evidence that only others have.

Institutional reforms of science may diminish but can not obviate the need for reliance upon the character of testifiers. *There are no "people-proof" institutions.* And even if it *were* possible to fully police scientific research, it would still be necessary to rely on the integrity of the newly created "science cops" and the reliability of *their* testimony.[9]

Every human institution is composed of people working in roles that intersect and are interdependent. The institution has policies and checks and balances. If necessary, special attention can be paid to possibilities of cheating, fraud, and dishonesty. But any implementation of policies in these areas will, in turn, depend on the competent and honest functioning of people who are checking. There is no way to eliminate our dependence on each other, and the need to trust.[10]

Barber argues that scientists' commitment to public welfare is suspect because they are too prone to assume that what *can* be done *must* be done. Even the hydrogen bomb was pursued partly because it was "technically sweet." Scientists often seem arrogant in their presumption of definitive knowledge and elitist in their unwillingness to submit professional plans and practices to the scrutiny of outsiders. Many move from their love of science to *scientism*, the belief that only pure mathematics and theoretical research science provide beliefs worth having. Arrogant about what their own subject and methods have to offer, dismissive of claims from non-scientific sources, insensitive to the fact that there are better and worse arguments on controversial topics, scientists may become oblivious of public concerns about funding and priorities or the social effects of their research and potential spin-off technology. Both engineers and scientists have been cavalier about hazards to the public in such areas as the development of nuclear energy.

Scientists and engineers also function as professors. The role of professor is one combining teaching and research, but the job security, promotion, and prestige of most professors depends more on publishing professional papers and books than on teaching and nurturing students. This inconsistency creates many tensions. Professors, especially those holding administrative positions or large grants, have considerable power over students and junior faculty, and that power can be abused.

An especially dramatic and tragic case occurred in the engineering faculty at Concordia University in Montreal, where Valery Fabrikant, an engineering professor who had repeatedly charged corruption in the administration, appears to have been driven mad with frustration. Fabrikant became so enraged by his colleagues that he embarked on a crazed rampage and killed four people on 24 August 1992. A prickly and difficult personality, Fabrikant had been embroiled in disputes with the engineering administration for years. On 30 April 1992 he sent electronic-mail messages to colleagues in computing science and engineering department across North America, charging that there had been financial fraud in contracts between Concordia and the Quebec government and that top members of the faculty were guilty of academic fraud and wanted to get rid of him because he could expose them.

A major charge was that the dean of engineering, Srikanta Swamy, and the former head of the mechanical engineering department, T.S. Sankar, had abused their power in order to have themselves listed as co-authors of academic papers to which they had not been genuine contributors. Graduate students and junior colleagues were compelled to list Swamy and Sankar as co-authors even when they had done no more than accept the title of co-supervisor or contribute grant money, had virtually no involvement in the actual research or writing, and did not even understand the subject-matter. Fabrikant wrote:

Absolute power corrupts absolutely, and this is exactly what happened to the moral standards of the "senior" members of the Department. Everyone knew that in order to get promotion, tenure, or just to keep the job, they had to include T.S. Sankar as co-author in their scientific papers, and they did. While being a Chairman, he averaged twelve papers a year plus even more conference presentations. I have included him in sixteen papers and eighteen conference presentations and his scientific contribution to all of them was exactly zero, more than that, he could not understand a single thing in any of my works.[11]

An investigation by a Canadian weekly magazine, *Maclean's*, concluded that on this matter of coerced co-authorship Fabrikant's charges were plausible. Apart from corroborating testimony by former professors and graduate students, the sheer number of papers written by two administrators was suspect in itself:

A search of several library indexes revealed that Swamy has written more than 385 journal and conference papers since 1958. For his part, Sankar lists 334 conference and journal papers over the past 26 years. That record of publication clearly places Swamy and Sankar in a league of their own – above even that of Albert Einstein, the most celebrated scientist of the century. Einstein's bibliography includes 238 conference and journal papers, and these were produced over a much longer period – a career spanning 53 years. Swamy's rate of publication actually increased after he took on an added workload as dean of engineering 15 years ago. Previous to that appointment, Swamy averaged about seven papers annually. Afterwards, his rate of publication more than doubled, reaching a high of 26 papers in 1982 alone.[12]

Suspect, to put it mildly. A follow-up report on integrity in scholarship, by H.W. Arthurs, Roger A. Blais, and Jon Thompson, concluded that while Fabrikant himself had abused the publication system, it was unlikely that Sankar could have made a substantive contribution to the papers he "co-authored" with Fabrikant.[13]

Though brilliant, Fabrikant was obviously an unstable personality. Pain and paranoia cry out from his messages. He was clearly an extraordinarily difficult person to deal with. But on the issue of coerced co-authorship, Fabrikant appears to have been basically right. Those who protested the practices were urged not to make trouble and led to believe that were they to do so, grant money or even graduation might be the price. Carl Goldman, a civil engineering professor at Concordia, said in an interview with *Maclean's* that the abuse at Concordia was unusual in degree but not in kind: "They go to the government to get money for research, hire juniors to do the work, and then put their names down on the papers. It is a practice that has corrupted the entire educational system across Canada, but Concordia engineering is probably the worst example you can find."

The problem is one of abuse of power in the quest for personal gain, and the credibility of the entire system of education, training, and credentials is eroded by it. A person is assumed to know a considerable amount about a subject in which he or she has co-authored a research publication. Reputations are based in large part on publications; grants, contracts, and administrative power are awarded on this basis; and talented students may make career decisions accordingly. (One man, who had travelled from China to Concordia to study with him, was bitterly disappointed to find that a prominent professor seemed to know little or nothing about the research area in which he had co-authored many papers.) This lack of integrity in scientific research puts the credibility of scientific findings and reputations in question.

RESPONSES TO PROFESSIONAL DILEMMAS OF DISTRUST

There are two sides to the relationship between professionals and their clients. Not only do clients need to trust professionals, but professionals must be able to trust their clients – to give accurate information and to follow advice. If a dentist is to do effective work, his patient must follow such advice as to refrain from eating toffees when new fillings have been installed and to floss regularly. A doctor's work is often similarly dependent on her patient's compliance. If a two-hundred-and-fifty-pound diabetic patient insists on eating fudge, there is little her doctor can do to maintain her health. If a patient is trying to maintain lower blood pressure, in order to help her the doctor has to have reliable reports about blood-pressure readings outside the office. If a lawyer is to defend an accused person successfully , he must know what that person's actions and circumstances really were – and in most cases must depend on his client to give him an accurate account. Such is the theme of many a Perry Mason novel. Scientists, who do not so obviously have clients, are dependent on the press to give a tolerably accurate account of their goals and results, and on policy-makers to act reasonably in their inevitably selective funding of scientific work. Teachers and professors count on their students to study and practise: without effort on the student's part, learning is unlikely to occur.

There are also ways in which various professionals are vulnerable to clients. A male physician who seeks to help a woman patient can be seriously compromised if she falsely charges him with sexual assault. In accepting her as a patient, he implicitly assumes that she has come to him in that role, not as a prospective victor in a legal battle, seductress, or spy. A scientist who agrees to testify on behalf of one side in a court battle must trust her clients to give her accurate information about the dispute and to provide good lawyers, translators, press agents, and so on. Analogous points can be made about other professions. Trust is needed on both sides of professional-client relationships. Clients share responsibility for the lack of trust in relationships with professionals.

Clients also bear some responsibility to be alert consumers of professional services. If they do not understand why certain procedures are being implemented, they should ask. With medications, for instance, patients should be attentive enough to ask doctors why the medication is being prescribed, what its known side-effects are, and whether it could interact negatively with another medication already being taken. Dental patients who are being prescribed expensive orthodontic or cosmetic procedures should ask how necessary those procedures are and how their health might be affected were they to choose not to undergo them. People embarking on lawsuits should be aware that lawyers may have adversarial tendencies and inquire about the possibility of alternative means of resolving disputes, and the cost and duration of a lawsuit. Those seeking to take advantage of scientific expertise should do their best to understand which area of scientific knowledge is relevant to their problem and whether scientists in that area agree on the matter in question. Consumer alertness is part of the answer to the problem of trusting experts and professionals.

However, the responsibility for consumer alertness does not go so far that it removes responsibility from professionals themselves. The specialized knowledge, high socio-economic status, and unique powers of professionals make the relationship between them and their clients asymmetrical. It is the client who is more vulnerable, and for this reason it is the professional who bears prime responsibility for competent and ethical practice. In an ideal world clients and professionals would be perfectly trustworthy and there would be no warrant for fear, suspicion, or unease. But obviously the real world is not characterized by ideal trusting relationships between professionals and clients. Clients bear some responsibility for these problems, but that says nothing about the issues of professional trustworthiness as such. For professionals to respond to issues of trust by accusing their clients is to evade the issue of their own integrity, and to shirk responsibility.

Professionals may proclaim from the rooftops that they are knowledgeable, responsible, and dedicated to the public good. They may exhort the public to trust them, insisting that they "deserve" trust because of their education and well-regulated character. They may insist, often correctly, that most of their members are persons of integrity and competence and that abuses are exceptional. They may believe that, because they are professionals, others should not criticize their actions and policies, and that lay persons could not possibly know enough to articulate valid complaints. They may respond to accusations by saying, in effect, "Trust us; we're professionals." But here as elsewhere, the "trust me" approach is unlikely to be effective. It is a manipulative appeal that stops short of supplying any real basis for trust. When distrust in a profession exists, there is nearly always a reason for it. A mere *appeal* to change attitudes is not enough. Why are people unwilling to trust? They may have experienced abuse, faulty information, callousness, lack of common sense, bad management, lying, unkept promises, gossip, intimidation, and plain incompetence. A mere appeal to *trust* does not address these concerns. Nor does the insistence that practitioners merit trust "because we are professionals."

Professionals upset about their image and reputation may rightly feel that the actions of the few unjustly affect the morals and prospects of the many. There are many thousands of competent and caring doctors, lawyers who serve their clients well without overcharging or embezzling funds, psychiatrists who do not sexually exploit their patients, clergy who do not sexually molest children, and rigorous scientists and hard-working professors who nurture student talent and honestly write their own papers on the basis of their own knowledge. The image of a profession is tarnished by the aberrant few, especially those aberrant few whose misdeeds are sufficiently spectacular to be covered by the media.

Be this as it may, the response from professionals must go beyond appeals, pleas, and exhortations. The best response is greater trustworthiness. Trust in a professional has two aspects: respect for the credentials and self-regulation of the profession and a sense that the individual practitioner is trustworthy. For clients the latter aspect is based on individual encounter, and in this area the practitioner is on his own. To establish trust at this point is basic. The professional must listen attentively to the client and try to understand his or her interests and needs; not try to manipulate, exploit, or deceive the client; admit the fact if he or she does not have sufficient knowledge to deal properly with the client's case; and perform necessary tasks in a reliable and competent way. In these contexts as elsewhere, the best way to seem trustworthy is to be trustworthy. So far as trust in the professions goes, this is the simplest and best solution to the problem of greater confidence from clients. Professionals will get the trust they and their clients need in the relationship when they deserve it – when they really are trustworthy and convey a sense of their trustworthiness to clients and the public at large.

Since a major factor in distrust of professionals is their tendency to band together, cover for each other, and see the world through the same limited spectacles, professional self-regulation often works imperfectly. Increasingly, lay people suspect that a regulatory body of professionals will be unwilling or unable to censure a qualified member of that profession, and this makes lay complainants uneasy about bringing cases forward, even in instances where abuse is clear. This sort of problem can be mitigated by broadening participation in regulatory bodies. Another approach is to appoint an ombudsman or intermediary to hear appeals. Such a person should be knowledgeable and autonomous – ideally not a member of the profession and not dependent on it for position and salary. If an ombudsman can deal with complaints fairly and effectively and is known to do so, public confidence in the profession will be enhanced. Some professionals who might otherwise have been tempted to abuse their knowledge and power will be deterred from doing so. The ombudsman technique, however, is appropriate only when there is already some public distrust of the profession. If a profession – dentistry, for example – about which there have been relatively few complaints were suddenly to appoint an ombudsman, the move could inspire distrust on the part of the public. Not thinking much was wrong, people might start to wonder why an ombudsman was necessary and begin to question their previous confidence in the profession.

The ethics code is also a common device. Many professions and semi-professions have worked out codes of ethics. But such codes have important limitations. Professionals have to be capable of exercising good judgment about knowledge and behaviour. And just as actions cannot be constantly monitored, neither can compliance with a code of ethics. If Concordia deans and professors were not (on the whole) sufficiently competent and responsible to teach, do research, and publish papers in a morally responsible manner without a code of ethics, providing them with an ethics code would be unlikely to solve the problem. Similar arguments apply to other professional groups; no ethical code can remove the need for judgment. No matter how sensitive the authors of a code try to be, its rules are necessarily couched in general terms and cannot cover every dimension of every circumstance. Ethical codes and principles must be applied to the real world. The general rule does not apply itself; some person must apply it. Some person must see that the case in question is one to which a rule or several rules apply and must determine whether the prescriptions made by those rules are coherent and sensible in the given case. That application requires sound judgment, integrity, and common sense. In professional ethics as elsewhere, rules cannot do the whole job: people need the commitment to try to abide by them and the judgment and discretion to interpret and apply them sensibly.

A professional code of ethics can be useful in addressing the image problems of a profession only if its members take the code seriously and the public believe that they are doing so. A profession with an especially serious image problem may find that its efforts to publicize a code are met with scepticism and cynicism – regarded as insincere whitewash efforts. Some codes of ethics are couched in vague and rhetorical language. Others are poorly circulated and may be virtually unknown to practitioners. People outside the profession may suspect that the code is a kind of cover-up – something professionals can point to if they are accused of abusing their knowledge and power ("But look, our code says ... we would never do anything like this").

Clearly the ethics code is not a complete response for the profession beset by problems of distrust. If a practitioner is set upon stealing funds from a client or using his professional relationships as a way of finding sexual partners, the adoption by his profession of a code labelling such behaviour as "wrong" is unlikely to deter him. Still, codes have their uses. They articulate a core professional consensus about right and wrong behaviour. That consensus can serve as a solid basis for the decision of a regulatory board or ombudsman in the event of complaints. If clients are informed of the code, they may be encouraged to take action when wrongs are done. Provided that an ethics code is worded accurately so that it has meaningful implications regarding professional action and is taken seriously by members of a profession, it can be helpful in establishing trustworthy behaviour by professionals and a good basis for trust on the part of their clients.

SEMI-PROFESSIONS AND NON-PROFESSIONS

Trust issues regarding professions have an especially high profile, but there are also significant issues of trust regarding people in semi-professional and non-professional roles. We are vulnerable to doctors and we are aware of this vulnerability, especially in situations of crisis. However we are also vulnerable to airplane pilots, hairdressers, automobile mechanics, taxi drivers, physiotherapists, nurses, teachers, and countless other people in semi-professional and non-professional occupations. If they are incompetent, our lives may quite literally be at stake. And if they were intent on harming us, the same would be true. Consider, for instance, the automobile mechanic. He is in an ideal position to perform acts of sabotage or terrorism. We are vulnerable to such semi-professionals as journalists, nurses, teachers, mediators, and counsellors. We depend on these people in many ways and would be in a highly precarious position were they not generally competent and well intentioned.

A taxi driver who commits sexual assault can injure his victim as much as a doctor. On entering a taxi we assume that the driver will remain "in role," just as we assume that our physician will remain in role and not turn into a seducer when we reveal ourselves in his examining room. So far as immediate physical harm and vulnerability are concerned, we are as dependent on the integrity and competence of the taxi driver as on that of the doctor.

Given these obvious facts, it is in some ways anomalous that professional ethics and professional trustworthiness receive so much attention while comparable aspects of semi-professional and non-professional occupations tend to be ignored. Why this disparity in attention? No doubt it is due to the power and relatively high socio-economic status of professionals; their resulting high public profile; their possession of esoteric knowledge, which makes clients relatively incapable of assessing their pronouncements and performance; and their quasi-autonomous status. Such professionals as doctors, judges, lawyers, scientists, and professors occupy roles that generally merit respect; when they lapse, they tend to lapse conspicuously. Because expectations for these professionals are high, abuses shock, and are treated accordingly.

These factors apply in lesser degrees to semi-professionals. Their income, power, and profile are less; the expectations of their specialized knowledge tend to be less; their knowledge is less specialized and more accessible to the lay person; and they are generally less autonomous in regulating themselves. For these reasons it is understandable that we hear less about "journalism ethics" or "teacher's ethics" than about medical and legal ethics, less about the social worker's responsibility than about the scientist's. We tend to be unaware that we need to trust journalists and teachers just as we do doctors and lawyers. The relationship is different; it tends to be more diffuse and may (as in the case of journalists) only rarely involve face-to-face meetings between professional and client. Still, if these people do not do their jobs well, we are vulnerable. Dishonest and incompetent journalists jeopardize public welfare and public policy at least as much as dishonest doctors or unduly adversarial lawyers.

In many respects semi-professional and non-professional occupations are as important and meritorious as professional ones. Modern society cannot function without teachers, journalists, air-traffic controllers, lifeguards, nurses, sales personnel, computer technicians, mechanics, real-estate agents, file clerks, income-tax auditors, and a host of other occupations. For things to work, these people must generally do their jobs competently and with integrity. If they do not, we are all vulnerable. We have specific expectations about what the occupants of these roles will do, and we depend on their living up to our expectations.

5 Trusting Strangers?

In daily life we depend on each other to act in standard predictable ways. By acting "normally" and finding that others act "normally" too we are able to know what gestures and actions mean, carry out mundane activities, and, simply, get through the day. We construct the normal world by focusing our attention and acting in similar and expected ways. Without ever thinking about it, we count on other people to do this, and are shocked if they do not.

COMMON-SENSE MEANING AND NASTY SURPRISES

Suppose that two people play a simple game together – say, tic-tac-toe. The game has rules, and to play it, people must abide by them. Each player knows how to play according to the rules, expects to abide by them, and expects the other player to abide by them too. Each player expects that the other expects him to abide by the rules. Some rules are typically stated when the game is taught: "take turns," "each player marks either x or o," "the first player to get three x's or three o's in a straight line – vertical, horizontal or diagonal – wins." Others are unspoken rules, which come to attention mostly when broken. If a player insists on two turns in a row and throws a tantrum when she is not allowed to have them, refuses to stick to either x or o, drawing happy faces and cartoon characters all over the grid, or puts her x on a line instead of in a space, the game cannot go on.

Sociologist Harold Garfinkel uses ideas about our mutual expectations to offer an account of how shared beliefs and attitudes construct the commonsense social world.[1] We make *reciprocal* assumptions about actions, motives, and standpoints. Though other people are different from ourselves in experience, emotions, and viewpoint, we nevertheless operate with them in a shared world of common objects; events and actions are given a common meaning. For instance, one who asks a question assumes that the person asked can understand, may know the answer, and – if he does – will tell it. Though such rules and expectations are looser in everyday life than in games, they are taken very seriously. We discover this when violations occur.

What an action means is not something a person can determine by himself. Suppose, for instance, we try to thank another person and she does not respond in the normal way. Instead of saying "Oh, you're welcome" or "I'm glad you liked it," she appears puzzled, says nothing, and then walks away; looks at us and says we should not be thanking her for *that*; or gruffly tells us that what she did was not the kind of thing we should thank anybody for. In such cases we are likely to feel that we have not succeeded in thanking her. We have said "thank you" and we wanted to thank this person, but because she did not respond appropriately, we did not succeed in doing so. The social world works smoothly only in so far as we can count on each other to make it work. We have webs of commonsense expectations, and for the most part those expectations are met.

Garfinkel sought to illustrate these basic expectations by setting up experimental situations in which he instructed his students to behave in unexpected ways and report reactions. The experiments embarrassed, confused, and annoyed most people who were subjected to them. The strong responses to the deviations serve to illustrate the strength of the expectation that people will behave normally. Social competence depends on events possessing a commonsense character, meaning that others must share in assigning meaning and relevance to events. There are things people are supposed to do and not do. For actions and events to be intelligible, we count on other people to do what we expect.

In Garfinkel's experiments, sociology students presented unsuspecting subjects with "nasty surprises." Here is a description from one participating student:

One evening, while shopping at Sears with a friend I (male) found myself next to a woman shopping at the copper-clad pan section. The store was busy ... and clerks were hard to find. The woman was just a couple of feet away and my friend was behind me. Pointing to a tea kettle, I asked the woman if she did not think the price was rather high. I asked in a friendly tone ... She looked at me and then at the kettle and said "yes." I then said I was going to take it anyway. She said, "oh," and started to move sideways away from me. I quickly asked her if she was not going to wrap it for me and take my cash. Still moving slowly away and glancing first at me, then at the kettle, then at the other pans farther away from me, she said the clerk was "over there," pointing off somewhere. In a harsh tone, I asked if she was not going to wait on me. She said, "no, no, I'm not the saleslady. There she is." I said that I knew the extra help was inexperienced, but that was no reason not to wait on a customer. "Just wait on me. I'll be patient." With that she flushed with anger and walked rapidly away, looking back once as if to ask if it could really be true.[2]

What tacit norms were violated in this case? The student experimenter failed to take the woman's moving away as an indication that she did not wish to be involved in further conversation. He ignored her statements that the clerk was somewhere else and she was not a salesperson. He insisted that another shopper relate to him as "help," calling her "extra help" in a demeaning and patronizing way. The unwitting victim of this sociological experiment was angry and astonished at his refusal to abide by the cues and customs of ordinary life.

In another Garfinkel exercise, students tried to adopt an attitude of deliberate and strong distrust towards others with whom they were conversing. Several reported that it was such an effort to try to disbelieve everything that they could scarcely follow the conversation. To their unwitting subjects these students were unreliable social actors; they seemed untrustworthy in bizarre and peculiar ways. In the context of the experiments the students destroyed interactive trust because they failed to comply with the tacit rules of mundane interactions.

Although there are contexts in which the rules and expectations of social interaction are altered, there are none with no rules at all. Consider the case of the theatre. Events transpiring on stage are to be taken seriously but are understood not to have the implications of real events. A character who is suffering from cancer in a play does not thereby run a risk of death from the disease in his non-theatrical life. Those who commit murders or robberies as part of the theatrical act are not pursued by police. Characters may do things that in ordinary life would be shocking; some such actions (urinating on stage, simulating gay intercourse, etc.) convey a message about what kind of play this is. Playwrights toy with the boundary between audience and play, sometimes writing audience action into the script – as in one case where audience members had to leave their shoes outside the theatre, and the resulting scramble to find their shoes at the end was part of the play.

But none of this means that theatre is lacking in constitutive rules. There are quite definite expectations and limits. The various theatrical innovations are undertaken by playwrights, directors, producers – not by the audience. In the Polish play *Marriage Blanc* the action begins with two young women in a large double bed together, centre-stage. They are wearing old-fashioned nightgowns and talking about their fears and feelings on the matter of sex and marriage. If a member of the audience were, on a sudden whim, to climb out of his seat, stride on to the stage, climb into bed with the young women, and begin to caress them, the result would be fear and havoc. Even in *avant garde* forms of theatre, actors and producers depend on the audience to behave appropriately. It is actors and producers, not the audience, who have permission to initiate disturbing innovations. The audience is supposed to watch and participate only when invited.

Games, theatre, and ordinary life in its many strands all feature a tacit co-operation where people in effect collude to uphold a social meaning. Whether playing a game, attending the theatre, acting in a play, thanking someone, shopping, conversing, or eating a family meal, we count on each other to do the "right" thing. Spontaneity and creativity arise within a range set by custom, wherein actions and events are given a common meaning. We do not think much about it, taking the customary social world for granted unless we run into nasty surprises.

Such expectations have been called trust. Garfinkel used the term in his early experiments, saying that trust in other people is necessary for grasping both the events in games and those of daily life. One person trusts another in that she confidently expects the other to produce or respect the normal, desired events – what Garfinkel calls reproducing the "normative order of events." Trusting in this context amounts to confidently expecting the other to act in an appropriate way. What is appropriate is defined by social custom and tacit rules. Such trust is typically unconscious and presumes no personal knowledge of the people trusted. It emerges from social experience. This is how "everybody does it," as we have simply learned. It is how "people like us" behave.

Someone might object that this is a thin and insignificant sort of trust, one that has little to do with care, non-manipulativeness, personal connection, knowledge, or emotion. And that is true in a way. Still, there are good reasons to think of these expectations as constituting trust. As in other cases of trust, our expectations are open-ended. We are interdependent and vulnerable to each other's actions. We have confident expectations that others will conform to norms; we predict and interpret the others' behaviour accordingly. It is an unpleasant surprise, a shock, if others do not act as expected. We are vulnerable and feel let down. We were counting or depending on the other to act appropriately, and confidently expecting that she would, whether we were aware of it or not.

SCATTER TRUST

Trust may exist as an attitude towards people with whom we have only a slight personal relationship or none at all: those whom we pass on streets and shops and with whom we engage in the many impersonal relationships of modern life. Although such impersonal contacts have less emotional depth and richness than those of friendship, love, or collegiality and are obviously based on limited experience, they are fundamentally similar in involving open-ended expectations of positive action, dependence, and vulnerability. In modern life people are interdependent to an extraordinary extent. We are dependent upon people whom we do not know, whom, in many cases, we do not even see.

Consider, for instance, the everyday activity of shopping. In small villages or towns people tend to know shopkeepers and producers and to feel confident buying things on the basis of personal connection. In modern societies, however, our confidence typically has a more abstract and institutional basis. We go to a large supermarket and purchase a number of items – bread, meat, fruits, vegetables, packaged cereal, sugar, flour, eggs – for the most part assuming unhesitatingly that they will be safe to eat. That means taking for granted that they have been grown, processed, transported, and stored in a safe way. Hundreds, perhaps even thousands of people will have been involved in such processes.

Given the intricate vulnerabilities of modern life, exceptions are serious. An example is the Tylenol case in the early eighties, in which someone deliberately put poison into some bottles of Tylenol pills, resulting in the death of several consumers. Such instances expose our vulnerability to the countless unknown people who could be involved in the anonymous processes that bring products to us. Quite literally, poisoning drugs amounts to terrorism. We might ourselves be victims. The case was frightening because it revealed to many who had not thought about it before that our vulnerability does not end with Tylenol or other bottled medications. It extends to any substance we consume. If enough people wanted to harm, kill, or terrorize others by poisoning drugs and foods, it would be extremely difficult to prevent them from doing so. The Tylenol case illustrates just how dependent we are on the competence and goodwill of countless strangers and how vulnerable we would be if even a minute proportion of these people sought to harm us.

From another point of view, what is amazing is that such things happen so seldom. There is a substantial underclass of people who are poor and alienated and may feel hostile to those who lead more affluent lives and purchase such things as Tylenol. Millions of people fall into this class. Hundreds of thousands resort to crime, but few to substance terrorism. Why not? There is ample opportunity.

Farmers, farm workers, transport workers, processing personnel, packagers, wholesalers, processors, buyers, and clerks – vast numbers of people are involved in bringing products to the shops of the industrialized world. Yet when we shop, we assume we are buying food that is safe to eat. One can call this attitude *scatter trust* because our trust is spread out, scattered.[3] We trust in a whole range of people, most of whom we do not know and never encounter. Our trust is, as it were, scattered over these various people whom we assume are performing their designated function in a competent and honest way. Ann-Mari Sellerberg, a Swedish sociologist who has explored personal trust and system trust, found that shoppers were confident about the safety and quality of goods in Sweden but that the source of their confidence was different in rural and urban contexts. Village people felt confident due to their personal knowledge of shop-owners and tradespeople. City shoppers, by contrast, based their attitude on institutional factors: consumer legislation, declarations on packages, and the self-service system. When we can pick out goods for ourselves, it seems that vendors have nothing to hide. A sense that things are well-regulated and functioning properly means that most consumers have a basic attitude of trust and confidence, believing that on the whole things function properly. Unless something happens to put them off, shoppers tend to retain this attitude of trust and confidence.[4]

Modern shopping assumes that we are able to use credit or cash to buy goods. Credit obviously presumes trust, both in individuals and in institutions. If a shopkeeper accepts a credit card, he is assuming that the customer legitimately possesses the card, that the credit-card company will pay him, and that the customer has not overdrawn on his credit and will pay the bill. Less obvious is the fact that cash too is based on trust. If, for instance, the shopkeeper accepts a twenty-dollar bill, he is implicitly assuming that he can exchange that bill for goods and services of a value equivalent to the goods he sold to his customer. Such confidence is based on a tacit faith in the ongoing workings of the relevant monetary system.

The relation between money and trust is explored by S. Herbert Frankl, who derives many of his ideas from the German sociologist George Simmel. Frankl begins by observing that money is nothing apart from the objects, services, or rights to which it gives access. To accept money in the form of bills, or even gold, is to assume that we can exchange it for something else – that it will give us access to goods and services. To perform this function, the money must be accepted by others. And they in turn accept it only because they believe that it will be accepted by still others. The value of money is a matter of general confidence. As Simmel observed: "Modern man requires the services and co-operation of innumerable others and would be quite helpless without them. Money ... connects him with them in a non-personal way, and thus gives him a feeling of not being beholden to them. In fact, the development of civilization has made him more dependent than ever before on the objective bonds with them."[5] The pervasive use of money is not without its hazards. Its anonymity makes us less aware that we remain dependent on other people and perhaps less inclined to build up personal relationships when we are doing business. Also, we tend to reduce other values to monetary ones, which distorts our sense of values. Still, money vastly increases our freedom. We need not possess an object that the supermarket will accept in order to acquire meat or lettuce; we can pay by cash or credit card.

In a reasonably sound economy people assume that the money is good; they will give goods and services in exchange, assuming that they in turn will be able to use that money to meet their needs. The viability of a currency depends on a web of expectations about what people will accept and do.[6] Trust and confidence, which are in the final resort "unprovable," are the essence of money. To use money we must trust that an indefinitely large number of other people will continue to accept that money as viable. Should they not, our own well-being is at risk. The trust on which money is founded is scatter trust.

Driving provides another illustration of scatter trust. When driving, we in effect trust that other drivers are trying to reach their various destinations, not intent on committing murder or suicide. We come to a red light and stop, assuming that others will stop too. We assume that other drivers will generally abide by speed limits, that they will not deliberately aim their car trying to kill us or pedestrians, that they will turn right after signalling right. Not, of course, that people drive perfectly. They sometimes break rules, and they do unwise things like passing on icy winding roads, tailgating, or speed-ing to get through orange lights. Some drive when intoxicated. Some waver from lane to lane, turn without signalling, or perform illegal U-turns.

At worst, there are drivers out to commit murder. In the late 1980s two young men went out in their car on the freeway between Los Angeles and Palo Alto and, at random, shot people driving on the freeway. But even in this extraordinary and appalling circumstance there were fourteen murders among an estimated 14 million com-muters. One's chance of being deliberately murdered by another dri-ver on the freeway was one in a million. In such a situation, knowing that there were drivers capable of murder and intent upon it, drivers would surely feel some unease and a lessening of trust. Could the chap in the white Toyota ahead be one of these? Yet, in the millions, people continued to drive on the freeway.

If we did not assume that other drivers were moderately compe-tent and moderately well-intentioned, driving would be a terrifying experience:"Since any collision is likely to result in substantial incon-venience, and any high speed collision in serious, permanent injury or death, this implicit trust carries very high stakes. Although one may flinch at the idea of driving alongside a barrage of oncoming machine-gun bullets, an equivalent risk is common to the experience of traffic."[7] Driving may seem to carry such high risks that we might as well drive through gunfire. Yet often we are barely aware of them. We do not know other drivers on the roads. We see them barely at all: they are enclosed in thousands of pounds of metal. Yet we are vul-nerable to them and count on them to drive competently.

We have this confidence in other drivers partly because we have driven frequently without coming to serious harm. Despite some vio-lations, aggression and outright malevolence on the part of other dri-vers are statistically rare. Carelessness, while far more common, rarely leads to accident and injury. In addition, for most adults it would be massively time-consuming and inconvenient not to drive. We have a powerful incentive to ignore our vulnerability to the com-petence and goodwill of others who are on the road. In many cir-cumstances, were we not to drive ourselves, we would be passen-gers. We would still have to rely on drivers in surrounding cars, and we would simply be placing our trust in another driver instead of ourselves. As passengers we depend not only on the driver's compe-tence but on his good, or moderately decent, will. We assume that he will take us to our destination and not abduct, rob, assault, or mur-der us. Such confidence in drivers is based on tacit trust, partly grounded in experience, partly based on belief willed by need. In

modern societies most adults feel a need to drive and a corresponding need to trust other drivers to be at least minimally decent.

In flying, scatter trust is still more obvious. To fly we must implicitly trust the pilot and co-pilot, the ground people who service the
airplane, the pilots and personnel of other planes flying in the area,
the engineers who built the plane, the computer personnel who
design and service the programs used for steering and other functions, those who prepare and store food, and the other passengers.
And that is not the end of it. Since a situation in which we cruise
thousands of meters above ground is unusual, people tend to be
aware of these vulnerabilities when flying, and as a result some
refuse to fly.

A down-to-earth example of scatter trust is provided by Annette
Baier, who writes of using a library:

Suppose I look quickly around me before proceeding into the dark street or
library stacks where my business takes me, judge the few people I discern
there to be nondangerous, and so go ahead. We can say that my bodily safety, and perhaps my pocketbook, are the goods I am allowing these people to
be in a position to threaten. I trust them, it seems, merely to leave me alone.
But this is not quite right, for should a piece of falling masonry or toppling
books threaten to fall on my head, and one of these persons leap into action
and shove me out of this danger, I would regard that as rather more than less
than I had trusted these strangers to do – a case for gratitude.[8]

My sense of this case differs slightly from Baier's. I agree that mostly
I would want other users to respect my physical security by simply
leaving me alone. But I would be pleased, not disturbed, if someone
also tried to protect me from danger. The key point, though, is that as
a library user Baier *assumes* that other users (whoever they may be)
will act in the appropriate way. If Baier were to lose her confidence
that the library is a safe place, she would be handicapped in doing
her teaching and research. Baier does not mention another kind of
trust involved in using the library: trust in the testimony and expertise of the authors of the books and articles we are seeking and the
care and integrity of the publishers who made these books and articles available.

Laurence Thomas defines *basic trust* as the confidence that others,
on whom we are dependent in a wide variety of social interactions,
will treat us in accordance with the basic precepts of morality. Basic
trust in this sense is an expectation that others whom we do not know
are not deliberately setting out to harm us by lying, wounding, robbing, or killing.[9] What Thomas calls basic trust overlaps significantly

with what is here called scatter trust. Its object is an indeterminate range of other people, mostly unknown to us, on whose actions and functioning we are dependent in the course of ordinary modern life. We assume quite confidently, without ever thinking much about it, that others do not set out to poison drugs or foods, that they drive with a basic respect for rules of the road, use libraries to find books, and, in general, do not intend to harm other human beings.

Countless people on whom we regularly depend are complete strangers. Thomas argues that if even 1 per cent of those with whom we distantly interact while driving, shopping, watching a play, or eating in a restaurant were "out to get us," or *were believed to be so*, life would be intolerable. Our attitude towards complete strangers is fundamental to our well-being and our general sense of the world in which we live:

In a basically moral society, trust is an integral part of the social and moral fabric of life. We trust people to be honest with us and with others about us. We trust that people will not desire our harm or death or the harm or death of others generally, that the reason why it does not occur to people to kill someone is not because they generally have too much on their minds but because they do not in fact want to be murderers. We would scarcely order a meal in a restaurant or ask a stranger for the time or walk down the street without wearing a bullet-proof vest if we thought for a moment that every stranger in life was out to kill us.[10]

We do not merely rely on the fact that most people we have encountered have not tried to murder us. We rely with confidence, assuming that people will not do this in the future. This confidence is based on our sense that other people are, for the most part, moral and law-abiding fellow citizens who choose to act responsibly. Most people find the idea of murdering another human being abhorrent and would not do it, whether or not they thought they would be caught. That we do not in general seek to deliberately damage or kill each other expresses our acceptance of the moral worth of persons. We contribute to each other's flourishing by affirming each other's worth. And one way we do that is by refraining from harming each other even when we have ample opportunity and power to do so.[11]

Evidence of the everyday reality of scatter trust can be seen in the following comments, drawn from interviews.

Going to a hospital? "You expect people to know how to treat your injury; you trust that society developed institutions for that purpose and maintains them. You are trusting the whole institution, that each person does what they are supposed to do, and to some extent you also trust what each individual is supposed to do. You have to trust that someone is keeping track of what needs to be done, trust that they are in control, that there is enough equipment available to deal with everyone equitably."[12]

Going to a hospital? "When you are a patient, you hand over your rights of decision to medical personnel. You enter a system where you lose control, so your trust has to increase. How much trust you need depends on how serious the situation is. The more technology that is involved, the more you have to trust. As your knowledge decreases, the more you must increase your level of trust; you must trust that the people involved are competent. The loss of control is very uncomfortable." [13]

Sending children to school? "You have to trust a lot to send your children to school. Obviously the teacher; you have to trust that they will not intimidate and harass your child, that they will actually teach them something and do it right; also you have to have confidence that they are going to convey other things the child needs, such as self-esteem and confidence ... The whole values framework and milieu of the school is something you pretty well immerse your children in, sending them there, and this certainly involves a lot of trust. Of course for most of us we do not have a whole lot of choice about whether to do this."[14]

Watching television news? "I trust it as one viewpoint, not that it's exactly right, because parts could be omitted or the interpretation could be something other than what I would come up with. They are honestly doing their best to tell us what is happening. You could trust it for a basic fact ... But not for further nuances. You can't even name whom you would be trusting – presumably reporters, cameramen, editors, announcers."[15]

Mailing a letter? "You trust that your letter will arrive, and sometimes you find out that it didn't. You trust the pick-up person, the sorters, the mailman. A major point is that these people are going to do their job and are not going to steal the mail. There is that feeling when you drop your letter in the box: it's gone."[16]

Going to a restaurant? "Definitely trust is involved in using restaurants. Meat has to be properly cleaned, stored, prepared, and cooked. You certainly have to trust the kitchen staff in a restaurant, and you never see them. They are in the background. It is not the waiter and waitresses you meet whom you mainly need to trust. Yet in Canada you don't think much about this usually. In Mexico I did not have such general confidence in restaurants; I watched where middle-class Mexican people went and followed, assuming they would know how to eat safely in their own country."[17]

Police? "Yes, I guess basically I trust them. I have called them to my house three times over the years and each time felt better when they came. When my son was a teenager the house was broken into, and the officer who came said it was probably a friend or acquaintance of my son, doing petty theft. This turned out to be true. But chases and other police activities reported in the media make me mad with the police. My husband was a fireman for forty years, and he saw quite some circumstances ... He really sides with the police, and he tells me I don't know what they are up against. But I think some chases are unnecessary and dangerous. And there is a definite tendency for a certain sort of guy to choose to become a policeman."[18]

In a reasonably well-run society we are able to maintain confidence and trust in the functioning of thousands of people on whom we depend when undertaking familiar activities: shopping, driving, using libraries, hospitals, schools, flying on airplanes, using banks, credit cards, the postal system, the media, and so on. Despite aberrations and occasional failures, we continue to rely on these institutions and those who function within them. To a large extent scatter trust is founded on relevant past experience. Most people in Western industrialized countries have purchased and consumed meat many times without becoming ill, driven many times without accident, successfully used public transit, the postal system, schools, libraries, and so on without serious mishap. Experience has taught us that the people whose work and actions support these institutions are sufficiently competent and well motivated to be reliable. Disturbances are rare enough to count as "nasty surprises."

Society is, after all, policed and regulated. There are laws against speeding, running red lights, driving when uninsured, murder, assault, robbery, and so on. There are regulations about the production, transport, storing, and marketing of foodstuffs, the licensing of teachers and principals, and virtually every mundane activity in the complex modern world. In a well-regulated modern society people do not operate restaurants in which the kitchen is unclean and the meat and potato salad are not properly refrigerated: they need a licence to open the restaurant and are subject to government inspection. (The system is not infallible, of course, but it is highly effective.) Trust is based on the sense that there is a reasonably effective system in which things run as they are supposed to, in part because policing, licensing, and inspection services run as they are supposed to. In the case of many goods and services, over the long term there is no opposition in interests between those who are protected and those from whom they are protected. For instance, in the case of a restaurant, it would not be in the long-term interest of the owner to economize by serving slightly spoiled meat or the previous day's potato salad. Were customers to suffer food poisoning, business would suffer as a result. Similarly manufacturers, retailers, airlines, and other services to the public must, over the long term, satisfy their customers in order to survive. Adverse publicity will expose failures. Most businesses are subject to long-term control by customers who can withdraw their patronage.

In complex urban societies we are rarely acquainted with the mailman or a clerk in the supermarket, still less with the mechanic who checks an airplane before it takes off, or those who restack books in libraries, put pills into sealed bottles, or clear snow off the streets. We do not typically make a conscious decision to entrust our well-being or goods to these people. Usually we are unaware of our vulnerability and tacitly assume that things will simply work.

One might question the conception of scatter trust by claiming that we merely *rely* on the functioning of others in situations where we have little choice but to do so. Or one might grant that people feel *confidence* in such contexts as shopping, driving, and the use of schools and hospitals but insist that such confidence does not merit the name of trust. However, such objections to the notion of scatter trust are not convincing. In the contexts considered for scatter trust we find more than reliance. For the most part, if we feel vulnerable, we do not rely on others. We assume that most people will act effectively, competently, and ethically most of the time – and that it is this proper functioning that makes things work. We feel confident. Consider the mail, for instance. To rely without confidence would make no sense. If we believed that those who deliver and sort mail have no competence at all or wilfully lose or steal items, we would believe that mailed items had little chance of reaching the destinations we intend for them. In that case, mailing a letter would make little sense. Generally, we mail a letter believing that it will be reliably delivered to its intended recipient. As with countless other everyday actions, we assume that others will act reliably and competently to make our own actions feasible. In effect, we trust the service.

In many contexts of scatter trust our vulnerability is a matter of choice. Did we not feel confident that restaurant food would be safe, we could prepare our own meals instead of eating out. Nor do we need to fly on airplanes, attend events in crowded theatres, or take thrilling rides at amusement parks. We depend on anonymous persons to carry out particular roles and functions. We assume they will do so with competence and integrity, though they could evidently choose to act otherwise. The comfort level that people feel, carrying out mundane activities in a reasonably well-run modern society, and the choices we make in those societies would be inexplicable on the hypothesis of mere *reliance* alone. Most of the time, most of us feel considerable *confidence* in the workings of other people and basic social institutions.

But does such confidence amount to trust? Confidence is a firm expectation that things will go well; we predict that they will, based on what we have experienced in the past. To trust others is to believe that they behave appropriately because they habitually behave in an ethical way and have no special desire to harm us. If people were to act as they do *only* because they are pursuing their own self-interest, they would readily maim, kidnap, plunder, or kill one another whenever it became convenient to do so. On this view, the fact that a stranger in the street does not assault or rob us would be attributable merely to his desire to stay out of prison, not to any idea that we are moral beings worthy of consideration. Trust implies a sense that others are motivated in part by a concern and care for their fellow human beings, that they have basic integrity and a commitment to abide by moral norms.

In contexts of scatter trust, do we *trust* or do we *confidently rely* on these people simply to act in a predictable fashion and pursue their self-interest within the limits of the law? It can be argued that people who do not assault, murder, run red lights, or sell contaminated foodstuffs have only their own interests at heart and for this reason do not deserve to be trusted. To believe that self-interest alone explains the fact that strangers refrain from harming us is to assume that people have no native sympathy or concern for each other and conform to basic moral precepts only because doing so is in their own best interests. It is often argued, and still more often assumed, that people are rational calculators who seek to maximize the satisfaction of their own preferences, attending to the needs and wants of others only because they are required to do so by moral and legal codes that they cannot violate without penalty. Whether this "rational actor" model is correct has been debated by many theorists.[19]

It cannot be denied that some people, some of the time, abide by moral restrictions only out of self-interest. And when people do not seem to be acting out of self-interest, it is always possible to make out an interpretation of their behaviour according to which they will be doing so. These possibilities, however, do not mean that the so-called "rational actor" or "rational interest" model gives a complete and adequate explanation of human behaviour. In the first place, it overestimates calculation and thought: in routine aspects of life people act out of custom and habit, not rational calculation. Customs and habits have their roots in moral practices and moral beliefs. Furthermore, unless it is made tautological (the defender of the "rational actor" model implicitly redefining preference so that people just "prefer" to do things like giving to charities, caring for handicapped children, and rescuing drowning victims from lakes), the view that people necessarily act to maximize the satisfaction of their own preferences is easy to refute. Any non-tautological version neglects important relevant elements of human motivation and behaviour such as generosity, kindness, sympathy, volunteerism, and sacrifice, and is almost certain to be counter-productive because it discourages us from empathy, generosity, and altruistic action. With few exceptions, it is not the view we take for granted in conducting our everyday lives; there we suppose that people have multiple motivations for their actions and do many actions out of habit and not as a result of calculation.

The "rational interest" model can be imposed on the phenomena, and it can be defended because it can be made tautological. But there is no good reason to adopt the view, and there are several reasons against it. Apart from its neglect of custom and habit and its lapse into vacuousness against pressure from counter-examples, the view is a counter-productive one that urges an unnecessarily selfish and limited picture of human nature.

Without specific counter-evidence we tend to believe that those we trust have no *desire* to harm us. This goes deeper than merely the belief that (for whatever reason) they *will not* harm us. In situations better than riot, anarchy, concentration camp, or war, our confidence in our fellow human beings is real. And it is characteristically based on trust, the supposition that most people most of the time are not disposed to harm us wilfully. Such trust is fundamental for our psychological well-being.

THE UNKNOWN OTHER

Scatter trust is an impersonal relation: the people in whom we trust or have confidence are strangers, many of whom we never even encounter. The unknown other is also a factor in a different kind of trust situation, when we have to decide whether to trust a particular person whom we do not know. Though this trust is interpersonal and the other person is encountered as an individual, he is not known. The difference between scatter trust and anonymous interpersonal trust can be illustrated with reference to the case of driving. When driving, we generally have positive expectations about the performance of other drivers, whoever they may be. This is scatter trust. But if one is offered a ride by a stranger, one must decide whether to entrust one's personal safety to a particular unknown individual. In such a case we are then likely to be aware of our vulnerability and confront the issue of trust. But there is little relevant experience or information on which to base the decision.

Examples in which people face decisions about trusting strangers are easy to find:

Mrs Olsen, a woman in her eighties, who is quite frail, is waiting for the bus when it begins to rain very heavily. She moves into a mall to wait and sees there a middle-aged woman just packing up a few grocery purchases. Mrs Olsen mentions that she is going to get drenched walking home from the bus stop. The woman looks concerned and offers to drive her home. Mrs Olsen takes the ride and gets home safely.

A vulnerable elderly woman accepts a ride from a complete stranger. It appears that the ride is offered out of concern and kindness. Mrs Olsen herself initiated conversation, giving some evidence that this woman was not lurking in quest of elderly ladies to rob or kidnap. She took a ride with a stranger and everything was all right.

The story of Mrs Olsen is a real one – only the name is changed. The real Mrs Olsen was fascinated by issues of trust. She used to ask repeatedly, "Can you really trust people?" and sometimes described herself as "hardly trusting anyone any more." Mrs Olsen was in her eighties, and since her younger days society seemed to have become a fearful place. Because she read newspapers assiduously, she was exposed to grim details about robbery, violence, child abuse, and corruption. Yet her action showed that she was ready to entrust herself to a stranger. On one significant occasion she accepted the ride and got home safe and sound – and dry. Others asked about the case said they would have done the same.[20] Middle-aged women buying groceries are not, apparently, particularly suspicious characters. People assumed a spontaneous offer to help should, in this case, be understood as being just that.

When we suddenly must decide whether to trust a stranger, we have little or no knowledge of character and background. We resort to rough generalizations based on such things as gender, social class, occupation, age, or race. Generally, women tend to be trusted more than men, being generally weaker, less aggressive, and less likely to commit criminal acts. (Men commit over 90 per cent of criminal acts.) Typically women have less social power than men; they more rarely occupy positions of wealth and influence. Women are thus seen as less dangerous than men and as easier to trust.[21] In addition, they are assumed to be more caring than men, more disposed to listen and be helpful, less competitive, and more sympathetic and empathetic.

These gender stereotypes persist because they have a basis in fact – although there are notable exceptions to them.

In addition, the middle-aged or elderly are likely to be trusted more than the young, those with a professional or middle-class style of dress more than the working class or poor, and whites more than blacks or natives. Needless to say, such rough generalizations are stereotypical and harmful to those whose race, gender, personal style, or economic class constitutes a handicap.

Laurence Thomas has complained that racism makes him a distrusted stranger. Thomas, an African-American philosopher and professor, has never committed a crime, is of modest size, and dresses conservatively. Yet on one occasion he had only to stand wearing a tweed jacket, tie, and wool slacks, reading a university bulletin board, to have four police officers come to check on him. Many white people seem to infer lack of trustworthiness merely from his race and gender, a fact that Thomas bitterly resents:

My sheer presence has reminded more white people – female and male alike – to lock their car doors than I care to think about. I suppose it can be said that I make an unwitting contribution to public safety.

I rarely enjoy what is properly called the public trust of whites. That is to say, the white person on the street who does not know me from Adam or Eve is much more likely to judge me negatively on account of my skin color, however much my attire and mannerisms (including gait) conform to the traditional standards of well-off white males.

I was recently walking down a supermarket aisle with a hand-basket full of groceries, one in each hand. A white woman saw me and rushed for her pocketbook, which she had left in her cart. I would have had to put my own groceries down to take her pocketbook.

No doubt she thought to herself, "He won't fool me with that old basket-in-each-hand trick." By contrast, I suspect that there are very few white males who, when traditionally attired and mannered, fail to enjoy the trust of other white males, or anyone else for that matter.[22]

Thomas suggests that if he had been dressed as a punk or acting disruptively, it would have been reasonable for others to be suspicious. He argues that his personal style provides more reliable indicators of his character than does his race. A man in a tweed jacket standing looking at a university bulletin board is not likely to be a punk, mugger, or pimp. Self-presentation is the most relevant thing; and in contemporary culture *dress* is a key element in self-presentation: "If you have nothing else concrete to go on, how a person dresses makes all the difference in the world ... One could insist that black people are the exception to this saying. But I take it to be obvious that such a move would be just so much nonsense ... very few people can report having been robbed or otherwise harmed on the street by a black male youth sporting a tweed coat ... A sports coat, after all, is markedly different in appearance from a ... black leather jacket of the sort that is often associated, rightly or wrongly, with gangs."[23] On this view, a black man in a sports coat should not be the object of suspicion. But a black man in a motorcycle jacket? Perhaps. Sadly, stereotypes persist in Thomas's proposal. Contrary to what he suggests, some trustworthy people do wear motorcycle jackets.

Clearly, the best basis for judging trustworthiness is actual knowledge of the character and actions of another person. We should know the other for what she is, her likes and dislikes, beliefs, passions, actions, motivations, and tendencies. Ideally we should know her personality and moral character. Clues regarding gender, race, dress, occupation, or social class are just that: clues. People of either gender, any race, style, occupation or social class can be dishonest, insincere, manipulative, exploitative, or brutal; or they can be loving, caring, helpful, honest, conscientious, and law-abiding. The problem is, with strangers we have no relevant knowledge and must have recourse to irrelevant or only marginally relevant characteristics as a basis for judgment. Although race and gender are gross categorizations that cannot possibly capture the essence of a person's character, we tend to use them in such contexts.

We can scarcely avoid categorizing or labelling people, especially when we have only limited and superficial evidence about them. There are many categories, some more specific and "self-presentational" than others. Who is that person? A black? An African-American? A guy in a motorcycle jacket? A floosie? A native? A white? A yuppie? A senior citizen? A cowboy? A Jew? A member of the blue-rinse crowd? A peacenik? A punk? A wasp? A "suit"? A little old lady? Every description has its associations and implications. Such categorizations use race, gender, age, dress, and self-presentation. Though not all are racist, all are in various ways stereotypical and expressive of various biases and prejudices. What we want and need in such contexts is knowledge of the particular individual. We have to get beyond thinking of a little old lady, a cowboy, a wasp, or a redneck. Or a black, a punk, or a yuppie. Yet with strangers we do not have the experience or knowledge to go beyond such superficial characteristics. The only solution is to use stereotypical generalizations with caution, as the basis for hypotheses that we know could be wrong. Whether another person strikes us as a "cowboy" or a "yuppie," we can try to keep our mind open to possibilities of character and style other than those implied by the category that first comes to mind.

In addition to inferences based on various cues, people are also more or less trusting depending on experience and upbringing. Most children are taught "never trust a stranger" – advice that could not be followed literally in modern society, though it makes sense in many situations. Some people pride themselves on having a casual, open, trusting style and on taking risks. Some even believe that an attitude of deliberate innocence and openness is protective in a way, innocent acceptance inspiring in the other a reciprocal attitude of goodwill and affection.

Somehow we have beliefs about human nature in general; people seem to have greater or lesser faith in human nature. Those attitudes emerge from experience and custom and are subject to alteration by events. Someone whose house is burglarized or who is the victim of a criminal attack is likely to find her faith in human nature diminished, especially if she is unable to explain the attack and is left thinking that anyone could have done it, or could do it again, at any time. By contrast, we may be the object of benevolent action by other people who are total strangers. Anyone who has had the experience of leaving a wallet or purse on a subway or in a store and having it returned, money intact, will know the boost of optimism such an experience can bring.

Cases are always interesting, but still more interesting would be a general theory about when to trust strangers. Clearly, such a theory would be incomplete. But two things are fairly obvious: we should be more cautious when more is at stake, and we will necessarily take more risks when we have less choice. For strangers, expectations of reliability and integrity can be based only on self-presentational cues, stereotypical beliefs, background experience, and general assumptions about human nature at large. Obviously, grounds for trust and suspicion in such cases are weak at best.

When our life, physical safety, loved ones, or prized goods are vulnerable, we should not trust a stranger. At best, only slight trust could be warranted by the evidence. If our vulnerability is slight, less trust is needed; trusting a stranger may be perfectly reasonable. Suppose we ask a stranger to mail a postcard, save us a place in line, or give directions to the nearest convenience store. A slight degree of trust is required in such situations, and we are not likely to be vulnerable. Should the stranger be unreliable, it will not matter very much. Because there is little risk, there is little objection to trusting strangers in such contexts. We have at best only superficial evidence of the stranger's trustworthiness, but at the same time we need trust him only slightly.

There are innumerable stories that can be told about trusting strangers. The recent telling of stories of "random acts of kindness" is a positive phenomenon. Some daily papers include an episode each day. Many involve people who experience car trouble and are assisted by strangers, who drive them to find help, boost cables, push their car out of snowdrifts, or even perform on-the-spot repair jobs. Others are about strangers who retrieve or rescue lost children, assist stranded travellers, or find and return lost wallets containing considerable sums of money. The beneficiaries of such acts are moved by the spontaneous generosity and report that their whole picture of human nature has been brightened as a result. By contrast, there are also random acts of appalling and extraordinary unkindness. We read terrible stories of people who admit strangers to their homes, ostensibly to use the bathroom or the telephone, and are robbed, assaulted, or brutally murdered as a result. We can find stories to support whatever claim we want to make about trusting the stranger, and the issue of whether, when, and how much we "should" trust strangers admits of little in the way of a general answer. Sometimes we trust strangers quite reasonably; sometimes we take irresponsible risks and get away with it; sometimes we take risks and pay dearly in personal security.

In the nature of the case we have little relevant knowledge and must base our decision on cues of limited relevance and reliability, stereotypical categorizations of "people like this," or hazy beliefs about human nature in general. How should we decide whether and when to trust an individual whom we encounter but do not know?

With individual strangers (as contrasted with cases of scatter trust) we are often well aware of the issue of trust and of *deciding* whether to trust. Trust seems to be a discrete act of *entrusting something* (often our physical security or very life) to another about whom we have no established expectations or feelings of confidence. And about this act, we face a decision. Acts that seem to express trust may not do so: they can be undertaken for a variety of other reasons. We might allow a stranger to come in and use the phone because we are embarrassed to refuse him, or accept a ride from a stranger because we do not want to appear ungrateful for the offer. The results are often positive, but occasionally disastrous. Despite their sometimes fascinating character, specific stories and dilemmas of trusting strangers seem to tell us little.

Whether to trust a stranger? In a sense the issue is one of interpersonal trust, because two individuals are involved. Yet that interpersonal trust is not founded on friendship, collegiality, kinship, meaningful encounter, or any other reliable and relevant relationship. The other who is a stranger is a person with whom we have an *impersonal* yet *interpersonal* relationship.

HIGH TRUST AND LOW TRUST

Individuals and perhaps whole societies and cultures may be more or less trusting of anonymous strangers. Scales for "faith in people" or "inter-personal trust" have been devised by social psychologists to indicate attitudes to human nature in general, which would presumably affect decisions about how much to trust individual strangers. One such scale, devised by Morris Rosenberg, was intended as "an empirical measure of faith in people." Rosenberg regarded faith in people, or the lack thereof, as a "basic interpersonal attitude."[24] The people he interviewed differed in this respect, some tending to have more "faith in human nature" than others. To rate respondents (college students) Rosenberg posed the following questions:

1. Some people say that most people can be trusted. Others say you can't be too careful in your dealings with people. How do you feel about it?
2. Would you say that most people are more inclined to help others, or more inclined to look out for themselves?
3. If you don't watch yourself, people will take advantage of you.
4. No one is going to care much what happens to you, when you get right down to it.
5. Human nature is fundamentally cooperative.

These matters seem so general, and the questions so vague, that it is hard to imagine a respondent replying with confidence. However Rosenberg reported that the scale was reliable and gave reproducible results. Apparently college students responded without objection, and the results show an appropriate degree of repeatability. Even those with little "faith" in fellow human beings seem generally to have been willing to assume that the researchers knew what they were doing and posed questions that deserved an answer.

Another effort to measure confidence in human nature is that of the social psychologist Julian Rotter. Rotter's Interpersonal Trust Scale (ITS) was intended to measure "a generalized expectancy held by an individual that the word, promise, or written statement of another individual or group can be relied upon."[25] Rotter used the scale to distinguish between high-trusting and low-trusting subjects.

People high in trust were disposed to be more trusting of people they did not know than were people low in trust. Rotter's scale ranges more widely than his definition of trust would suggest.[26] Respondents were asked to strongly agree, agree, neither agree nor disagree, disagree, or strongly disagree with twenty-five statements. Some representative statements:

Most idealists are sincere and usually practice what they preach [strong agreement indicates high trust].

In dealing with strangers, one is better off to be cautious until they have provided evidence that they are trustworthy [strong agreement indicates low trust].

Using the honor system of not having a teacher present during exams would probably result in increased cheating among students [strong agreement indicates low trust].

In these competitive times, one has to be alert, or someone is likely to take advantage of you [strong agreement indicates low trust].

It is safe to believe that, in spite of what people say, most people are primarily interested in their own welfare [strong agreement indicates low trust].

Most repairmen will not overcharge even if they think you are ignorant of their specialty [strong agreement indicates low trust].

Hypocrisy is on the increase in our society [strong agreement indicates low trust].

As noted in chapter 1, Rotter's understanding of trust was broader than his definition in terms of the reliability of statements. Issues such as cheating, honesty, concern, exploitation, and personal safety are raised. One of the most important aspects of trust is its open-ended character: we trust the other to do what is right or appropriate. Trust is rarely based on an explicit verbal commitment, a fact that constitutes an important objection to Rotter's account. Trusting, we feel confident that the other will do what is appropriate, that the full range is not easily capturable in language, much less typically promised in advance. We do not verbally promise to care for each other, be honest, abide by the rules, and do our jobs. In the circumstances of ordinary life most of us simply do these things as a matter of custom and habit and assume that others will do likewise.

The Rotter ITS scale was used with apparent success by various social psychologists over a twenty-year period.[27] In a 1971 article Rotter reported support for a number of interesting conclusions about the relationship between high or low trust and other personal characteristics. Being intelligent did not necessarily make people more suspicious of their fellows. Having less control over one's life was associated with lower trust. A lower socio-economic status tended to be correlated with lower trust. Youngest children in the family tended to be less trusting than only, older, or middle children. College students who described themselves as agnostics or atheists were generally less trusting than those with a religious affiliation. Having a more trusting attitude did not imply either being gullible or being too dependent on others.

Rotter published further results in 1980. He repeated his conviction that high or low trust was "a relatively stable personality characteristic." The ITS scale was designed to deal only with generalized expectancies. It was relevant to the issue of trusting an individual stranger about whom we know practically nothing. Studies based on this scale had nothing to do with trust in lovers, friends, children, colleagues, and professionals, and only an indirect bearing on scatter trust, trust in political figures, and institutional trust.

So far as the unknown individual is concerned, "high trusters" have a normal or default attitude of slight trust and "low trusters" one of slight or moderate distrust. Both deviate from their starting or normal attitude in the light of evidence and developing events: "It seems that high trusters can read the cues as well or as poorly as low trusters. They differ, however, in their willingness to trust the stranger where there are no clear-cut data. The high truster says to himself or herself, I will trust the person until I have clear evidence that he or she can't be trusted. The low truster says, I will not trust the person until there is clear evidence that he or she can be trusted."[28] The high truster, knowing nothing specific and having no cues, would be inclined (slightly) to trust the other; the low truster would be inclined in such a case (slightly) to distrust him or her. In any specific situation there are strands of background knowledge, contextual considerations about choice and degree of vulnerability, and cues from self-presentation. But we start from our standing attitude, which for high trusters presumes trust and for low trusters, distrust.

Rotter found that high trusters were more trustworthy than lower-trust subjects. They were more likely to respect others' privacy, to refrain from cheating and lying, and to perform tasks conscientiously. He also found that "everyone likes a high truster." People viewed high trusters as happier, more ethical, more attractive to the opposite sex, more desirable as close friends, and more likely to have had a happy childhood than low trusters. Having a tendency to trust did not indicate gullibility. On the contrary, there was some indication that high trusters were less gullible than low trusters because they were more sensitive to cues. Somewhat paradoxically, low trusters were more easily taken in by con artists than high trusters, being in this respect more vulnerable to their own failures of judgment.

This result is important and merits attention. A possible explanation (one not mentioned by Rotter himself) is that, compared to high trusters, lower trusters are *more* dependent on *fewer* sources of information. Being more suspicious does not generally protect us from error; it makes us more prone to error. We need other people as sources of evidence because we do not and cannot experience everything for ourselves. If we are generally suspicious, we close ourselves off from many sources of information. Cut off from most sources, we are left highly dependent on the few we are willing to rely on. We have fewer sources of information and fewer resources to analyse these sources critically. In addition, attitudes of distrust and suspicion will tend to make us less sensitive to other persons and less able to spot specific cues that something is wrong. Ironically, being suspicious can ultimately render us uncritical and more vulnerable to error.

The point is amply illustrated in a book on spies by Philip Knightley. Knightley gives many examples of fantastic bungling by intelligence services. Among the causes of this bungling, two seem to be primary: the tendency of agents to have an unrealistic, conspiratorial, virtually paranoid view of the world, and the tendency of politicians and bureaucrats not to believe these agents when they occasionally report solid and correct but surprising information, information that, though vital for the national interest, does not fit established views. The two phenomena are connected; the fixed negative view of outsiders requires a limited outlook insensitive to new information. In the spy world people must frequently lie about themselves and act out false roles. Knowing that they do this, knowing that many others must do it, spies and their administrative bosses become extraordinarily suspicious. Those who seem to be fellow spies might be double agents; sources might be trying to double-cross a person. They are under tremendous stress and do not know whom to believe. There is a kind of "obligatory paranoia" that goes with the role: "The CIA believes that this is healthy on the job and will help an officer to survive in a hostile environment. But once established, it is difficult to eliminate and separates the officer still further from the outside world. He begins to grow suspicious of it: is it plotting against him, as he has plotted against it? Finally, no one can be trusted, the enemy is everywhere."[29] Obviously such attitudes are apt to cause personal and interpersonal difficulties. In addition, they lead to *mistakes*. Their high level of suspicion makes these people reject new information because they do not trust the sources, and that disposition to reject new information makes them cling inflexibly to their fixed picture of the world. According to Knightley, closed-minded attitudes are a major cause of crucial and devastating mistakes within intelligence services. He describes many occasions when people had evidence of novel or surprising developments, sometimes of developments of tremendous significance, but were too rigid and suspicious to accept the information and consider its implications.

Rotter's conclusion that high-trust people tend to fare better in life than low-trust people is plausible and could be used as the basis for an argument that we should try to trust others more than we do, as was claimed by Alex Michalos. However, Rotter notes the limitations of his samples; most of the studies were done with American college students. Caveats aside, he summarizes his results as follows:

First a strong statement can be made about the consequences to the society of people being more trusting. People who trust more are less likely to lie and are possibly less likely to cheat or steal. They are more likely to give others a second chance and to respect the rights of others.

Second, the personal consequences for the high truster also seem beneficial. The high truster is less likely to be unhappy, conflicted, or maladjusted; he or she is liked more and is sought out by a friend more often, both by low-trusting and by high-trusting others.

Third, the high truster is no less capable of determining who should be trusted and who should not be trusted, although in novel situations he or she may be more likely to trust others than is the low truster.[30]

In addition, being open to friendship and intimacy, accepting of others, relaxed about the implications of others' actions and initiatives, and ready to establish relationships with strangers makes for a less stressful life than being fearful, competitive, and hostile.

Francis Fukuyama also argues for the benefits of trust. His account is more broadly based than that of Rotter in that he considers many countries and cultures. Yet in another respect, it is narrower: Fukuyama concentrates almost entirely on the economic effects of higher and lower trust. Fukuyama attends in particular to the size of firms and corporations generated within a society and the character of its worker-management relations. Contrasting "high trust" and "low trust" societies, Fukuyama attends primarily to relatively advanced societies: Japan, Germany, the United States, France, Italy, China, Taiwan, Hong Kong, and Korea. According to Fukuyama, Japan and Germany are high-trust societies in which people readily form relationships with strangers and are able to work and associate with them in a comfortable and flexible way. France is a less trusting society, with a lower level of spontaneous sociability. Southern Italy and Chinese societies (whether the People's Republic, Taiwan, Hong Kong, or Singapore) he regards as low trust. Korea is also a relatively low-trust society. Fukuyama claims that the United States has historically been a high-trust society but is at present a mixed case. Describing the economic arrangements in each country and culture at some length, Fukuyama argues that only in high-trust societies are people able to form, manage, and preserve extremely large corporations.[31]

In low trust-societies people are unwilling or unable to trust others outside the family. Familial corporate arrangements mean smaller firms. Handicapped by their unwillingness to supplement family efforts and talents by using professional managers, such firms rarely last more than two generations and often do not thrive after the death of the family founder. The phenomenon is so well-known that it has a name of its own: the Buddenbrooks effect. Fukuyama recognizes that for some purposes small firms have advantages over large ones: for instance, they tend to be more flexible. In the global marketplace, he argues, they are at some disadvantage. For this reason, from an economic point of view, low-trust societies are at some disadvantage compared to high-trust ones. Fukuyama also argues persuasively that economic arrangements do not emerge purely from material circumstances and the self-interested decisions of "rational actors." Rather, they are enormously affected by history, culture, and social ethics. To the extent that people share a core of moral beliefs and can trust each other to conform to basic moral precepts, they are more able to work with strangers, and the society is characterized by spontaneous sociability, which is advantageous for getting together in large organizations.

High trust, Fukuyama argues, facilitates more enduring and larger corporations. In societies not characterized by high trust, such as France and Korea, such corporations require considerable support and impetus from the state. In societies with a relatively high level of trust relationships between firms are also eased; there is less need for contracts that attempt to spell out every detail of arrangements, and relationships are more likely to persist in the face of hurdles and problems. Worker-management relations, and hence productivity, are vastly improved when people are able to trust each other without being members of the same family. If we accept his very general contrast between high-trust and low-trust societies, Fukuyama's arguments seem to show that high trust pays off from an economic point of view.

Should we be more trusting and try to adopt a more positive attitude towards human nature? To what extent does it make sense to urge people to trust more? We can try to be more trusting if we try to see the positive side of people and situations, avoid leaping to negative conclusions, cultivate our awareness of possible benevolent interpretations of what people say and do, and avoid dwelling on our negative emotions and beliefs. We have some choice about where we focus our attention and which feelings and sentiments we cultivate. Thus trust can be cultivated and distrust downplayed. The advice to "trust more" or "cultivate trust" or "try to be a high-trust person" makes some sense on this interpretation. We can also trust more by being more trustworthy.

A person who is trusted more is more likely to behave in a trustworthy way, as was indicated by the psychological research summarized by Mark Snyder. We can look at the matter either individually or socially. If an individual senses that she is, in general, regarded as a suspect and immoral character by society at large, she is unlikely to develop virtue and integrity; these are effects on individuals. In addition there are effects on society at large. People in general are affected by prevailing attitudes to human nature in general. If we live within a culture with a negative image of human nature, one that perpetuates and encourages the belief that human beings are by nature competitive and selfish and everyone is "out for number one," we are likely to behave accordingly and expect others to do likewise. The "rational interest" view has considerable opportunities to perpetuate itself, and the results are not, on the whole, beneficial. In fact, if Fukuyama is right, those results are counter-productive, even when judged from a purely economic point of view.

In so many ways a high-trust individual or society is better off than a low-trust one. High trust is better for individuals who trust more because it is conducive to relaxation, improved health, attractiveness, more friendships, and a better intimate life. It is individually better for those who are trusted more because it offers to them a more hopeful and inspiring model of their motivation and action. Socially, higher trust is better for all because it helps us to construct a social world where we see each other as morally valuable and responsible beings. We can mutually benefit from cultivating moral dispositions and habits and confirming our own positive and confident expectations. And, if Fukuyama is right, there are considerable economic benefits to living in a high-trust culture. Distrust, he argues, limits economic opportunities and has real economic costs.

What these arguments do not recall is our vulnerability when we trust. Both Rotter and Fukuyama seem wilfully insensitive to the existence of cases in which distrust is warranted or people are greatly harmed because they have trusted. In some contexts we risk life itself. Having a high-trust attitude to other people may be generally beneficial, but there are some contexts, and indeed some whole societies, in which trusting strangers is too risky to be sensible. What people expect of others depends on their culture, religion, and material and political circumstances. If relatives simply disappear, if one is starved, beaten, and tortured, if friends and colleagues may be spies for a brutal regime, people are unlikely to be high trusters, and a recommendation to trust more makes little sense. Although there are no societies without trust and none without interdependence, the webs and patterns of trust and the sorts of trust that are productive and sensible vary enormously from one type of society to another.

6 Lower-Trust Societies

Thus far we have considered trust as fundamental to knowledge and belief in modern societies, to effective working and professional relationships in those societies, and to their very functioning. In Western industrial societies people who are inclined to trust others, including strangers, seem to fare better than those who are mistrustful and suspicious. But such benefits may not hold in other sorts of societies. Are there societies where being generally inclined to trust others would be a handicap? Where social trust is virtually absent? Some writings suggest that impoverished peasant societies fit this description, offering evidence that trust in others is limited because of the bleak circumstances in which people live. Pervasive distrust is understandable in such circumstances. When distrust is generalized and substantial, it constitutes a considerable obstacle to material and social progress.

REFLECTIONS ON PEASANT SOCIETIES

Many observers have seen fearfulness, suspicion, and competitiveness as characteristic of peasant societies. In what respects are peasant societies "low trust?" Would peasant communities fare better if they were able to be trusting enough to co-operate and carry out community projects?

A peasant village or community is agrarian, typically small, and relatively isolated. Peasants work the land for their own subsistence.[1] A peasant society at a low level of material development is not just any society at such a level; it contrasts, for instance, with the nomadic society of the traditional Inuit, African Bushman, or nomadic horsemen of Mongolia. In nomadic cultures people lead a simple life that is certainly pre-industrial, but they are not peasants because they do not engage in agriculture. The peasant conception of a good life characteristically involves productive work raising animals and crops on a small amount of land, and marriage, with children who are brought up to help work the land. A fervent attachment to land and ancestral ways is typical of peasant societies. In terms of social trust, it is noteworthy that in impoverished peasant communities suspicion is so ubiquitous that it is difficult to carry out co-operative community projects.

George Foster, an anthropologist who has studied a number of peasant societies, suggests that many peasant cultures have an Image of Limited Good: "Peasants view their social, economic, and natural universes – their total environment – as one in which all of the desired things in life, such as land, wealth, health, friendship, and love, manliness and honour, respect and status, power and influence, security and safety, exist in finite quantity and are always in short supply ... there is no way directly within peasant power to increase the available quantities."[2] The peasant's world is a competitive one in which every other person is an actual or potential opponent because what one takes is not there for another. There is not enough for all. Even sexual pleasure, maternal love, energy, and honour are thought to exist in finite quantities according to the Limited Good view of the world. Any status and well-being achieved by others constitutes a threat to oneself and one's family. To preserve *machismo* a man has to keep on winning battles, which others will have to lose. Given a fixed quantity of goods, if one person receives more, others will receive less. In this zero-sum game other people are potentially a threat and will be regarded with suspicion.

While the notion that there are fixed quantities in friendship, talent, or reputation may strike us as implausible to the point of being bizarre, it is nevertheless understandable that the Limited Good hypothesis is plausible to impoverished peasants engaged in subsistence farming. Land is absolutely fundamental to peasant peoples; it is the very basis of their livelihood. And the quantity of land is fixed. Peasant economies are characteristically poor and unproductive, and it is often difficult to improve production levels or to establish material security. In harsh circumstances it is natural to pursue first the material interests of one's own family. Without special persuasion and especially favourable circumstances, that will mean a reluctance to participate in co-operative economic endeavours outside it. This ethos has been termed *familism*, *amoral familism*, or *familial individual-ism*. It is the doctrine that what counts, what should be pursued, is the interests of oneself and one's own immediate family. Ethical obligations do not exist outside the family circle.

Familism seems a viable approach to life for many agrarian people living under harsh material circumstances: "Economic activities in peasant societies require only limited cooperation. As family units, peasant families can typically produce most of their own food with-out extra help, build their houses, weave cloth for their clothes, carry their own product to market and sell it – in short, they can take care of themselves with a degree of independence impossible in an indus-trial society and difficult in nomadic or hunter-gatherer societies."[3]

This is not to say that family units in subsistence agricultural soci-eties are completely independent; they are merely closer to being so than are families in many other societies. In an impoverished peasant society each family unit tends to see itself as contending with others for the bare necessities of existence. The head of the family (the man) must compete with other men to provide for his family in harsh cir-cumstances.

Many observers report that in such circumstances people tend to use caution and reserve, even secrecy, to hide important economic resources from others seen as actual or potential competitors. "Toward those who are not of the family the reasonable attitude is suspicion."[4] An unusually prosperous peasant family will be regard-ed as a threat to others and may suffer backbiting, or even accusa-tions of witchcraft as a result. The ritual-consumption characteristic of many peasant societies (in huge wedding or funeral feasts, for example) can be understood as a redistributive mechanism, com-pelling those who have amassed resources to expend them. In such societies the socially acceptable paths to material improvement are those that depend more on luck than on effort. A peasant family might receive goods from outside, emigrate, have a rich patron, find buried treasure, or win a prize or a lottery; that sort of improvement in its fortunes would be socially acceptable because it would not threaten others. Like manna from heaven, such goods acquired come from outside the system, and one person's good luck does not repre-sent bad luck for another.

Life is competitive and difficult, and hard work often brings little progress. Sometimes things are so hopeless that thrift and hard work seem to have limited functional value; it may seem as though it is impossible for things to change. When impoverished peasants have a bleak and fatalistic outlook, that outlook is based on their own expe-rience of the world, which seems to confirm it. In the precarious world of subsistence farming, life is difficult; merely surviving takes a lot of energy, and few manage to improve their situation by their own efforts. As we might expect, such fatalism tends to be counter-productive, but it cannot be deemed entirely irrational, given the harsh circumstances in which many subsistence farmers live. Their overriding goal is their own simple survival and that of their children, so *amoral familism* is a natural ethos in these circumstances. Yet that ethos stands in the way of material and social progress because it makes co-operation difficult by making social trust impossible. When everyone is understood to be working only for himself and his immediate family, anyone who would seek a co-operative venture is immediately suspect of wanting to exploit others for purposes of his own.

The classic work on amoral familism is Edward Banfield's *The Moral Basis of a Backward Society*. It is based on the interviews, observations, and experiences of Edward and Laura Banfield in the southern Italian village of Montegrano in the mid-1950s. In Montegrano the Banfields found a culture in which distrust of people outside the immediate family was a strong norm. When people married, they tended to break off from their family of origin and did not engage in shared activities even with their parents and siblings. The family in Montegrano was the nuclear family (parents and their children), not the more extended family including aunts, uncles, grandparents, and cousins. Despite its ethical centrality, this nuclear family was a small and weak social unit. The family provided a sense of what life was all about. Individuals were expected to define themselves in a family role (ideally that of parent), work to keep the family going, set their children off on the right road to life, and protect the family unit against calamity.

Banfield describes life in Montegrano as harsh and empty of joys, and the people as too distrustful to engage in collective community improvement. Peasant life was difficult: "a mountain of woe hangs over it by a single thread."[5] Banfield asked the inhabitants of Montegrano to tell him stories. Of three hundred twenty stories told, only two or three had a happy tone. Peasants were fearful of what life held in store, and fatalistic, viewing events as largely beyond their control. Success, if experienced at all, would result from luck or the favour of the saints, not individual effort and certainly not co-operation. Men and women were to do their best to protect the short-term material advantage of the family and keep on reasonably good terms with their neighbours. No further action was feasible. Suspicions ran deep; people were characteristically distrustful of others.

With wealth limited and fellow villagers cast in the role of competitors, the peasants of Montegrano were unwilling to reveal the extent of their economic resources. A favourite story:

a peasant father ... throws his hat on the ground. "What did I do?" he asks one of his sons. "You threw your hat upon the ground," the son answers, whereupon the father strikes him down. He picks up his hat and asks another son, "What did I do?" "You picked up your hat," the son replies, and gets a blow in his turn. "What did I do?" the father asks the third son. "I don't know," the smart one replies. "Remember sons," the father concludes, "if someone asks you how many goats your father has, the answer is, you don't know."[6]

Lying was viewed as normal. You had to lie because, if you told other people the truth, they might use that knowledge against you. But somehow it was still a fault in others that they lied. You lied because you distrusted others, and then you distrusted them all the more because of the things they did to you, including lying. Thus the custom of lying served to increase the distrust on which it was founded. People were suspicious of each other, unwilling to reveal information, so they lied; then, lying, they were unwilling to believe each other, so their suspicion was enhanced.

Economic insecurity and the conviction that resources are finite entailed harsh competition and distrust. In their competition for survival people measured their progress by comparing themselves with others, fearing anxiously that others were doing better than they. In the bitter competition each family was implicitly a threat to every other. The people of Montegrano were nominally Christian, but religious beliefs seem to have had little effect on their daily life or moral attitudes. Nor was there any faith that God could be counted on to make life better some day. A southern Italian peasant might hope for a little help from the saints or the Madonna, but he regarded God as a capricious, unreliable being. Under the ethos of amoral familism, goodness had little to do with religion and everything to do with support of the family.

The peasants of Montegrano were sorely affected by poverty, ignorance, and low social status. The nuclear family was the dominant social unit, and each family was essentially isolated. Of course people had occasional friends, and there were some temporary political alliances, but nothing at the group level lasted long. The few organizations that existed – burial societies and festival committees – were not very important in the total scheme of community life. As a structural unit, the community was simply weak.

Southern Italy had been governed by absolutist monarchical

regimes since the Middle Ages. In no period had there been autonomy for communities and regions, and the peasants who worked the
land did not typically own it, or even occupy it for very long. Even
the institutions of the church were felt by people to be a burden and
did little to support any sense of community. Unlike the north and
centre of Italy, in which there had been city-states that formed
republics whose history included many vibrant social organizations,
the south had virtually no tradition of civic associations. Southern
Italy had preserved feudal practices as late as Napoleonic times, and
this history did much to discourage people from associating with
strangers and trying to work co-operatively for the community. The
prevailing assumption was that political power was elsewhere.
Extreme centralization had contributed to the ethos of suspicion
because these people had little or no experience of doing anything
together.

The people of Montegrano appeared to have no conception of community interest or public good and would take no initiative to make
even minor improvements in their village. "It is precisely their inability to act in the public interest which is the problem," Banfield concluded, contrasting Montegrano with a comparably sized town in
Utah where people worked together to organize sports and cultural
groups and there were many and varied civic organizations.[7] In the
small Utah town people were able to collaborate on various community projects, something that never happened in Montegrano. Banfield was convinced that if the people of Montegrano had worked
together, the quality of their lives could have been improved by cultural and sports activities, better school and medical facilities, the
sharing of agricultural equipment, and the formation of economic
enterprises – not to mention more friendly associations, generally
improved relationships, and a higher degree of social trust.

Montegrano was, of course, affected by poor material conditions:
overpopulation, underemployment, land hunger, and unproductive
agriculture. But Banfield saw the distrustful social outlook as an
enormous obstacle to progress. To overcome the moral limitations of
amoral familism, Banfield thought three things would have to
change. First, the interest of the family, defined exclusively in short-
term material terms, would have to be understood to include some
non-material aspects such as prestige or reputation. Second, some
people would have to gain the capacity to act as leaders. Third, the
people would have to refrain from gratuitously seeking to destroy
social organizations. Banfield's second and third points are directly
related to trust. For people to gain the capacity to act as leaders, others must trust them in the role of leader; in the Montegrano that Ban-

field observed this was not the case. And people need a sense that they can work together with others who are not members of their family, collaborating in pursuit of a common goal.

Some twenty years before the Banfields visited Montegrano, an Italian doctor, Carlo Levi, was banished to the small and poor village of Gagliano in the county of Luciano, also in southern Italy. Levi was a painter, doctor, and writer, an uncompromising opponent of fascism; he was exiled to village life for his anti-fascist views. Levi describes Gagliano as a place whose way of life had been essentially the same for nearly five thousand years. Neither Greeks nor Romans nor Christian missionaries had really penetrated the isolated area. The inhabitants themselves said that Christ had stopped at Eboli, to the north. In some ways Levi's description of village life is similar to Banfield's. He emphasizes the suspiciousness of the people of Gagliano. He was warned right away by the mayor that "there were many tongues. I had better trust no one."[8] He was told not to accept food from inhabitants, especially women, who, he was told, would give him love potions made of disgusting substances. (Levi ignored this advice and came to no harm.)

The village of Gagliano had experienced considerable emigration to America. When Levi lived there in the mid-thirties, although there were only 1,200 inhabitants, over 2,000 men from Gagliano were living in America. Second-hand clothing from America was sold at conveniently cheap prices, and many inhabitants had household objects sent by relatives. America had some potential to improve one's prospects in life. Peasant homes with pictures on the wall showed two figures: "On one side was the black, scowling face, with its large inhuman eyes, of the Madonna of Viggiano; on the other a coloured print of the sparkling eyes, behind gleaming glasses, and the hearty grin of President Roosevelt."[9] The Black Madonna struck Levi as an ancient earth goddess, President Roosevelt as an all-powerful Zeus. The Madonna might bring luck – or, more probably, benefits might come from Roosevelt's New Deal America. To Gagliano at this time the outside world was, for all practical purposes, America. The Italian state was absent so far as any contribution to daily life or hope of material improvement was concerned. Like Banfield, Levi observed that the state was seen as something remote, a locus of power but not a centre from which one could expect anything good. Power was in the far-away state; the people of Gagliano certainly did not have it. They had no notion of doing much themselves, but they did not think the state would do much good either: "To the peasants the State is more distant than heaven and far more of a scourge, because it is always against them."[10]

The prevailing attitude in Gagliano was one of resignation and fatalism. There was little public spirit or community effort. But the tone of Levi's description is different from that of Banfield. He did not see the peasants as desperately competitive or suspicious. Unlike Banfield, he came to love them. They had complete confidence in his concern for their well-being and his abilities as a doctor. When Levi broke the law in order to see needy patients, he "had complete faith in their loyalty and discretion; they would have died rather than betray me."[11] Levi found among these people a kind of passive solidarity. It was not an activist one, not a solidarity based on any sense that they could work together to get anything done. What the people of Gagliano seemed to share was a comradely, age-old patience and sense of suffering together. What would happen to them and their community depended on Fate: "They live submerged in a world that rolls independent of their will, where man is in no way separate from his sun, his beast, his malaria, where there can be neither happiness ... nor hope, because these two are adjuncts of personality and here there is only the grim passivity of a sorrowful Nature."[12]

In the end Levi found a harsh beauty in this limited world. When he was permitted to leave, he was sorry in a way. Levi saw the hopelessness of peasant life as due in part to the abyss separating people from the state, in which they had no share, and in part to the middle-class village tyrants who lived off petty thievery and a bastardized tradition of feudal rights. For material progress to be possible, he thought, the people needed some autonomy and a stake in affairs of state.

Frank Canciun, who has studied Banfield's work, rejects the theory that a backward ethic of amoral familism explains the lack of community spirit among southern Italian peasants. Canciun does not dispute Banfield's general description of the bleakness of peasant life and attitudes of suspicion and hopelessness. But he rejects the idea that those phenomena should be explained by appealing to an ethos of amoral familism and a generalized condition of distrust. Rather, Canciun argues that the causes were the peasants' fatalism and lack of confidence in their ability to change their environment. The peasants, on his understanding, did not trust themselves to be able to do anything to improve their condition. Canciun argues that it was the people's deep conviction that they could not do anything and were not responsible to try that accounts for the lack of co-operative effort. In contemporary parlance we would say that these people were not "empowered." They had no trust or faith in themselves and little sense that they could do something about their circumstances. To work together on any community project that might improve their condition, they would first need a sense that it was possible for them, collectively, to accomplish something. They would need to counter fatalism with energy and hope.

Canciun disagrees with Banfield in some respects, but he does not really challenge Banfield's claim that trust was low in Montegrano and similar places. He disagrees with Banfield in regarding low trust as the *cause* of a general lack of collaboration and passivity. He sees these as resulting from the lack of any sense of responsibility or capacity to initiate change. Empowerment would require that these peasants believe they could do something. Indeed, people in impoverished circumstances have sometimes worked together to change their circumstances.

Canciun sees distrustful and fatalistic peasant attitudes as a natural effect of their way of life. These attitudes are based on decades, even centuries, of hard experience that seem to prove that peasants are basically vulnerable to forces of nature and far-away governments. Peasants tend to see the world as a stratified place wherein people in different social positions have different responsibilities. The government, though distant and distrusted, is regarded as responsible for solving any problem that is not specifically within one family or another. In Canciun's experience, when a problem was discovered, people would invariably say the government should do something about it. Yet they would add that there was little hope the government would act effectively. Canciun believes that that attitude was often historically and politically realistic: history has given peasants many reasons to distrust government actions. But somewhat perversely, these people, who had learned to consider the government their worst enemy, at the same time expected it to solve all social problems. The people were "disempowered" in the sense that neither individually nor collectively could they see themselves as potential agents of social and political change. What was happening? What was going wrong? What could be done about it? The duty to think about and do something was assigned elsewhere, to an alien agency. To bring about constructive change, these people would need some experience of their own competence, responsibility, and agency.[13]

Southern Italy is apparently not unique in these respects. Observers have made similar comments on peasant life and attitudes in other parts of the world. George Westacott and Lawrence Williams, for instance, worked in Peru, where they studied trust among 2,715 villagers. Like Banfield, Westacott and Williams assumed that trust is a key element in co-operative action, which is necessary for development and positive social change. They hypothesized that the ability to place one's trust in strangers is necessary in order to co-operate and "modernize." And they found their hypothesis confirmed.[14] Like Rotter, Michalos, and Fukuyama, Westacott and Williams hold that higher trust is an advantage when it comes to economic and social development. To the extent that people can "trust more" and can readily form associations and bonds outside their immediate family, they will be able to make arrangements that contribute to a better society. On this view, a greater willingness to trust people outside the immediate family and to rely on strangers will tend to make people more progressive, more open to change, and more oriented towards the future.

Westacott and Williams define trust as the expectation that others will interact in a positive manner, and a confidence in one's fellows. With such confidence a person will be ready to entrust aspects of his or her own welfare to other people. Westacott and Williams expected low trust in a situation of scarcity and rigid social stratification. Indeed, the Peruvian villagers who were their subjects tested low in trust and were unwilling to work with others. They had little belief in their own efficacy, little flexibility in the face of change, and little positive orientation towards the future.

John Aquilar commented on similar attitudes when he studied an Indian peasant community in Mexico.[15] Aquilar found chronic mistrust to be pervasive in the lives of the Indian peasant people. He believed that this attitude was an understandable adaptation to harsh economic conditions and a history of exploitation. But even though there was a sense in which the attitude was realistically grounded, generalized distrust was a serious social handicap in this Mexican village, just as it was in Banfield's Montegrano. Here too, generalized distrust prevented people from working together to improve their condition. Some of the effects of general distrust in this Indian village were insecurity, secrecy about resources, lying, a tendency to disbelieve others, and a conception of life as fundamentally competitive. There was considerable backbiting, envy, and gossip. One person's gains were assumed to be another's losses. The social landscape was bleak, forbidding, and ruled by selfishness.[16]

Though acknowledging that life was hard and hazardous, Aquilar thought that the distrust of the Indian villagers went beyond what circumstances warranted and was too generalized and rigid to be helpful as an attitude to life. He found some co-operation between villagers on routine household affairs but virtually none in the area of commercial or community activity. Villagers said that co-operative activities would not work because people were "too bad-hearted." And the lack of trust and desire for secrecy made even social visiting seem risky and difficult: "People say they do not visit others because they might be thought to be spying on them and they dread the visits of others, who they feel may take away information about their possessions and activities which might become the topic of general gossip. Self-disclosure (of sentiments, ambitions, etc.) is particularly avoided because this is simply another way of arming others."[17] A relaxed and friendly chat could be dangerous, revealing information that could cost economically or could lead to ridicule or betrayal. If you told someone something, he could use it against you. In conversation, meaningful interpersonal contact was kept to a minimum.

In this society people were aware of trust ("confianza") as an issue, and they did trust neighbours to offer help in emergencies. They valued close friends whom they trusted. (Banfield does not comment on friendship in Montegrano; we are left with the impression that friendships outside the family did not exist.) In the Mexican village there was an additional kind of trust in exchange arrangements, where people would tacitly contract to help each other in certain ways. (I'll help you with the vegetables; you look after my child.) There were particular strategies to be used in developing such relationships: gifts of food, presuming allegiance through exchanges of gossip, inviting another to a feast, extending unsolicited aid, and publicly greeting another with special enthusiasm. Such partners in social exchange were sometimes intimate friends. Thus, within a situation of generalized mistrust, some relationships of trust were created.[18] Even so, Aquilar's analysis gives an impression similar to Banfield's: the difficulty of subsistence farming made for secrecy, limited trust, and a general lack of optimism.

In a small community or peasant society the vast majority of people deal only with familiar people in familiar situations. One author estimates that in peasant life of the Middle Ages the average person did not encounter more than one hundred different individuals during a lifetime.[19] Thus, even in those small peasant societies where there is trust, people tend to base it on personal knowledge, not on any sense of how government, institutions, or social roles function to create a reliable infrastructure. It is individual, based on personal experience. (I have known this man for years; I know how he care for his animals; I can safely buy meat from him.) By contrast, a modern economy and a viable democracy require acceptance of the idea that there are reasonably functioning institutions, bureaucracies, and checking procedures and that we can deal reliably with strangers.

As is immediately obvious when we consider the many phenomena of scatter trust, complex modern societies presume that people are generally able to trust strangers and feel some obligation to act in trustworthy ways towards them – especially when they are doing their job. Modernization, bureaucracy, and social roles presuppose that most of the time, most people in a society are both trusting and trustworthy. It is on the basis of such accounts as Banfield's that many observers have seen lack of trust or "low trust" as an obstacle to social and economic development. There appears to be a certain chicken and egg problem here. Does low trust cause material poverty? Or does material poverty cause low trust? The competitiveness that is characteristic of some bleak peasant societies is in all likelihood itself the result of material poverty. It is not unreasonable to expect that having more abundant resources would lessen this desperate competitiveness, making people less fearful and more inclined to trust each other enough to work together. Perhaps an improved level of material development would *produce* greater trust rather than being an *effect* of it.

Does greater trust facilitate material development? Or do material development and increased economic security facilitate greater trust?[20] The most reasonable interpretation, I think, is that there is influence in both directions. As we have seen, unwillingness or inability to trust people outside narrow family circles works against civic association, community improvement, and economic growth. The attitudes and practices of amoral familism result from historical and cultural forces going back many centuries, have their social and economic costs, and are an obstacle to constructive development. But these attitudes and practices are to some extent the result of material deprivation as well as its contributory cause. If material conditions and cultural attitudes could be changed, opportunities would emerge from a situation in which a genuine civil society developed. To change either materially or culturally, people need to associate and work with strangers and others outside the family.

Even cultural and historical patterns do not make suspiciousness inevitable. Generalized social distrust persists as it does because it is an attitude that seems natural and is corroborated by circumstances and because of the history of the society. Confidence in the human environment is correlated with increased education and economic privilege and with experience of voluntary civic organizations. Peasants in bleak circumstances turn out to be relatively low in trust – for good reason.[21]

PATRON AND CLIENT

A device that partially compensates for lack of formal bureaucratic regularity and generalized trust in others is the patron-client relationship. In this relationship a relatively vulnerable and low-status member of a society establishes a special connection with someone of higher status, more wealth, and greater power. The client shows the patron deference and performs various services for him or her, expecting protection and favours in return. These relationships are *particularized, hierarchical,* and *diffuse.* They are particularized in so far as they depend on the history of these particular individuals and their interactions; they are not based on generalized social roles but on the specific people involved. The client relies on this "big man" to help him because he has made specific arrangements and has had specific experiences and exchanges with just this "big man." The relationships are hierarchical because they are constructed on the presumption that the patron is definitely the social and economic superior of his client. And they are diffuse because they extend without clear boundaries over many areas of life. The patron may find a job and shelter for his client, name the client's children, receive gifts from him on Christmas, call the client in to assist in sudden domestic emergencies, get him to take over when a servant leaves, and so on. There is no single specific job the client does for the patron and no single specific area in which he receives benefits from the patron.

In such arrangements the client buys protection and in return accepts the patron's control. What the client receives is a kind of unofficial insurance. He depends on the patron, to whom he is morally indebted and whom he tends to honour and sentimentalize. Trust in a clientelistic relationship is based on personal ties and obligations, not on positive expectations about social roles and institutions.[22]

In this sort of system, if an official treats a person well, it is because of a personal relationship, not because officials as such can be counted on to do the decent thing. A person who gets decent treatment will generalize not by role or function but across *time* and *personal identity* to further actions by the same person. If a patron has treated him well in the past, the client comes to trust him in this respect and will rely on favourable treatment from him in the future. He thus generalizes about what *this person over time* will do, not what the next person he encounters in the *same role* (clerk, doctor, teacher, official, etc.) will do. The patron-client relation epitomizes an individualized bond, which is a thin form of trust and provides little basis for more generalized social trust. Under a system of clientelism, people trust not roles or institutions but individuals to whom they owe things, and who owe them in return.[23]

In societies where formal norms regulating bureaucracy tend to be weak, client-patron relationships perform the social function of offering some protection to weaker members of society. However, the

problem of transferring trust to new actors in similar roles and stations is not addressed by this kind of system. Patron-client trust is
entirely dependent on what has happened in the particular relationship between the client and his patron. What helped the client was
his own patron, not the system at large nor even anyone of a kind.
There is no prospect of mastering uncertainty through institutional
means: there is no system in which job-holders perform reliably and
offer services and opportunities on the basis of universal criteria. To
cope with the world, vulnerable persons must involve themselves in
a dependent (and potentially humiliating) personal relationship with
some individual benefactor attached to "the system." Entitlements
are special, not conferred by citizenship itself: "People expect to be
treated not as citizens, equal before the law, but as individuals having special links with other persons, either the bureaucrats themselves or certain intercessors who mediate in otherwise impersonal
contacts with a bureaucrat, so that the latter will play his role in a
more interested manner and accelerate administrative procedures."[24]
A weak individual should look for a patron; otherwise he or she will
have no hope of protection.

Even by those who participate in them, patron-client relationships
are seen as somewhat corrupt. There is little boundary between economic, religious, political, or social arrangements, and the personal
nature of the bond shows a lack of open access in a society to important goods and opportunities. Even to one who benefits from patronage, it feels slightly wrong: "Patronage has a contradictory nature,
being hierarchical but mutually beneficial, somehow combining
inequality andpromised reciprocity, voluntarism and coercion, symbolic and instrumental resources."[25] In clientelistic societies, political
and administrative posts are regarded as starting-points to personal
enrichment and benefiting one's dependents. Particularized, non-
institutional trust tends to be fragile and limited. This is not the system of trust Luhmann describes as characteristic of a modern society;
nor is it the trust Fukuyama argues to be of such importance in productive economies: "The trust that underlies clientelistic relations
cannot easily be extended and does not confer system reliability – not
even the obligations between client and patron are relatively long-
term. Instead, this sort of individualized trust reinforces the low level
of institutional trust and reproduces the divisiveness and weak internal solidarity of the lower strata, the elites, and the entrepreneurs,
leading people to establish clientelistic arrangements for the mastering of future interactions."[26] Vulnerable people who accept the role
of client are likely to receive benefits and decent treatment from a
patron. But they will quite rightly attribute them only to the

favourable disposition of the patron, with whom they maintain that special and somewhat undignified relationship. Their security, such as it is, will not be credited to institutions or the social system but only to their subservience and loyalty to well-placed individuals from whom they can solicit and obtain favours.

The system of clientelism is one in which participants have unequal power and unequal social dignity. The client needs favours from the patron, who is powerful enough to dispense them. Even in a system that does not work on the basis of universalistic criteria, many people seem to preserve a moral conviction that greater equality would be better and that some people should not have such power to dispense benefits and offices to others. Thus, even in contexts where it is pervasive, clientelism tends to carry with it a certain aura of improper partiality and corruption. With a particularistic basis of distribution (under clientelism, it is definitely not *what* you know but *who* you know) a distrust in the occupants of various social offices is a natural consequence. People know that these roles have been filled by the relatives and clients of powerful people, whose selection has had nothing to do with either honesty or competence. If their own friends and relations are not in power, they are likely to feel vulnerable and insecure. (One would expect clientelism to aggravate ethnic, religious, or tribal conflict for this very reason.) A kind of trust has been established outside the family, but it is a precarious one, and not a building-block for confidence in social roles and institutions. Client-patron relationships are based on a tenuous kind of trust, set in a context of flawed social justice. Its limitations may be indicated by the notes of insincerity characteristic in some compulsory transactions – as when a client in considerable poverty has to supply gifts to the patron, ostensibly as a gesture of friendliness and gratitude or, worse yet, in the feudal tradition of the right of the seigneur to take the virginity of the tenant's bride.

According to Luis Roniger, who has written extensively on the subject, patron-client relations are common in Mediterranean cultures, the Middle East, Southeast Asia, and Latin America. Under clientelism there is a tension between potentially universal criteria for allotment of jobs and benefits and the limitation of free access by particular relationships. The former are the basis for modern institutions requiring trust in strangers; the latter are typical of clientelism. Roniger comments that societies that rely on personalized trust and exchange tend to have economies characterized by a sharp contrast between rich and poor, a low level of local autonomy, and a tendency towards passivity.[27]

These features produce in turn a low level of societal trust. To the extent that there is trust between people who are not in the same family, that trust is in the patron or in a small range of people whom one knows well, and it does not transfer easily to broader settings.[28] There is no act or set of actors that is effective and perceived as legitimate. There is no sense of equal opportunity, or of offices and roles filled by people selected because they are competent. Social agents are seen as immoral or amoral, featuring "a continuous manipulation and perpetual imbalance."[29]

Inequality, hierarchy, lack of dignity, and a sense of partiality and corruption make the system seem less than good even to participants. Patron-client relationships are necessary to people made insecure in the continual struggle for scarce resources, but they are unreliable and only marginally an improvement on amoral familism so far as trust and sociability are concerned.

Millions – perhaps billions – of human beings in peasant or pre-modern cultures live in circumstances where distrust is the norm and there is little social solidarity. But this is not to say that they live in societies where there is no trust at all.[30] Such people tend not to trust strangers any more than they have to, and they have little confidence in government, institutions, or generalized social roles. Instead they place their confidence in family members and, to a limited extent, in a few neighbours, friends, or powerful people outside the family. Client-patron relationships offer a partial substitute for generalized social trust. These lower-trust societies are by no means societies with no trust. People associate, connect, and are interdependent, even if they try to limit their dependency to a small circle of others whom they know. In these societies there is social trust, but it is limited in scope, and its limitations are accompanied by significant social, political, and economic handicaps.

TRUST AS SOCIAL CAPITAL

In his recent book *Making Democracy Work* Robert Putnam offers a detailed and rigorous study of government institutions in the various regions of Italy. In 1970 the central Italian government established fifteen new regional governments. Five had been established somewhat earlier, so there were twenty regional governments in all. They had the same structure and a similar financial basis. Yet by the late 1980s these governments varied considerably in effectiveness. In northern and central Italy regional governments were far more effective than in the south with respect to their internal operations, policy initiatives, and implementation of policy. On the basis of extensive empirical studies Putnam concludes that the primary factor behind this variation is the degree to which the various regions have a vibrant civic life. In voluntary civic associations – whether these are choirs, bird-watching clubs, or sports groups – people have an opportunity to interact as equals. They are in a context where they can be comrades, colleagues, or friends, not competitors, not patrons or clients: "Citizens in a civil community, though not selfless saints, regard the public domain as more than a battleground for pursuing personal interest ... Citizens in a civic community, on most accounts, are more than merely active, public-spirited, and equal. Virtuous citizens are helpful, respectful, and trustful toward one another, even when they differ on matters of substance."[31]

What is most needed for civic participation is a sense of social trust, a sense that we can work with others, who will do their part to participate and take projects forward. Experience in civic associations can help to develop and extend this sort of trust, building a sense of solidarity and co-operative public-spiritedness. Although social trust is immensely significant from a political point of view, it need not develop in political associations. Any form of getting together outside the family to participate in common activities or work towards a common goal will build trust and a sense of community and empowerment. Putnam argues persuasively that in contemporary Italy, the more "civic" a region is, the more effective is its regional government. Though it is more than forty years since the Banfields studied Montegrano, Putnam's results are consistent with their observations. Southern Italy is still a region where there is little social trust; it is still handicapped by a low level of civic participation and a weak sense of community, and these differences between it and other regions of Italy have a clear impact on the effectiveness of regional governments: "The performance of a regional government is somehow very closely related to the civic character of social and political life within the region. Regions with many civic associations, many newspaper readers, many issue-oriented voters, and few patron-client networks seem to nourish more effective governments."[32]

In a society where there are strong civic associations, politics tends to be less elitist, more horizontal. Representatives and leaders come from a wider slice of society, and privilege, including educational privilege, counts for less. Where there are civic associations, there tends to be a greater sense of political equality. Citizens of less civic regions tend to feel exploited, alienated, and powerless. In a civic community, where many people have the experience of participating in groups where work must be shared, there is greater understanding that you cannot ride for free. Putnam found that the least civic areas of Italy are the traditional, small southern villages, where social trust is low or absent. His description of these regions, based on observations in the 1980s, recalls Banfield's description of Montegrano:

Few people aspire to partake in deliberations about the commonweal, and few such opportunities present themselves. Political participation is triggered by personal dependency or private greed, not by collective purpose. Engagement in social and cultural organizations is meager. Private piety stands in for public purpose. Corruption is widely regarded as the norm, even by politicians themselves, and they are cynical about democratic principles. "Compromise" has only negative overtones. Laws (almost everyone agrees) are made to be broken, but fearing others' lawlessness, people demand sterner discipline. Trapped in these interlocking vicious circles, nearly everyone feels powerless, exploited, and unhappy.[33]

Why are there so few civic associations in southern Italy, as contrasted with north and central Italy? Putnam traces the difference to historical factors going back ten centuries, to conquest and feudal traditions in the south and the absence of guilds and republicanism, which were characteristic of the north. The greater social trust in north and central Italy has been advantageous economically; with the impact of regional government, allowing local culture more influence on development, income differences grew from 50 per cent higher for the north in 1911 to 80 per cent higher for the north in the 1980s.

Voluntary co-operation is much easier in a community that has inherited a substantial stock of *social capital* in the form of norms of reciprocity and networks of civic engagement. By "social capital" Putnam refers to features of social organization, such as trust, norms, and networks, that can improve the efficiency of a society because they make co-ordinated action easier.[34] When a society has social capital, just about everything is easier, because people can turn to others for information and assistance. As an example of social capital and trust, consider a person beginning a new book. Suppose she has a friend who in turn has several acquaintances with knowledge relevant to the project. The writer can thus readily make connections, meeting people who provide information, tell her about sources, and themselves provide further names of people who can assist. With a single phone call the beginnings of an information network can be established. All this gets started only because the writer trusts her friend, and then trusts the introduced semi-strangers enough to meet with them and follow up on their suggestions. The same sort of story could be told of a person with an entrepreneurial interest: a new business proposition could be developed much more readily with a social network ready to offer information, suggestions, and advice.

Social capital is a *moral resource* and a *public good*, Putnam claims. A fascinating and distinctive aspect of social capital is that unlike other forms of capital, when it is used, the supply tends to increase rather than diminish: "The more two people display trust towards one another, the greater their mutual confidence." Social capital is intensely sensitive to virtuous circles (trust builds on trust) and vicious circles (distrust builds on distrust). In a rosy spiral, or virtuous circle, there is a benign equilibrium: we find high levels of co-operation, trust, reciprocity, civic engagement, and collective well-being. In a vicious circle there is a stagnant equilibrium: defection, distrust, shirking, isolation, exploitation, and disorder. The people of Montegrano were not irrational to distrust: they were merely functioning in a context of vicious equilibrium. It is easier to co-operate when there is social trust, and the experience of successful co-operation will make future co-operation more likely. Thus social capital tends to perpetuate itself: "Trust lubricates cooperation. The greater the level of trust within a community, the greater the likelihood of cooperation. And cooperation itself breeds trust. The steady accumulation of social capital is a crucial part of the story behind the virtuous circles of civic Italy."[35]

Social trust is not blind. It emerges from experience: personal experience in friendships, and experience in the informal groups of civic life. Whether a civic association is cultural, athletic, or political, it is likely to embody norms of reciprocity (you do this and I'll do that) and may extend to networks of further social engagement. People involved in such associations are relatively unlikely to let each other down: they have an experience of reciprocal co-operative assistance and a stake in their personal reputation, which would suffer if they defected on an obligation. Civic associations not only make communication easier; they facilitate the transfer of information about the trustworthiness of individuals and make an enormous contribution to social capital. For politics, economics, and personal well-being, social trust is a valuable resource.

7 Totalitarianism and Civil Society

In the peasant societies described by Banfield and others there was little social organization between the level of the family and that of the state. Community projects were difficult or impossible because of extreme competitiveness and a lack of social trust. A civil society based on free association of people for mutual social and public ends seems scarcely to have existed. The state was alien and far away, often assigned responsibility for rectifying problems but regarded with hostility and cynicism.

Stalinist and post-Stalinist societies present a striking contrast. The state is not far away and ineffective; it has been all too present. In fact it has permeated every level of life and association. Civil society has scarcely existed because associations between people have been rendered nearly impossible by states seeking to dominate every aspect of life. No association independent of the official ideology was legal in Stalinist societies, no area of life immune from state governance. The situation in which a monolithic state intervenes in virtually every area of life is the structural opposite of one in which the state is far away and appears to do nothing. But so far as civil society is concerned, there is a paradoxical similarity between the two. In both sorts of societies, unchosen conditions tend to separate people from each other and work against spontaneous sociability. In peasant societies the causes include harsh material conditions and historical factors. In Stalinist societies the main factor is the state's presumption that it can dictate values in every domain. State surveillance keeps people apart.

TRUST IN STALINIST SOCIETIES

Stalinist societies were modelled on Marxist-Leninist principles and featured vast state power concentrated in a small group or a single figure. They were built on an official ideology of equality of persons, said to be ensured by people's ownership of the means of production. Stalinist societies were totalitarian: the state sought authority over every area of work, culture, and life. The ideology dictated "scientific" responses to all problems, and there was an official recipe for truth that had to be followed. Deviation came at a high cost. Stalinism was Marxist-Leninism of a particularly authoritarian and brutal type.[1] Authority was centralized and coercive, conformity at all levels mandated, deviation punished, often brutally. These societies illustrate a contradictory combination of egalitarianism and authoritarianism. All human beings were theoretically equal – but in practice some had unqualified power over others.

Totalitarianism in the Soviet Union under Stalin was a system of mass terror in which even the Communist Party was effectively extinguished as a genuine political movement. Personal dictatorship was extreme. State goals were to improve economic status and enhance military power. To Marxist ideology was joined the belief that the General Secretary was infallible. People had to profess this and try to believe it, though the effort had an Alice-in-Wonderland quality. Reasonable people were scarcely capable of accepting such a thing, or even of seriously believing that other people did so. V. Tismaneanu, an expatriate Romanian analyst, called Stalinist societies mythocratic. There seemed to be no rationality or meaning. People felt lost and hopeless, eternally vulnerable to the wayward decisions of an insane despot.[2]

Even in Stalin's inner circles of power, anyone could be labelled a traitor at any time; no member of the gang felt secure. Stalin was to replace not only God himself but all the links between people and their own history, culture, traditions, and feelings. The language of domination was internalized even by many of Stalin's victims, until a dissenting thought became almost impossible. Such totalitarianism almost eradicated spontaneity and informal communication. But there were always hidden thoughts, processes, and groups carrying a subterranean germ of free thought; independent judgment, courage, and dissent were not eliminated.

After Stalin's death and Krushchev's 1956 speech exposing some of the worst abuses of power, overt terror in most of the Soviet Union and East-Central Europe was followed by less grossly dictatorial practices. But the infrastructure of Stalinism was preserved. There was always a risk of lapsing back into Stalinist terror, a fact painfully understood by people who feared that the old brutality could return at any moment. Stalinist society did not depend solely on Stalin as an individual, and it did not die with him. The same patterns existed, with local variations, in China under Mao, Albania under Hoxha, Romania under Ceauşescu, and (with Mid-East variations) Iraq under Saddam Hussein.

To the extent that totalitarian domination of thought, expression, and association succeeds, there is a destruction of civil society. The connections between people, the nature of public space, are destroyed. People cannot confidently share their feelings and opinions because any potential friend or lover is also a potential betrayer. Thus there emerges an artificial personal loneliness. Stalinist and post-Stalinist societies sought to control education and thought as well as speech, publication, and broadcasting. Freedom of association could not be granted because any group of people – even a chess club – might organize to work against the state. The most significant feature of Stalinist societies was the attempt to control thought and speech so as to eliminate a free social space. Stalinist states were based on surveillance, spying, and fear. The pervasive possibility of betrayal affected every aspect of individual and social life, ranging from family and personal development to education, work, culture, and attitudes to leadership. "No communication was possible between terrified social atoms," one commentator has said.[3]

In the early stages of what later became Stalinist societies, there was support for the official ideology, and genuine progress was made in some areas. Many people believed what they were taught in education groups and regarded Marxist governments as a likely improvement on their predecessors.[4] Later, doubts set in, and there was widespread, but unacknowledged, disbelief. V. Stojanovic, a Yugoslav philosopher theorizing about the demise of Stalinist and post-Stalinist states in East-Central Europe, describes three phases of their development. The first was an idealistic phase, in which people genuinely subscribed to the Marxist-Leninist ideology, seeing it as a source of equitable material progress and social development. The second phase was based on a realistic pragmatism: some defects were acknowledged, but the system struck many as having workable aspects and a broader pragmatic justification. In the third phase, one of "mendacity," people no longer believed in the system either for idealistic or for pragmatic reasons. They had to distort their words and thoughts in order to pretend to take it seriously. Many did so, and as a result there was some appearance of support for the system, but in reality the ideology was preserved only by hypocrisy and false consciousness.[5]

Vaçlav Havel's writings reflect this third phase. Describing Czechoslovakia in the 1970s, Havel called it a post-totalitarian society in which people were "living a lie." Though less gross in its forms of domination and punishments than were Stalin's USSR and Mao's China, the Czechoslovakian state at this time rigidly enforced conformity to the official ideology. People lived in an atmosphere of fear and lack of freedom. Hardly anyone believed in the tired slogans about class consciousness, the inevitable triumph of communism, Marxist truths, and the leadership of the working class. Oppression made hypocrisy and deception the normal course of life. Consumer products were shoddy, telephones and airports unreliable, the currency nearly worthless. Yet people had to profess belief in the inferiority of Western industrial societies and the inevitable triumph of socialism. Voting in elections was compulsory, but in these elections there was no choice of candidates. Still, this was supposed to be real democracy. In the name of equality there were deprivation and privilege; in the name of democracy, single-party elections.

Most significant from the point of view of trust was the ever-present possibility of surveillance. In Stalinist and post-Stalinist societies a wrong step, a true word to a false friend, could literally be fatal. A single political dogma permeated virtually every aspect of social, economic, and political life. Orthodoxy and conformity were demanded of citizens. There were countless occasions for surveillance and betrayal. Nothing was immune from state scrutiny and interference – not family relationships, sexual love, friendship, reading and writing, shopping, work, career, travel, sport, housing, or culture. The state was everywhere, and virtually everyone was afraid to say what he thought about it. Most went along with tired slogans expressing a stagnant orthodoxy. Although the defects and inconsistencies of the system were transparent, people had to pretend otherwise.

Stalinist societies were characterized by terror, post-Stalinist societies by grey pretence, enforced conformity, lack of truth, and lack of belief. There was physical power – the state apparatus, the army, the police, the prison system. There was, apparently, some legitimacy residing in the state, which controlled the system and, in a manner of speaking, kept things running. But there was scarcely any viable civil society.

The appearance of state legitimacy in these societies was illusory, and it was the purely illusory nature of this legitimacy that made possible the sudden fall of the communist regimes in 1989. Because post-Stalinist societies appeared to have some legitimacy and considerable strength at the centre, many military theorists and strategic analysts assumed, in effect, that they would last indefinitely. Many strategic analysts of the "realist" school predicted an ongoing Cold War and a standing nuclear threat for the indefinite future. They were wrong. When opportunities for public expression and action arose, the governing elite, and the state system, become completely vulnerable.

Hypocrisy, false consciousness, and pretence had come to such a point that Vaçlav Havel, in his New Year's speech of 1990, described the Czechoslovakia that had just emerged from a communist period as one whose people were morally ill: "The worst thing is that we live in a contaminated moral environment. We feel morally ill because we became used to saying something different from what we think. We learned not to believe in anything, to ignore each other, to care only about ourselves. Concepts such as love, friendship, compassion, humility or forgiveness lost their depth and dimensions and for many of us they represent only psychological peculiarities."[6] People could not say what they thought, and mouthed political orthodoxies that had no bearing on their genuine feelings, instincts, or personal experience. The moral illness was the effect of forced pretence at the very core of life. What is meaning, when it has so little to do with saying? One looks at another, listens to another, hears the same tired phrases and words. Who can be trusted when words cannot be believed, roles are false, and anyone might turn out to be a spy? "All these societies had been plagued by corruption, cultural despair, economic decay, and more than anything else, an abysmal decline in the sense of social solidarity. Suspicion was rampant. With its compulsive drive toward conformity and uniformity, communism went out of its way to destroy all intermediate institutions that could become the pillars of a revived civil society."[7] In the strictest totalitarian societies of East-Central Europe – Romania, East Germany, Albania, and Bulgaria – there was little in the way of social organization and free association between the level of family and that of the state. People were unable to communicate honestly and associate freely; all their relationships were affected, and there were scarcely any social associations apart from family relationships and the closest friendships.

When an ideologically totalitarian society makes its people live a lie, more than politics is compromised. The very social fibre is ruptured: people are held apart by the omnipresent state. They cannot say what they think, must hide many aspects of themselves from others, and cannot fully develop relationships or even their own thoughts and emotions. People present themselves as loyal to the regime and its ideology; they must so present themselves in order to survive. But are they what they seem to be? If loyal to the regime, they may be informers; if disloyal, they are not as they pretend, and may also be a threat. There is no way reality and appearance can coincide and be comfortable. For good reason people are nervous, fearful, and suspicious until they know each other very well.

Ceauşescu's Romania was an especially terrible case. Throughout the 1980s, life there was brutal and terrifying for most inhabitants. The population was virtually under attack from its own government due to the widespread lack of food and heating and the deterioration of medical services, accompanied by a refusal to treat many people. The centre of Bucharest had been razed to make space for grotesquely huge and expensive monuments to the dictator. Pollution reached extraordinary levels. Villages were destroyed. Forced labour existed: semi-starved men worked long, harsh hours to construct nuclear-power stations. The Securitate taped sexual encounters, apparently for the enjoyment of Elena Ceauşescu. The population policy, making birth control and abortion illegal and requiring every woman to produce five children, meant that the state intruded into every area of life. Women of child-bearing age were checked regularly at factories to determine whether they were pregnant. According to one young woman, if you were pregnant "you were followed to make sure you didn't do anything about it." The harsh pro-natal regime resulted in many children being abandoned and brought up in grossly inadequate state orphanages.[8]

Throughout all this, there was very little civil society in Romania. Even the church counselled loyalty to the regime. Ceauşescu was only one man, after all. Why did the people not revolt? Why did they not come together, share their fears, dissatisfactions, and power, and co-operate to bring an end to the brutal regime? Pavel Campeanu, an exiled Romanian political commentator, argues that fear kept people apart and was the key factor preventing the overthrow of the regime. The state sought to keep people from associating freely in ways that would threaten a regime or undermine its (near) monopoly on information and cultural life. The Securitate was for decades extremely successful in accomplishing this goal. It had a vast number of agents and informers. They were thought by people to be everywhere, and this intense suspicion could not be downplayed as paranoia.

After the changes of December 1989, some pertinent information about the strength of the Securitate emerged. In the town of Focsani, north of Bucharest, there were files on half the adult male population. One man, Doru Pavaloie, whose second wife was Jewish, had once told an old schoolmate that he might like to move abroad. The schoolmate turned out to be an informant. In 1990 Pavaloie was able to see his file, which was some fifteen inches thick. Eight people had been informing on him, and there was material from tapped telephone calls, copies of intercepted letters, clandestine photos, and descriptions of the sexual activities of his first wife.[9] In such a society people who fear that there may be a hidden camera in the bedroom, that whispered intimacies to a lover may go on tape, are not unduly suspicious but rather prudent and informed by evidence. It would be dangerous to be a "high trust" person in such circumstances. If a society like this is "low trust," there are compelling political reasons for it. At the end in Romania, people were infuriated not only with the Ceauşescu family and regime but with themselves for passively accepting so much humiliation. When change came, it was violent.

Romania is an extreme case, but it is not unique. Throughout the Soviet bloc the termination of Stalinist and post-Stalinist regimes led to astounding revelations about spying and betrayal. Spying by the Stasi and its informers in East Germany received considerable attention due to the unification of East and West Germany, and the exposure of some files to the glare of the West German press. There were Stasi files on one-third of the population of the former German Democratic Republic – that is to say, on six million East German citizens. One analyst estimates that East Germany must have had the highest per capita ratio of spies, tapped telephones, and bugged homes in the world.[10] Stretched out, the Stasi files were nearly two hundred kilometres in length, and there were 88 million pages of microfilm material. The network of betrayal was everywhere, extending from the schoolroom and pulpit to the bedroom and confessional. The net spread widely: to members of any opposition group, to all employees in national institutions, to church workers and members, artists and intellectuals, and anyone who had connections in the West or applied to go abroad. Homes, telephones, workplaces, cars, confessionals, and concert halls were bugged. Teachers filled out forms on children, some as young as nine years of age. The German Democratic Republic seemed to have been built on "lies, corruption, and terror" – and little else. In the aftermath of the regime one official charged with investigating and resolving problems of victims and former Stasi workers commented that the state had put every individual under tremendous pressure.[11]

By February 1992 more than three hundred thousand East Germans had applied to read their files. Those who gained access found evidence of treason by supposed friends, co-workers, and trusted professionals and, in some cases, brothers, sisters, and spouses. Vast numbers of prominent people in East German society turned out to

have been Stasi informers – dissidents, leaders in peace and environmental groups, writers, artists, counsellors, church workers, professors, and countless others. One prominent artist, ostensibly dissident
but really Stasi, was Sascha Anderson, who had associated with
human-rights activists. Another was Heinrich Fink, the dean of the-
ology at Humboldt University. Files show that Fink had been telling
stories to the Stasi for years, though he said he was not really an
informer. It later turned out that Fink was by no means unusual:
many faculty at Humboldt University were informing to the Stasi.

Heinz Egbert, a Lutheran minister, found 2,800 pages about himself in the Stasi files. Twenty of his supposed friends had been spying
on him. A trusted doctor pumped him full of drugs as part of a Stasi
plot. Gerd and Ulrike Poppe were members of Initiative for Peace
and Human Rights, a group in which there were fifteen members
who had been meeting in each other's living-rooms for years. It
turned out that of the fifteen, at least four were Stasi informers.
Christa Wolf, a writer, found six hundred names in her file. Just about
everyone she knew was either an informer or being watched. Truly,
the Stasi were "everyone and everywhere."[12] In such a society one
would feel nervous and suspicious, fearful and ill at ease, in virtually any environment.

The Stasi files even featured a library of suspect smells, composed
of numbered glass jars containing unwashed underwear and socks
stolen from the laundry hampers of suspect people. These were to be
used to assist dogs to identify those suspected of forbidden activities.
In the end the Stasi seems to have gone berserk in a combination of
lust for power and sick voyeurism. Much of the detail seems devoid
of significance, and there was so much material that one could make
little sense of it. Paradoxically, Stasi surveillance yielded so much
redundant and irrelevant information that the bureaucracy was col-
lapsing under its own weight. But this appalling overaccumulation
did not mean that the Stasi was harmless. People lost their jobs,
families, health, or liberty as a result of Stasi imprisonment, torture,
or exile. Informing on a friend, lover, colleague, or associate could
lead to extremely serious harm. Yet hundreds of thousands of people
did it.

Germany was thrown into a state of angst by these revelations and
the complex and devastating moral problems they posed. Few who
worked for the Stasi were willing to admit wrongdoing, even after
reunification had officially rendered the GDR morally and economically bankrupt. Some informers claimed not to have given any useful
information; others said they had used Stasi connections to protect
dissidents, inhibit especially risky opposition actions, and save vul-

nerable people from harm. Still others argued that they had had no choice and were forced to inform. From a moral point of view there were various types of cases, including many where victimizers were themselves also victims in one way or another.

With the termination of the East German state, Stasi officials and employees usually lost their jobs, and casual informers were harshly judged in the press and in the courts. But the moral questions were far from simple. Who was guilty? Who was victimized? Who was most guilty and who most victimized? Who should forgive? And why? The Stasi problem was merely the surface of the moral and political problems confronting the former East Germany. In some way or other nearly every adult person in the GDR had colluded in making the totalitarian regime possible. The context of the Stasi agent and his victims has a superficial and misleading moral simplicity. The real issue is how such a regime can function, and what people do that makes it possible.[13]

In such circumstances every sort of trust is adversely affected: friendships, relations within the family, relations with colleagues and professionals, anonymous strangers, and people in every social role. Nothing is safe. The state, in which most people have no confidence, intrudes everywhere and infects everything, insinuating its mandated conformity with the associated dynamic of hypocrisy, possible betrayal, and insecurity into every corner of life. One must either pretend allegiance to the disbelieved ideology or risk fearful consequences. People may trust friends and family members and develop coping strategies, but the omnipresent possibility of spying still produces stress, fear, and atomization. People are kept apart; they pretend, feel they must pretend. Many act in ways they feel to be dishonourable. Self-trust and a sense of one's own integrity are hard to preserve. Only a strong individual, or one with special advantages, could retain a sense of independent judgment in such circumstances.

"I know I did things that were not right. I know I told lies for the state," said a Romanian television announcer interviewed on Canadian television in January 1990. "Now I must reorder my whole life and all my relationships. Who am I? What sort of person am I? What am I going to do?"

For all this, it would be an overstatement to say that the Stalinist societies of post-war Europe were absolutely without trust. There were order and regularity in many areas of social and economic life, and thus a kind of reliability and limited confidence. In areas such as use of the subway, driving, and purchase of food, there was scatter trust. People knew they had guaranteed employment and a guaranteed pension, and expected prices of goods to be maintained at an artificially low level. Maternity and day-care benefits encouraged women to combine the roles of worker and mother. Such social guarantees came to seem precious when, after the changes, they disappeared. Though people did not, on the whole, believe the rhetoric of class struggle and socialist progress, they did count on the government to supply them with jobs, education, medical care, housing, and basic foodstuffs. Quality was poor and was mocked, but the guarantee was there.

Deficiencies in the economy were filled, in many cases, by black-market arrangements, which were largely tolerated by authorities who knew that they helped the economy to function. One might argue that such arrangements presuppose some degree of trust or confidence. In some instances both buyer and seller depend on the other not to betray him to the authorities. In others, both have a confident expectation that the authorities will not pursue black marketeers because they are tolerating the black market for reasons of their own.

In post-Stalinist societies many people sought solace in warm and intimate relationships with family and friends. Not pursuing happiness through careers or the accumulation of material goods, alienated from state power and the professed ideology forced upon their society, they looked for meaning in close relationships with a few cherished other people. Until the Stasi revelations some Western observers of East-Central Europe believed that these cultural values could be significant for people in the West, so many of whom seem compulsively ambitious, consumerist, and materialistic.

The experience of spy states does not show that human nature is inevitably self-interested, competitive, and vicious – only that human beings are capable of treachery and betrayal in desperate circumstances. As the Stasi files so dramatically reveal, a state can warp and corrupt many human relationships, resulting in a failure of truth, authenticity, and integrity. The eventual non-violent overthrow of post-Stalinist regimes in Europe is a testament to the staying power of people who were able to preserve and reassert their integrity and solidarity and to withstand adversity, overcoming a heavy sense of powerlessness, suspicion, and cynicism to come together and achieve change.

OTHER TRAGIC CASES: CHINA AND IRAQ

Stalinist and post-Stalinist societies are by no means the only examples of states in which totalitarianism has nearly wiped out civil society. There are many other societies in which free relationships and associations among people are flawed due to heavy intervention by the state. And within the category of Stalinist and post-Stalinist societies, there are considerable variations. China during the Cultural Revolution is one such. Though Maoism had many of the features of Stalinism, the Cultural Revolution falls into a category of its own in its combination of ideological totalitarianism, routine surveillance of citizen over citizen, and the extraordinary disruption of daily life. There are many descriptions of experiences from the period, all giving a terrifying picture of betrayal, suffering, chaos, and brutality.

Bette Bao Lord, a Chinese American who lived for three and a half years in Beijing while her husband was ambassador from Washington, described the terrible stories people told her of the Cultural Revolution and the general distrust that remained a full decade later:

Inevitably old friends had chosen to sit together. Chinese, unlike Americans, were wary of making new friends. Old ones were safe. New ones were risky: betrayal had been a daily occurrence during the Cultural Revolution; caution had become habitual. Still, I never grew accustomed to how frequently, how sincerely, how urgently one good friend of mind would warn me about another good friend of mine.

"Watch out, that one reports everything to Public Security."
"Watch out, that one is disloyal."
"Watch out, that one abuses friendship."
"Watch out, that one violates confidences."
"Watch out, that one is an out-and-out spy."[14]

Lord found that bitter memories of betrayals and brutality during the Cultural Revolution had made these people extremely suspicious of each other.

An especially moving and pertinent collection of short stories is *The Execution of Mayor Yin* by Chen Jo Hsi.[15] Chen is a Taiwanese woman, educated in the United States, who returned with her husband to mainland China in 19XX. As "returned Chinese" she and her family were suspect people in China, especially vulnerable during the Cultural Revolution, and her stories offer poignant depictions of the attitudes and struggles of the period. A number of central characters in the stories are given the "returned Chinese" identity.

A major theme of the collection is the early stage of faith in the Communist Party and its actions and policies. In the early phases of Maoism – as in the early phases of Stalinism in Europe – people typically believed in the ideology and saw it as a path to development, nation-building, and personal growth. They were taught to trust party doctrines and edicts more than their own judgment and conscience. In Chen's early stories people who begin to doubt party dogma struggle internally to question and resist their own doubt, feeling that they must be in error if they cannot understand the edicts of the party to be correct. Such faith in the party diminishes as the book continues. Faith becomes progressively harder to maintain as the turmoil, anti-intellectualism, destruction, and chaos of the Cultural Revolution continue. Eventually the early faith is destroyed.

Throughout the terror, misery, and near-anarchy that characterized China at the time of the Cultural Revolution there were, of course, instances of individual trust and co-operation. But people tended to be extremely cautious about others and tried to reveal as little as possible. They were especially cautious of people close to party officials, Red Guards, and others positioned with special powers. But they were suspicious of everyone, even family members. The family was by no means an island of trust and safety where people could be protected from the vicissitudes of the Cultural Revolution. Many people divorced their spouses to try to protect themselves from class contamination, and in some cases people turned in their brothers, sisters, parents, or other relatives for interrogation.[16]

Chen Jo Hsi's story "Chairman Mao is a Rotten Egg" depicts a woman whose three-year-old son attends a state kindergarten. Rumour has it that her son has said "Chairman Mao is a rotten egg" and been reported to authorities for doing so. Such a report would almost certainly result in his being labelled an enemy of the state and deprived of opportunities for the rest of his life. The mother is terribly afraid of a neighbour who works at the kindergarten and might have heard the rotten-egg remark. When she finds out the neighbour too has an "imperfect" class background and a child who has said "improper" things, she is deeply relieved and gains an extra confidence in her.

There is a gently ironic tone in some of Chen Jo Hsi's stories, as if to reflect her distance from characters who are still trying desperately to adjust to the terrible times. In "Residency Check" a promiscuous wife offers another woman a chicken. The second woman refuses it because she has been forced to accept the role of informant and will have to report on the other, whose promiscuous behaviour cannot escape comment. Thus there opens a gap between the women: a gesture towards friendship must be rejected.[17] The system of surveillance holds the women apart.

Saddam Hussein's regime in Iraq is another example of state domination keeping people apart and virtually eliminating any possibility of civil society. The suspicion and fear that characterize the regime and the impossibility, in such circumstances, of civil society, are vividly described by Samir Al Khalil in *Republic of Fear: The Inside Story of Saddam's Iraq*. Al Khalil, an Iraqi dissident and political analyst living abroad, describes Iraq as a society based to an extraordinary degree on institutionalized violence. A vast apparatus of army, police, and state officials, conjoined with the phenomenon of conspicuous public executions, strike terror into the hearts of the population. One diplomat estimated that 3 million Iraqis were engaged in watching 11 million others, and remarked that many diplomats had lived three years in the country without being able to know a single Iraqi citizen. But anxieties on the part of foreigners pale in comparison to the stress on Iraqis themselves. Masses of informers exist, and people can disappear suddenly after making perfectly innocent remarks that are interpreted as dissident. Suspicion and fear are rampant:

Nothing fragments group solidarity and self-confidence like the gnawing suspicion of having an informer in your midst. Therefore, to the extent that the public polices itself – a function of the number of informers – it (the public) *inevitably disintegrates as an entity in its own right*, separated from those who rule it. Informer networks invade privacy and choke off all willingness to act in public or reflect upon politics, replacing these urges with a now deeply instilled caution. In so doing they destroy the reality of the public domain, relegating what little remains to a dark and shadowy existence. In such a world the more well-known violence of state institutions – executions, "disappearances," murders, reprisals, torture – take on a new societal meaning. Nothing is as it seems, and nothing can be taken for granted.

The numbers of victims are not as important as the atmosphere constantly being invoked.[18]

Because the Iraqi people are constantly afraid of informers, they censor their own thoughts and instincts. They cannot express their real views – if, indeed, they allow themselves even to think them.

In such an environment there can be no genuine public discussion or reflection. Whatever critical thought exists has to be hidden away from the public eye and ear. Because of the fear of informers and the rampant distrust that it rightly inspires, any public space between individual and state has, in effect, disappeared. The distrust that is warranted by these circumstances has made a civil society impossible. The atmosphere is forbidding of trust, free association, and public discussion:

No one who has seen faces etched with the insecurity of it all could fail to understand the tragic depths of Iraqi self-withdrawal in the 1970's ... This kind of fear reduces human beings to a bundle of reactive sensations, all keyed up for the next blow. With its emergence, civic values, comradeship, nationalism, any sense of community, and even the private capacity to reflect disappear. These sensibilities do not gently fade away; they are obliterated the instant fear of this nature takes grip of the psyche, and irrespective of how highly cultivated they may once have been.[19]

Fear and suspicion render civil society non-existent. There are germs of dissent and disagreement, but in the context of overwhelming general fear and in the absence of public space, they are of little significance.

Reporting on family members is routine: Saddam Hussein has explicitly recommended it in public speeches. Children are taught to report to school officials on the doings and sayings of their parents. Even quite innocuous remarks, reported by young children with no intention of betraying their parents, can lead to the disappearance of parents for weeks or months. People feel isolated as individuals because they can communicate openly and honestly with only a very few people. There is a sense of fatalism: life will have to go on like this because there is no way anyone could change things. With every dimension of daily life under threat, and no realm of privacy, it is difficult to retain sufficient psychological balance for everyday living. To many, pretence is the best way of coping.

Perversely, the restricted thought and coerced professions of belief lead both to cynicism and to extreme gullibility. People cynically expect everything to be some kind of lie, but then gullibly fail to distinguish between the more and the less preposterous. The Leader can say anything and have it accepted, make any rule, break any of his own rules, and still be Great. He is Exalted, while ordinary people have lost any sense of confidence or capacity for independent judgment: "Saddam Hussein can now say anything with impunity ... Unlike outsiders, the mass of Iraqis have not been duped into this stance; they have arrived at it *by coming to believe in their own utter political worthlessness*, after having also experienced the same."[20] In this society people are fearful and perpetually insecure. They are at constant risk of brutality and violence, against which they appear to have no redress. They gain little or no capacity for independent reflection, and when they compare themselves with the Great Powerful Leader, they can only feel themselves to be nothing. They are extraordinarily vulnerable, treated as worthless, coming to believe they are worthless. The situation amounts to a political version of the battered-woman syndrome.

There are many other examples of people living with little or no community, solidarity, or civil society. In addition to totalitarian dictatorships of various descriptions and degrees of brutality, there are prison and concentration camps in which life is even more closely regulated. Perversely, thought may be freer, since people already in prison are already experiencing the worst their society has to offer and have little to fear. There are situations of anarchy or civil war. There is the case of the Ik, the alienated asocial people who lived in proximate territory but were so unsupportive of each other they can hardly be deemed a society at all.

Without exploring the details of all the horrible situations in which human beings may find themselves, it is nevertheless possible to make tentative generalizations about trust and distrust in adverse circumstances. In contexts of domination by alien authorities or extreme material hardship, distrust is the standing norm, and for good reason. Life is harsh, competition extreme, moral norms unreliable. Risks are huge, and to survive people must be very careful. People have to be extremely wary of trusting others because the hazards are simply too great.

Quite reasonably, given the circumstances, distrust must be the standing attitude, and widespread distrust nearly eradicates civil society, free thought, and autonomous judgment. Still, the existence of civil society is not the same as its visibility. Even in the most repressive regime, there are always germs of independent thought and voluntary association. No police state, no ideology, can annihilate the human need for autonomy, self-assertion, friendship, love and intimacy. Dictators tend to think they are omniscient and omnipotent. But such a belief is always a fallacy. Where there are human beings living together, trust is never entirely absent, and the connections that persist are more cherished than ever. Through solidarity and collective action, formerly isolated individuals may alter their desperate circumstances.

CIVIL SOCIETY AS A FORCE FOR CHANGE

The dramatic changes in some countries of East-Central Europe in 1989 were attributable in part to civil society. Theorists in Poland, Hungary, and the Soviet Union had developed a conception of change in which civil society would be both actor and object. People would work to develop independent associations with the hope of opening a public sphere and ending the atomization and depoliticization resulting from state domination. These conceptions of civil society were strongly oriented towards criticizing and reforming the post-Stalinist state. They were not revolutionary in the sense of seeking to usurp state power by violent means. Influential theorists of civil society such as Adam Michik and Vaçlav Havel explicitly renounced the use of violence against the state.

Under Gorbachev the historic dynamic of political power and initiative in the Soviet Union and East-Central Europe was dramatically changed. Instead of being a bulwark of communist conservatism, the Soviet Union of the late 1980s was suddenly placed in the new role of initiating social change. The forces of civil society were not insignificant in this configuration. Gorbachev himself did not emerge from nowhere; he was one of many reform communists within the Soviet bureaucracy. These people had been influenced by the relatively liberal Khrushchev period and by the Dubček movement in Czechoslovakia in the late 1960s. Gorbachev and his associates were themselves products of earlier civil-society developments in the Soviet Union of the late 1950s and the Czechoslovakia of the mid-and late 1960s.

Although the sudden and dramatic changes of 1989 will not be fully understood for many years, it is clear that the existence of civil society was an important factor inspiring change. In most cases, previously dissident independent groups provided a key basis for association, analysis, and action. They organized demonstrations against governments and undertook negotiations for compromise arrangements, sharing of power, or changes of power. In Czechoslovakia, society itself had become a legitimate actor on the political stage. All this confirmed in unexpected ways the theories underlying Czechoslovakia's Charter 77 movement, which had sought to restore the independent life of the society by cultural and moral reconstruction, creating bonds between people outside official channels. Charter 77 supporters sought an open society in which governments would genuinely respect the civil and human rights they had formally acknowledged in international agreements. The ideals of this group and similar ones in Poland and Hungary made possible a broader understanding of politics as concerned not solely with state power and policy but also as a realm in which citizens work together. The civil society in these countries was a non-official culture in which people could define their identity and accept some responsibility for practices and events. With the problem of legitimation, economic pressures, and the withdrawal of Soviet military power as a backing for the regimes, there was a vacuum at the top in East and Central Europe. Since there had been a development of civil society through dissident and opposition groups, there was a force for change.

In the context of East-Central Europe and the Soviet Union, civil society emerged as a social force in opposition to the state. Spontaneous grassroots initiatives from below loosened the ideological hold of ruling parties. Such groups were able to act spontaneously and flexibly when circumstances became favourable. After changes in Poland and Hungary and the opening of the Berlin Wall by a desperate regime in East Germany, the stage was set for dramatic shifts in Czechoslovakia, Bulgaria, Romania, and even Albania. Havel, a major player and theorist of civil society in Czechoslovakia, saw the new politics as based on morality and aiming to restore solidarity, trust, and hope. He spoke of restoring free public space.

Only a few months before the opening of the Berlin Wall on 9 November 1989 East Germany had seemed to have scarcely any civil society at all. The Stasi had estimated the numbers of active opponents of the socialist regime as in the hundreds. These people, members of unofficial peace, ecology, and human-rights groups, seemed to be despairing voices in the wilderness. The country seemed paralysed, and there was little detectable opposition, since so many opposed to the regime had left. But with East Germany losing people to the West at an increasing rate throughout the late summer and early fall of 1989, these unofficial groups banded together under the name New Forum to make demands on the increasingly vulnerable government. Demonstrations organized by the New Forum started to attract vast numbers: on 23 October there were hundreds of thousands of demonstrators in Leipzig, and on 4 November half a million in East Berlin. With marked absence of Soviet support for the regime, all this led to the resignation of the entire Politburo on 7 November and the opening of the Wall two days later.

Another country that appeared to have little in the way of civil society was Romania. Ceauşescu seemed to be in full control: just one week before the rebellion, at a Communist Party congress, he was unanimously re-elected and gave a long, dogmatic speech, applauded by a vast room full of apparently enthusiastic supporters. Both inside and outside Romania people seemed to think Ceauşescu could retain power. But what appeared to be support was not genuine; it was coerced. Ceauşescu apparently believed that compliance with his bizarre decrees signified that his regime had legitimate power and enough support to be secure. He put down a demonstration in Timisoara and proudly took personal responsibility for deaths and reprisals, announcing that participants in other demonstrations would be fired upon.

So convinced was Ceauşescu of his own power and security that he gave another speech in front of a huge crowd in Bucharest. It was broadcast live on television. As had been customary, people were shouting support ("Ceauşescu si poporul") as he spoke. Then someone yelled instead "Ceauşescu dictatorul." The tone of the crowd instantly changed. Virtually everyone began to yell against the dictator.

Ceauşescu's face suddenly crumpled; his demeanour of power and confidence shrivelled into one of fear. In an instant the terrifying dictator became a small, aging, and vulnerable man standing before thousands of furious people who were screaming against him. Power relations between the dictator and the crowd changed utterly, in a televised moment. People united in solidarity against a tyrant who epitomized brutal and irrational state power. Feeling the danger, Ceauşescu and his wife Elena escaped in a helicopter. They were captured several days later and executed by rebels. These events showed in an especially dramatic and compelling way just how political power ultimately presupposes popular consent. When such consent is clearly denied, everything changes.

When one person yelled that Ceauşescu was a dictator, others responded. Was this planned in advance, by Securitate who had decided to dump the leader? Planned in advance by dissidents? Or entirely spontaneous? Whatever the case may be, the solidarity and unity of the crowd was a genuine factor.[21] If only a few people had cried out against the dictator, they would have been brutally punished. The crowd came together and cried out together. As a result of this solidarity, the Ceauşescu regime was over. Whoever began the outcry took a chance and had to count on others to support him. The cry was perhaps an outburst by someone who could keep quiet no longer, perhaps a deliberate gesture of revolt, presuming a confidence that others must feel the same way and act too. Momentarily, Romanians were able to act together, and that solidarity brought about the end of the Ceauşescu regime.

But the unity of the Romanian people proved to be a fragile thing. People could briefly unite *against* a dictator but had tremendous difficulty uniting *for* anything. Tragically, within days of Ceauşescu's downfall, distrust of the successor group asserted itself, and stories of lying and corruption were rampant. Romanian commentator Vladimir Tismaneanu said, "Politics is perceived as the market-place of social climbers, opportunists, imposters, and adventurers." There was a deep suspicion of government and of the political process itself. Though open dialogue was beginning, civil society in Romania was embryonic.[22]

CIVIL SOCIETIES IN THE WEST

In contexts such as that of eastern Europe, where totalitarian governments have been overthrown by people's groups organizing non-violent demonstrations, it is natural to think of civil society as something that had to be developed in opposition to a totalitarian or post-total-itarian state. This way of thinking of civil society might suggest that the liberal democratic countries of North America and Western Europe can take their civil society for granted. It seems to assume that people in Western industrial societies already have the kind of civil society that people elsewhere are still struggling to create and maintain.

This presumption of much post–Cold War theorizing recalls Banfield's contrasting of the distrust and amoralism familism of Montegrano with the volunteer activism of a small town in Utah. Western industrialized countries, it would seem, "have it all." Other peoples, less fortunate, must work to sustain the civil society that those in the West have developed over many years and can now take for granted. But to think this way would be to overstate the contrast between societies and to be too optimistic about the West.

Civil society in Western industrialized countries, though thriving in many respects, is threatened in others. Beliefs that there is no point in trying to work for social change, that things must be as they are, that people are best off to pursue family and relationships, that government is responsible for everything but will never do anything, that others cannot be trusted to work for desired change, that everything is hopeless, and that politics and politicians are not to be trusted are not found only in bleak peasant societies or under totalitarian governments. Such theories are likely to sound painfully familiar to political observers in Western industrialized countries. Despite superficial evidence to the contrary, there are in contemporary Western societies significant obstacles to the maintenance of civil society. Notable among them are consumerism, an ethos of privatization, materialism, careerism, lack of moral consensus, corporate greed and power, and sheer lack of time.

Anyone who needs to be convinced of this conclusion should read *Habits of the Heart*, by R. Bellah, R. Madsen, W. Sullivan, A. Swidler, and S. Tipton. Stressing the importance of co-operation and community, these five authors wrote a co-operative book. Their interview material and reflections show clearly that many Americans experience tremendous difficulty identifying their activities meaningfully with the efforts of others. In the contemporary mass culture of America there is no generally accepted conception of community involvement, responsibility, and identity that would lead them to do so. Most face a choice between a managerial-utilitarian view of the world, in which what matters are efficiency, having a good career, and making money; or a therapeutic understanding of life, in which one's purposes are to develop oneself and one's own interests. What may appear superficially to be communities are often only "lifestyle enclaves," in which people band together on the basis of similar lifestyle choices and exclude those who are different. In Western industrial societies there is a heavy concentration on self, competitive success, and material consumption, all of which work against a sense of community, or solidarity in trying to improve the society or state.[23]

This kind of competitive and individualistic ideology encourages people to ignore the fact that they will best discover and develop themselves when they can work along with others. To be effective and happy, to lead meaningful lives, we need to associate with others in groups and communities. The free and open association and solidarity that provide the basis of civil society are at the same time the basis of self-development. An ethos of privatization and competitively defined individual success prevents many of us from realizing this.

It is extraordinarily difficult to get a picture of the whole society and how one fits into it. This phenomenon has been referred to as the problem of invisible complexity. We tend to see, and are encouraged by many media accounts to see, only contending groups with contending claims based on rights, entitlements, and special interests. What should be – and in many ways is – a society of interdependent people is seen instead as a marketplace wherein people contribute only by competing with one another.

In the United States, Bellah and his co-authors argue, the individualist language of self-development and pursuit of interests is so prevalent that even those who find identity and purpose in community projects often have trouble putting their feelings and goals into words. The language of community, public good, and public space is disappearing.

In the mass culture of contemporary America, matters outside the area of individual choice can scarcely be conceptualized as meriting moral appraisal. After the fall of communist regimes in East-Central Europe in 1989, many people in former Stalinist societies looked to the West for their ideals and norms of success. But the emulation has its tragic side. Competition, consumerism, exaltation of the market, and the pursuit of individual material interest provide only the shakiest basis for community or for civil society. Writing in the mid-1980s Bellah and his colleagues spoke of the "extreme fragmentation of the modern world," claiming that American society was atomized. They called for its reconstitution by involvement of individuals in groups that could carry a moral tradition, reinforce individual aspirations, and nurture individual development. They did not advocate an ethos of self-development; rather, they argued that self develops in community, where people find historic roots and values and accept commitments and responsibilities. Politics, seen as a battleground of contending interests, might retrieve its dignity and legitimacy if it emerged from community work and association.

A community is a group that attempts to be an inclusive whole and can celebrate different callings and the interdependence of private and public life. People in a community mutually respect each other despite their differences, and are able to understand that the community has long-term interests and must provide for the needs of future generations. People in communities have commitments to each other and to common projects and causes. They have a kind of rootedness, a connection to the place where they live with others. A person rooted in a community knows that she is a participant in a form of life that, in turn, provides the basis for fulfilling her own identity. A member of a community is not a separate, independent individual. Contrary to popular opinion, the good life cannot be lived alone. A meaningful human life requires connectedness to others in work, love, and voluntary associations; this connectedness requires sociability and trust. Contrary to the propaganda of neo-conservatives, in a community, or civil society, "we the people" does not merely amount to another interest group.[24] Free associations of people who communicate openly and co-operatively dedicate their efforts to normatively grounded change in state policy and social practice are of key importance in Western democracies as well.

In their recent work *Civil Society and Political Theory* Jean Cohen and Andrew Amato seek a characterization of civil society that will be useful in understanding both post-communist societies and the contemporary West. They cite four basic characteristics of civil society: plurality, publicity, privacy, and legality. *Plurality* refers to the fact that in a civil society there are many sorts of individuals and many sorts of groups. These include families, informal groups, and various voluntary associations; people can freely associate together in various ways. By *publicity* it is understood that institutions of culture and communication exist to facilitate the wide dissemination and discussion of ideas. In a civil society there is a realm of *privacy*: there are areas of life in which people can develop themselves as individuals and make individual moral choices. *Legality* within civil society means that there are structures of general laws and basic rights that make plurality, privacy, and publicity free from interference by the state and (so far as is feasible) major players in the economy.[25]

We can think of civil society as a place for social and political dialogue between equal persons who behave and speak in a civilized way. One who advocates an ethical norm should be thought of not as a solitary agent but rather as a person in civil society who presents that principle to others in order to test it in open discussion and debate. On this model, reflection on moral norms and ideals, and by implication reflection on political policy, is not private; it is public. Rationality should be understood as the capacity and tendency to test beliefs and claims in a pluralistic public forum. This notion of a public discussion, derived from Habermas, points indirectly to the importance of trust in free association and civil society. The notion itself assumes that participating individuals are well-motivated and competent, and will participate with integrity and genuine substantive concern, not merely in order to pursue their own interests. If we suspiciously or cynically insist that claims and counter-claims amount merely to expressions of "special interest," we reduce civil society to a context of contention, interpreting it as a struggle for self-interest and neglecting the very possibility of sincere discussion and principled argument about what *should* be done in the public realm. The notion of public ethics grounded in public discussion presumes openness, honesty, mutual respect, publicity, and trust, all of which are essential in the voluntary associations of civil society and none of which have been proven to be utterly absent from public life. A wilfully cynical interpretation can argue such aspects out of existence, but there is no theoretical justification for doing so, and the practical consequences are negative.

Especially notable in civil society in Western industrial countries are the "new social movements" addressing issues of civil rights, feminism, peace, and environmental protection. These groups consider and advocate consideration of many issues on which they seek new laws and amended state policies. They rarely seek state power in their own right and are oriented as much towards the civil society as the state. Feminists, for instance, seek to change all social institutions based on patriarchal gender roles. They address issues of gender stereotyping in advertising, film, literature, and drama; issues of housework and child care; education; health issues; employment; foreign policy, and more. Other new social movements have a similarly broad focus. Peace groups seek to affect not only foreign policy, military expenditures, and weapons development, which are mainly matters of state, but also social attitudes towards violence and conflict, education about tolerance and human rights, war toys, child-rearing, and public beliefs about the legitimacy of violence, war, militarism, and nuclear weapons. Analogous points can be made about environmental and civil-rights groups. They are directed both at the state and at civil society itself.

We misunderstand the new social movements if we think of them solely as being in confrontation with the state. Such movements are not simply *against*; they are *within*. They are an important part of civil society and seek to influence people within society by communicating positive messages about how things should be changed. With few exceptions, new social movements do not seek state power. They seek to *influence* people outside and inside government. For new social movements civil society becomes not only the terrain of work for social change but its intended object. This sort of thinking is similar to that of Vaclav Havel, Adam Michnik, and other theorists of opposition movements in post-Stalinist Central Europe.

Bill Moyer, a long-time activist and theorist of social movements, emphasizes the many times in history when needed changes were brought about by an inspired citizenry working together as activists outside the main channels of electoral politics. His account shows that the word "new" in the phrase "new social movements" is decidedly inaccurate. Social movements have existed for centuries. There is a hidden history of unsung ordinary people behind the history of great men, parliaments, and wars. Often when the work of activists is at an end, a political decision will be taken by political figures, who may be simplistically credited for the entire reform. For instance, in Calgary activists campaigned for seventeen years to get a large area of Nose Hill, in the northwest part of the city, proclaimed as a park. After years of meetings, petitions, speeches, and submissions, they succeeded. The newspaper then reported that the mayor and the city council had declared the area to be a city park; the decision was reported to be theirs, and implicitly the credit for the creation of the park went to the politicians, the paper making little reference to the work of the activists. It is through such constructions that grassroots campaigns and the efforts of ordinary people outside official politics are underemphasized in history. But the fact that descriptions and labellings omit ordinary people certainly does not mean that they play no role. Part of human history is the history of moral and social accomplishment on the part of groups who work for idealistic social causes. Many reforms have resulted from the commitment of citizens working in informal associations outside established political institutions. Through their efforts, Western countries virtually eliminated child labour, established free public elementary education, imposed a minimum wage and limitations on the work week, extended the franchise to women and men without property, legalized unions, and much else.[26] What seems to be new about social movements is not their existence but the willingness of contemporary political commentators, analysts, and theorists to pay attention to them – an interest attributable, I think, to their desire to understand the sudden demise of communist governments in the Soviet Union and East-Central Europe.

In the 1950s, Edmund Banfield contrasted small-town Utah with Montegrano and assumed that the United States was a environment in which voluntarism and a sense of community thrived. Yet in the 1980s, the authors of *Habits of the Heart* emphasized atomization, fragmentation, and failures of community in America. They called for nothing less than the reconstitution of the modern world, saying that "individuals need the nurture of groups that carry a moral tradition reinforcing their own aspirations" and regretfully concluding that such moral traditions were hard to come by. *Habits of the Heart* is an acclaimed and influential book. Yet we should not conclude from it that civil society in America is moribund. Clearly civil society does exist in the United States and other Western industrialized countries. There are effective norms of plurality, publicity, privacy, and legality. If we do not notice them, it is because we take them for granted. It remains true that countless people volunteer their time and energy to worthy causes. Their efforts make possible leisure and cultural activities, charitable institutions, and reformist social movements. The kinds of things that Banfield valued in a small Utah town still go on – even if our prevailing moral discourse does not permit us to describe them very well and the mass media, concentrating on tragedy and mishap, do not emphasize them. Civil society is fully alive, though there are powerful currents of materialism, individualism, and self-interest working against it.

In civil society we are able to associate freely with each other and undertake co-operative action. Such action requires mutual trust: we need to express our beliefs and feelings freely, listen to others and take their views into account, and do so without fear of betrayal. To act together we need to believe that we can achieve something by our individual and collective action, that we can act meaningfully to improve our material and social environment, that colleagues and fellow-citizens are reliable partners who can be counted on to do their share. In effect, we need a kind of trust or faith in our collective selves. In civil society, people cultivate respect for themselves and others and see human beings as capable of working for what is just and good. With mutual respect and trust much can be done by the ordinary citizens whose consent is ultimately needed for the legitimacy and durability of any state power.

8 Politics, Leadership, and Trust

In 1971 two social psychologists published a survey of public attitudes regarding the trustworthiness of twenty selected occupations. People were asked to rate various occupations in terms of honesty, competence, and altruism. Politicians ranked extremely low on all three counts: only used-car salesmen were deemed less trustworthy. The Americans surveyed rated those in public life poorly.[1] Although there are variations in different circumstances and countries, the notion that politicians are untrustworthy is too common to need documentation. Low regard for politicians and political leaders may make for good jokes, but it is a matter of serious concern. Politics is an essential and inescapable feature of human life in complex societies and will continue to be so for the foreseeable future. A widespread belief that politicians as such are incompetent and work only to serve themselves undermines governmental legitimacy, which is essential for workable systems.

GOOD REASONS TO DISTRUST POLITICIANS

The conspicuous and widely publicized promise-breaking of some politicians ("Read my lips: no new taxes") reflects on others. People tend to lump politicians together in one category and discredit all for the sins of some. The "whole lot" may come to be regarded as a suspect and sleazy group. The issue of trust arises when we are vulnerable, and we are certainly vulnerable to politicians. They can pass laws, consume public monies, raise taxes, and set policies that may lead nations into war, increase or decrease employment, and in other ways crucially affect our lives. A sense that politicians are not especially competent, are dishonest and corrupt – but nevertheless may dramatically alter our lives – leaves us feeling pessimistic and uneasy. Many people count on elected politicians to resolve key social and economic problems while at the same time holding them in low regard – an unstable combination of attitudes recalling the isolated peasants who expected government to solve all problems but at the same time thought it could do no good.

As a group politicians have royally earned the disrespect of the public by making false election promises, deceiving people about dealings and policies, engaging in corrupt practices, giving key appointments to relatives and friends, failing to practise what they preach, trading on image, evading substantive debate, and indulging themselves with the perks of power. Secrecy is another issue that renders many ordinary citizens suspicious – things are understood to be going on behind closed doors or in the "corridors of power," and we suspect that those unwilling to disclose their dealings are up to no good. Worse yet, well-placed politicians have on many occasions colluded in criminal dealings. To cite just one of innumerable possible examples, Japanese Prime Minister Hosokawa, elected on an anticorruption platform, was under investigation in February 1994 for having accepted a multi-million-dollar home-renovation package from a powerful trucking magnate hoping to exploit Hosokawa's connections with the Japanese royal family.

In recent years public debt has been a key matter in many industrialized countries. Spending cuts have been imposed with the professed goal of reducing debt and deficits, and members of the public have been lectured long and hard about the need for belt-tightening. When, in the midst of such "economies," politicians support generous increments for themselves, people feel angry and betrayed. They feel hardship and fear for their economic future; yet politicians – the very group whose spending has produced the problem in the first place – appear secure in their comforts and able to enhance their own security. If, as their personal behaviour suggests, political representatives are not committed to cutting back, they are misleading and manipulating the public. If they live luxuriously, spending lavishingly on themselves and using their power to enrich themselves and protect themselves from their own policies, political figures appear corrupt and hypocritical.

Accountability is another problem. Once elected, politicians seem beyond effective scrutiny. When they or staff members make mistakes, often nothing happens save a flurry in the media. In October

1993 the Reform Party of Canada achieved considerable success at the polls by urging greater accountability for politicians. But by February 1994 – having elected more than fifty new members to the federal House of Commons – they were already experiencing problems of their own. Reform MP Werner Schmidt was embarrassed by the fact that Adolf Hitler was quoted in his constituency newsletter, and Jewish constituents were frightened and alarmed. Apologies were made, but staff were not fired. Without accountability, the public may come to believe that there is no real check on the behaviour of elected officials between elections and that the lack of checks and sanctions licenses irresponsible behavior – at least until shortly before the next election.

Politicians are rarely able to live up to their own calls for a return to "traditional family values." In January 1994 Alberta Social Services Minister Mike Cardinal gave a speech in which he urged families to be responsible for their own children and get off government assistance. Cardinal asked plaintively, "Where are the fathers?" implying that single mothers would not need government assistance if fathers accepted their responsibilities. Within days it was revealed that Cardinal himself had fathered a child some twenty years before, that he had had no contact whatever with that child and had given extremely limited financial support to her mother. At the same time the Conservative government of John Major in Britain was encountering even more flagrant difficulties in the area of family values. Two ministers, Tim Yeo and Lord Caithness, had to resign in the wake of scandals about their private lives. Yeo had a mistress and an illegitimate child. Lady Caithness had committed suicide in the wake of claims that her husband was having an affair. Then, in February 1994, Steven Milligan, a Conservative MP, was found dead, clad in a woman's garter-belt and stockings, with a plastic bag over his head. Apart from the simplistic nature of much "family values" thinking, a major difficulty about promulgating basic family values as the basis of a political platform is that politicians seem unable to practise their own preachings in this area. Hypocrisy, failing to practise what one preaches, is a major basis for distrust. If members of political parties are (as it would appears) unable to practise traditional family values, they should be frank enough to admit it and honest enough not to preach them to the public.

Implicit recognition of the importance of trust in politics is found in one of the very things that tends to undermine it: concern for image. With the importance of television in campaigns, appearance and individual style are deemed critical to success. People who are heavy try to lose weight; those with nasal or high voices take speech lessons. Even those who might be judged reasonably good-looking in a conventional sense acquire new wardrobes and hairstyles contrived to make a good impression. Candidates seek a positive image as attractive, strong, confident persons capable of leadership. Absurdly, the details of image management may themselves be deemed newsworthy: when Reform leader Preston Manning adopted a newly "pouffed" hairdo in the fall of 1996, the new style did not pass without comment. It was news when Manitoba Liberal leader Sharon Carstairs took voice lessons and when Kim Campbell, briefly prime minister, publicly worried about the size of her hips. We may be briefly entertained or titillated at such "news," or feel a sense of relief that these people who look so glossy have to work to appear that way, but ultimately image management works against itself. The public feels manipulated and for that very reason will be less affected by the cosmetic alterations than political managers suppose.

Because politicians are known to cultivate an appealing and attractive image, people suspect that appearances do not represent the real person. This perceived lack of genuineness is a prime basis for distrust. Many politicians try to seem authentic, to appear as just one of us, an ordinary person. Women aspiring to office may be photographed in domestic scenes. A national network showed Audrey McLaughlin, leader of Canada's New Democratic Party, setting out her garbage just before the 1993 election campaign. One of the most famous photos of Margaret Thatcher portrays her in her kitchen, wearing an apron and drying dishes. The problem with all this supposed ordinariness is that it is fake and known to be so. The person who appears to the public may seem attractive in various ways. But many in the public will suspect, when they think at all, that this appearance is only for show and does not represent a real human being.

Staged events and contrived appearances tend to undermine trust. There is a kind of antinomy of trust here: politicians are working so hard to contrive a positive image that they miss – often precisely because of their cosmetic efforts. Those who struggle to contrive a credible *persona* produce an incredible one. They struggle so hard to achieve a good public image, and are so widely known to be doing so, that they seem inauthentic, contrived, and insincere. Among voters there is resistance to slickness and manipulation; they become suspicious that what is presented is too polished.

People seem to want something better. A poll taken in Calgary in the summer of 1993 indicated that what people sought most in politicians was integrity, honesty, reliability, and a willingness to work for others. People wanted politicians to be honest, dependable, and gen-

uinely altruistic. They wanted them to be trustworthy and to care –
and they felt that these attributes were missing.

BAD REASONS TO DISTRUST POLITICIANS

In a democracy politicians must be elected to hold public office. To
achieve this, they must curry favour with voters and try to win.
These aspects of politics necessarily require appealing to many voters. The common notion that many politicians have no principles, no
integrity, and do not really stand for anything is enhanced by the
need of mass parties to appeal to many different people and constituencies. Yet it is inevitable in a democratic system that people will
be elected only if they are able to have fairly wide appeal; some
degree of adaptation to one's audience is justifiable in response to
this need. Some matters "go with the territory," and for these we
should not discredit politicians individually or as a group. In so far
as these aspects of political life discredit politicians in the public eye,
the fault lies with public understanding (or misunderstanding) and
not with politicians themselves.

The competitiveness of politics may suggest that people take part
only because they want to win. From the idea that politicians are trying hard to win against their opponents it is only a short (though fallacious) step to the suspicion that they want *only* to win, and from
there only another short (but also fallacious) step to the suspicion that
they will do just about anything to win. One could scarcely survive
an electoral campaign without some strong competitive drives. But
because they must have some such drives, which "go with the territory," politicians are often seen as ruthless people with little care or
respect for others. This perception suggests that politicians are too
aggressive and corroborates the suspicion that they are merely
power-hungry. Those elected are often suspected of having won in an
unclean race, perpetrating some dirty tricks or making questionable
alliances along the way. Made in completely general terms, the accu-
sation is unfair.

In Western democracies such as Canada, the United States, and
Britain, mass political parties reconcile and represent many different
constituencies and interests. In the formulation of policy within such
parties as the Liberal, Conservative, or Reform in Canada, or the
Republicans or Democrats in the United States, many compromises
are necessary. In other democracies such as the Netherlands, Germany, and Italy, political parties represent more specialized interests
and convictions, and there is less need for compromise within such
parties. Compromise may be less within parties in these democracies,

but there is extensive compromise needed to form and maintain governments, which typically are coalition governments in which the elected members of several different parties must collaborate to govern.

For some the very word "compromise" has negative connotations; one who compromises has somehow compromised himself or herself, failing to be true to his or her principles. If compromise is something shameful and the essence of politics requires that people compromise, then politicians are going to be regarded as untrustworthy. But to think that politicians are untrustworthy merely because they sometimes qualify and compromise themselves and their principles is a mistake. Compromising may be less than the best that can be done, or may be the best, or may be reprehensible – depending on the circumstances. We should not assume that compromising is always wrong or that willingness to compromise indicates a lack of principles and an absence of integrity.[2] Society is composed of diverse groups with diverse and conflicting interests. To politics falls the job of working out policies and allocations that can be argued to be reasonable and are acceptable to as many citizens as possible. In situations of pluralism, where the absolute truth of what should be done is known to no one, there is no shame in adapting so as to make collaboration possible and work out jointly acceptable solutions, so long as concessions are made honestly and for good reason.

The idea that politicians have few principles and little gumption to stand up for them may seem to be confirmed by the practice of voting the party line, as is common in parliamentary democracies such as Canada. To citizens reflecting on politics, it may appear that there is little scope for politicians to be true to themselves – little territory in which they speak for and represent their own views on policy and governance. The notion that politicians are not true to themselves contributes to the sense that the role of politician is one characterized by little sincerity, authenticity, or integrity, and to the widespread public sense that politicians as a lot are untrustworthy. This common perception is based on a misunderstanding, however. Some amount of concession to one's political group and voting as a bloc is necessary in order to keep things going in a democracy. Voting with one's party and against one's personal convictions *some of the time* is essential for the maintenance of parliamentary systems and thus should not be interpreted as a sign of inauthenticity or lack of trustworthiness.

Distrust in politicians means many things and has many grounds. Deception, manipulation, exploitation, bribery, spying, and slandering opponents are objectionable practices found in politics. But they are not inevitable in politics. Anyone who distrusts politicians on the grounds that they contend with others to make a favourable impression, seek to win over their opponents, participate in the party system, which requires compromise and some concessions to group policy and interest, and seek a broad constituency among voters misunderstands the real nature of politics. Such phenomena are inevitable in a democracy, in which people stand for election to office. We can distinguish between an honest and fair campaign and one that is conducted in a dirty or ruthless fashion. Politicians should not be viewed as overly competitive solely because they engage in electoral politics.

If we fail to understand that such factors as competitiveness and compromise of principles are ineliminable in politics, we render the problem of political distrust incapable of solution. To be appalled or disgusted by such activities, or to understand them as incompatible with personal integrity, is to fail to understand democratic politics. Such a standpoint is worse than impractical: it is immature and founded upon untenable ideas about what democratic politics could be.

OBJECTS OF DISTRUST

Trust and distrust in politics or government can mean many things. Most discussions of such distrust focus on issues of integrity – honesty, reliability, promise-keeping, principled action, and lack of hypocrisy. These are *fiduciary* responsibilities; people in public office must be faithful to the duties and responsibilities of their office. But expectations of *competence* are also essential for trust, in politics as elsewhere. People sometimes distrust government action because they believe the requisite officials and civil servants are incompetent – too inefficient, or insufficiently knowledgeable to implement a task they have set for themselves. There are different people and institutions within politics and government, and we may distinguish among these on grounds of trust. At the national level, we might think of trusting the leader, the Cabinet, the governing party, the elected members from the governing party, the whole body of elected representatives, or our favourite political party or locally elected representative. Alternatively, we might concern ourselves with civil servants and governmental institutions as distinct from elected representatives. To speak of trusting or distrusting *politicians* is to focus on elected representatives and those who seek election. But to speak of trusting *government* can mean either politicians or civil servants and institutions. Those who are suspicious or cynical tend to be most critical of politicians as such. But the bureaucracy comes in for attack too, typically for rather different reasons.

In discussing trust in politics, Bernard Barber emphasizes the distinction between trust in competence and fiduciary trust. Barber argues that studies of trust in politics have been flawed by failing to take this distinction seriously.[3] But he tends to draw the line too sharply. We cannot easily separate competence and integrity, especially not in the area of politics. To acquire and apply knowledge in social affairs, a person needs to be conscious of his or her situation and have good judgment. Competence is not a purely intellectual or technical matter that can be separated from ethical aspects of character. And for integrity to be meaningful, one needs competence: one needs to be aware of how one is acting and what particular contexts demand. Moral integrity and trustworthiness presuppose this personal competence. Overall good judgment about priorities and personal qualities is tremendously important. In an age presuming the necessity of expert knowledge, politicians have to be generalists knowledgeable enough to debate a wide variety of public issues and good judges of character who can select reliable advisers.

SPURIOUS SIMPLICITY

Although it is the purest truism to say that modern societies and their problems are complex, it is common – particularly during electoral campaigns – for only the most simplistic approaches and solutions to be considered, and these only in the most superficial way. Something like "the economy" is seen as an entity that the government, or worse yet a single individual leader, can "manage" or "fix." Economic relations are based on millions of transactions, many occurring outside the border of a nation-state and beyond the control of its government. There are many similar examples of complex situations reduced to pseudo-entities: the educational system, the level of crime, international security issues, and so on. With the best will and competence in the world, no leader or party could simply "solve" unemployment, crime, racism, or ethnic conflict. To think otherwise is to fail to appreciate the complex and deeply rooted nature of these problems.

Seeing complex situations and interactions as single entities for which governments are straightforwardly responsible, and expecting political leaders to address and solve vast social problems in a short period of time, sets people up for disappointment. Yet such simplistic analysis is widely disseminated by the media, provides the very core of political discourse, and appears to be generally accepted not only by the public but by politicians themselves. Against their own long-term interest politicians create and exploit unrealistic expectations by endorsing misleading slogans, simplistic solutions, and careless reasoning about causes and responses to problems. They take credit for good things that happen during the tenure of their own party but refuse responsibility for the bad – and reason in the reverse way about their opponents.

An especially baneful aspect of contemporary political reasoning is exaggerated individualism. Campaigns typically focus a great deal of attention on specific individuals – usually leaders – and their personal style, past history, and moral attributes. Though counter-productive, this concentration of attention testifies implicitly to the importance of trust in contemporary democratic politics. People cannot understand – sometimes cannot even name – key issues of the day, which tend to be complex. They sense their lack of expertise and feel that they have to believe someone. But different people make different claims. The question of *what* to believe about the issues of the day becomes one of *which person* to believe. People try to appraise contending leaders for their personal qualities, attempting to get a sense of their character and competence from a television image. Knowing that one among these leaders will be the next president, prime minister, or premier, people try to ascertain their character and trustworthiness. Attention shifts from complex problems like social programs, environment, economic trends, and language rights to the clothing, personal style, or domestic and sexual habits of the candidates. Could these provide clues about who should be trusted and believed?[4]

Given the importance of trust and the complexity of substantive issues, this shift in public attention is understandable. But it perpetrates individualistic assumptions and unrealistic expectations. Debate turns to Clinton, Bush, or Perot – or to Manning, Mulroney, Campbell, Chretien, or Bouchard – and what *that person* might do to set things right. A short time-range – the so-called honeymoon period – is set. (One hundred days is a common norm in the United States; the Chretien government in Canada seems to have enjoyed a much longer period, perhaps because of the fact that neither of the two main opposition parties has a credible base across the country.) Typically, if the new leader and team have not been able to set major new directions by then, media pundits start to pronounce that they have failed. The public, having been encouraged to expect too much too soon from too few, then tends to flip from overly high expectations to bitter disappointment. Within months of taking office a government may be pronounced a failure. This shortened time-frame has been called the phenomenon of "media time."[5] The media demand constant change, will not stay fixed on an issue for long, and express a childish desire for quick and clear results. Inflated expectations can have tragic consequences, as when careers and lives are destroyed because people believe they have failed when they cannot measure up to unrealistic standards.

Unlike the dilemmas of television sitcoms, problems in the real world take a long time to solve – if, indeed, they can be solved at all. Politicians who contribute to simplistic reasoning and false expectations eventually fall victim to their own mythologies. The whole syndrome of oversimplification, exaggerated individualism, and media time contributes to the general lack of respect for politicians.

In many industrialized countries people have high expectations about what politicians leaders should do and what they personally can rightly expect in the line of material well-being. Global economic trends have led to declining standards of living and a dramatic contraction of job opportunities. In most Western countries, citizens have for decades assumed that they could anticipate lifetime jobs with good benefits and pensions, home ownership, a wide variety of consumer goods, college education, and continued material resources to support a high standard of living for their children and future generations. They expect elected politicians to deliver the goods. Given the current economic situation, this amounts to demanding the impossible. There is considerable unwillingness to re-examine life expectations, which may be unrealistic given the rapidly integrating global economy and the material aspirations of billions around the globe. To blame politicians or governments for declining home ownership or lower job prospects is simplistic. Such changes are due to many factors, including many beyond the control of national governments.[6]

THREE PERSPECTIVES ON ELITES

Reflecting on trust and politics, Barber draws a distinction between what he calls the *elitist* model and that of *realistic perceptions*. According to the elitist model, political leaders or elites expect and need the public trust because democratic government must be legitimate, and legitimacy presumes a degree of trust. The political elite sees itself as qualified to determine and implement policy; those in politics believe that people should trust them because they are qualified to govern: "The general public is likely to be ignorant and incompetent, unsatisfactory actors in a democratic society. Therefore ... an elite must be primarily responsible for taking action and leading the society. This elite ... even if wholly committed to democratic values, goals, and rules, still must have the trusting support of the general public in order to govern effectively. Such trust is the functional complement of democratic leadership in a viable democratic polity."[7] According to the elitist model, trust in elites must exist for democratic government to be possible. To ensure such trust in elites, people must be educated to have trusting beliefs. Children should be taught that institutions, officials, and leaders are worthy, reliable and trustworthy; widespread distrust would undermine effective governance. On this assumption, if ordinary people fail to trust their leaders, political representatives, and governing officials, something has gone wrong – and the fault is not with elites but with ordinary people. They have become alienated, cynical, or apathetic.

But in reaching such conclusions, elites and those who support them seem to have made some fundamental mistakes. The model combines insufficient respect for the competence and common sense of ordinary people with an exaggerated sense of the competence and integrity of elites. Most seriously, proponents of the elitist model seem arbitrarily oblivious that ruling elites are often distrusted for *good reasons*, ranging from demonstrated incompetence to lack of integrity to blatant corruption. Those who argue that government requires elites, whom the people must trust, assume that, since trust is necessary for governance, then ordinary people are failing in loyalty when they do not trust. Ironically, the elitist model of democratic loyalty reproduces the very self-satisfaction and isolation that so often characterize elites themselves. To say that, if the public distrusts the elite, there is something wrong with the public is to assume that when the public distrusts the elite it is *not* because there is anything wrong with the elite. Typically, elitists and their defenders admit failure only in the area of communication problems; if they could just communicate better and make people understand their policies and practices, those people would approve.

An illustration of the overconfidence of elites in Canadian affairs was apparent in the summer and fall of 1990. After the failure of the Meech Lake Accord, the Liberal Ontario government of David Peterson was suddenly and unexpectedly defeated in an early election, which he had called feeling sure that he would easily be re-elected. Columnist Jeffrey Simpson, who writes regularly for the prestigious *Globe and Mail* and is a frequent panelist on the CBC, is himself a member of the elite. Simpson, who had supported Meech and was only one of many highly placed observers who were horrified at its demise, attributed the surprising Ontario results to "cranky voters" and speculated just how the disgruntled public would deal with other provincial leaders seeking re-election. He categorized voters (most of whom are definitely non-elite) in terms appropriate to children needing a nap: they were cranky. The idea that voters might have genuine and valid misgivings about a provincial government that had supported a decentralizing constitutional accord and then called an unnecessary and expensive election after its demise was not one Simpson could take seriously.

An alternative to the elitist perspective on political distrust is that of accurate perceptions. According to this account politicians are distrusted by the public because the public accurately perceives their failings. It is both arrogant and mistaken for elites to blame the public for distrust – as is blatantly obvious from Vietnam, Watergate, and the Iran-Contra affair in the United States, the Meech Lake débacle and Oka crisis in Canada, and numerous scandals among politicians around the globe. Examples of dishonesty, manipulation, hypocrisy, promise-breaking, corruption, incompetence, and plain old immorality among politicians are easy enough to find. A single issue of any major newspaper is likely to provide at least four or five examples. People need not be crabby or cranky, alienated or cynical, to distrust some politicians some of the time. To a considerable extent, that politicians are distrusted is the logical result of their own practices and actions. They are distrusted because they have shown themselves to be untrustworthy. Plainly, this perspective of accurate perceptions is itself at least partly accurate, but it does not account for the fact that so often *all* politicians are tarred with the same brush. The failings of some tend to be imputed to all.

A plausible third perspective on distrust in politics places some responsibility on the public and some on politicians themselves, implying *shared responsibility*. Distrust of politicians is due both to their failings of competence and integrity and to simplistic understanding and implausible expectations common among the electorate and in the media. Many people, and much of the media from which they draw their impressions, are guilty of façile acceptance of simplistic analysis and unrealistic expectations. A survey in the summer of 1993 showed that most Americans would prefer spending two weeks in jail to spending one week as president in the Oval Office – a recognition, perhaps, that the post of president of the United States is defined in such an exalted and unrealistic way that no one could hope to fill it satisfactorily![8]

From this perspective, which seems to be by far the most reasonable one, distrust for politicians is attributable both to irresponsibility and unreliability among politicians and to unrealistic expectations on the part of the public. Solutions to the problem of suspicion in politics should be sought in several quarters. If this interpretation of political distrust is accurate, then the solution requires reform among politicians, greater sophistication among members of the public, and more subtle and substantive treatment of issues in the media.

Distrust of politicians and political life can go so far as to be counter-productive, but it would not be desirable to overcome all distrust in this area. Some degree of political distrust is healthy and necessary for democratic functioning. People need to question what politicians tell them, try to ascertain their character and motivation, and show a reasonable scepticism towards electoral promises and policy proposals. Since political leaders are charged with vast responsibility, it makes sense also to scrutinize their moral character. It is not that distrust in the area of politics should be replaced by an innocent willingness to take politicians and their statements at face value. There never was a golden age in which political office-holders and aspirants were beyond reproach and trusted by everyone in every respect. If there had been, it would not have been a utopia. Scepticism and critical thinking are essential in democratic politics. An unwillingness to take every statement and action at face value is absolutely necessary. But when qualified distrust becomes tantamount to a cavalier dismissal and rejection of "the lot" of politicians, when the very role of politician comes to connote sleaziness and the focus on personal failings replaces substantive debate, democratic politics is in trouble. Distrust may spread from a lack of confidence in some offending politicians and officials to alienation from the entire political system, which will be regarded as doomed. At this point, distrust has gone too far.

TRUST AND LEADERSHIP STYLES

In reflecting on trust and politics, we naturally come to the matter of leadership. In western industrial democracies the elected leader has been selected as leader of a political party that seeks an electoral mandate to govern. A political leader must lead in a variety of contexts, the most obvious and most important being the political party, the government, and the public itself. The political leader may be leader of a party, head of government, and, in a different and less formal sense, leader of the people. He or she has several distinct leadership roles, and different contexts call for different leadership skills. Approachability, public-speaking skills, and charisma are especially important in relating to the public, while facilitation, negotiation, and mediation skills are central in managing the caucus within the political party. Original ideas, understanding of issues, knowledge, and attention to detail are important in the actual running of government. Few individuals have all the qualities necessary for the many contexts in which a modern leader functions. Different people have different styles of leadership, which suit different situations. There is no one thing called leadership and no one way of doing it right. But no matter who and no matter how, effective leadership always requires a considerable degree of trust. Generally speaking, the greater the trust, the more effective the leader.

On a classic model of leadership, the leader is a strong and directive figure with considerable power and control. He has energy and good ideas, communicates these well to others, and inspires people to follow him and work for his policies. Such a person really *leads*, being in some sense "ahead" of his followers and able to get them to work together with him towards common goals. In democratic politics the two main goals are getting members of the party elected and then, if successful, governing to implement the policies of the party. The successful leader will first lead his party to electoral victory and then lead the country in the direction deemed most suitable. Leadership in this classic sense requires outstanding personal qualities. The model tends to fit male styles, and indeed most political leaders are men, though some women have filled traditional leadership roles effectively. Classic leadership is assumed in the rhetoric and practice of politics in Western industrialized countries. A person who seeks to be head of government is assumed to be a strong individual who will inspire others to follow and take charge and direct the party's efforts. Political debates nearly always pit leaders against each other. Other party representatives, identified and regarded as supporters, generally comply with the leader's policy and style. Trust in the leader is obviously crucial within the political party, for voters, and in the process of governing.

A person will not be chosen leader of a political party unless most party members have confidence in him or her. A key issue initially is whether a prospective leader could bring the party to electoral victory. Succeeding in electoral campaigns requires the ability to pick suitable advisers and managers, identify (with assistance) the key issues for the campaign, keep one's cool under scrutiny of the press, manage disagreements in upper circles of the party, handle public appearances, and perform well in debates, to name just a few. A leader will be well served by charisma – the ability to attract and inspire others – and by the sort of personality that is attractive to voters. Because trust is so fundamental for successful relations inside and outside the party, integrity factors are crucial. When choosing a leader, a party should look at moral character in virtually all contexts – both because key failings are likely to be caught by the media and because a dishonest and corrupt person cannot be relied upon to implement party policy. A leader will have the power to affect many lives and careers. Party members will be vulnerable to the leader's decisions and uncomfortable without confidence in his or her integrity and competence.

The need for trust is still more obvious when we consider some of the specific functions of a party leader. The leader chairs meetings and must be relied upon to include necessary items on the agenda and not to manipulate process so that some items are systematically dismissed or evaded. He must be trusted to let people speak and to strike a balance between expression of disagreement and avoidance of divisive or destructive conflict. Leaders also have a co-ordinating role. In the functioning of a political party, as with any large group, many matters will have been delegated to individuals and subcommittees. It is up to the leader to ensure that different subgroups are not setting off in incompatible directions, or working on incompatible timetables. People also must trust that matters referred to a small subcommittee will not simply disappear. Organization requires competence in co-ordination, which is absolutely fundamental in running a party, electoral campaign, or government. Organization is ultimately the responsibility of the leader. Here again, both integrity and competence are required.

With the public the party leader is a kind of key communicator for the party. Typically he or she entertains reporters' questions about central matters of policy, and states and defends the party's position in the all-important television debates. Effective leadership presumes that the leader is trusted by members of the party. They cannot feel comfortable with the selection of someone who speaks poorly, has difficulty responding to questions, easily becomes enraged with critical journalists, or seems boring, lethargic, or devoid of ideas. Anyone who is going to lead a political party to electoral victory and then conduct an effective government needs the trust of fellow party members. People who lack essential qualities of competence and integrity may fall into leadership positions due to special circumstances, but they have little chance of being effective leaders.

To be elected and run a government, a leader needs some degree of public trust. Unlike party co-workers and colleagues, most members of the public never encounter the leader in person and will not witness his or her day-to-day efforts in administrative and policy matters. They will hear about the leader through media reports, see that person on television, or hear him or her on radio or at public meetings. To govern effectively, the leader needs some public confidence.

Obviously, a leader can govern without *strong or deep* trust from a solid majority of the population. In fact, complete trust in a leader is unhealthy politically: policies and actions may be insufficiently scrutinized, and dictatorship could follow democracy. In democracies at present there is no problem of too much trust in political leaders. The problem is more likely to be a dramatic loss of confidence after an all-too-brief honeymoon period based on superficial identification and inflated expectations that have arisen from simplistic analysis and campaigning.

There are different styles and models of leadership, but I would argue that all leadership styles presuppose trust in the leader. On alternative models of leadership, trust is still needed but the details are different. Consider, for instance, a feminist model of leadership, according to which leaders are not perceived as "strong" individuals but rather as moderators and facilitators who work on the basis of consensus. On this understanding, a leader is not outstanding within a group but rather adopts the role of bringing out and reconciling the best ideas and abilities of members and nurturing their talent and initiative. She elicits ideas and information from others and works to achieve consensus and collaboration. For one who adopts the consensual style of leadership, some requirements of classic leadership drop out or diminish in significance. It is less necessary to be a dominant personality, to be charismatic, to have one's own conception of viable policies and directions, or to have apt judgment in selecting advisers and officers; there are more sources of input into decisions. Policy and personnel decisions will be worked out by a broad group; so too will agendas for political meetings and strategies for electoral campaigns. Consensual leadership puts less weight on individual talents and tendencies.

Indeed, this movement away from exaggerated individualism is a potential strength of the feminist model. With responsibilities shared by a substantial number of people, the idiosyncratic capabilities and failings of the leader matter less. He or she will elicit various opinions, facilitate discussion, synthesize ideas, nurture competence, and seek consensus.

But these very functions indicate why consensual leadership too presupposes trust. The consensual leader must conduct open discussions in which people genuinely express their feelings and beliefs, and those discussions must be conducted fairly, providing all with an opportunity to speak. People do not openly express their ideas and feelings about controversial and important matters unless they trust others to hear and respect them. Establishing consensus can be a slow and painful process, one that faces special obstacles in modern bureaucratic cultures that value efficiency and individual power. In a culture where the classic model of leadership is standard, consensual leadership is relatively unorthodox and likely to be regarded with some suspicion. Someone attempting to provide it may seem inefficient, vague, and indecisive, an obstacle encountered by Canadian New Democratic Party leader Audrey McLaughlin when she took over the party leadership and worked initially in a "feminist" style.

Another adaptation of leadership style expresses a still more radically non-individualist stance. It recommends separating various leadership functions and designating different people to fill them.[9] Such functions include: initiating new proposals and ideas, seeking information, seeking opinions, giving information, giving opinions, elaborating ideas, co-ordination, providing energy, and being a procedural technician or recorder. But even with divided leadership of this sort, the need for trust remains. Its location shifts, and less trust in any given person is required; trust is not so focused on one particular individual. And yet every one of the functions listed can be effectively performed only by a person trusted by his or her colleagues. Even something as apparently mundane as elaborating an idea can be done in a manipulatively selective or tendentious way. If a person is going to have another elaborate his favourite idea, he will want to think that the other person understands the idea and is articulate, imaginative, and honest. This requires trusting him or her in the relevant respects.

There are, then, different models of leadership, and different styles and contexts of leadership. But in politics as elsewhere, any effective leadership presupposes a considerable degree of trust. If those who come forward as political leaders cannot be trusted, the gap will be felt by party members and the public alike.

Distrust in politicians, leaders, political parties, and politics as a whole is fashionable and has some basis, but the phenomenon can become dangerous. When it is generalized, moving thoughtlessly from context to context and figure to figure, distrust can become pathological. In democratic societies there are of necessity people who seek election to office and others who take on leadership roles in politics. To understand the importance of trust for electoral politics, governance, and leadership is not to say that all these people are trustworthy all the time or that they merit the complete and unquestioning confidence and trust of the public. Notoriously, many do not, and obviously a working democracy requires doubt, scepticism, and distrust on many occasions. Yet without some trust in some politicians and leaders, our system cannot work, and the need for that trust points to the risks of generalized distrust and cynicism. We should do what we can to maintain warranted confidence in political figures because democracy cannot work well without it. Whatever the failings of politicians and leaders in democratic systems may be, dictators, militias, or war gangs are certain to be worse.

9 Trust and Distrust between Groups

Clearly individual attitudes count for a lot in politics. Among these trust and distrust are especially significant, whether we are thinking of public attitudes towards politicians in general or of contexts of leadership. In these cases the objects of trust and distrust are individuals. Typically, those who distrust politicians in general direct their attitude towards any individual who is a politician, not towards politicians as a collective. But it would be a misrepresentation and a gross oversimplification to think of trust and distrust in politics solely in terms of the attitudes of some individuals towards other individuals. Much of politics involves groups. Groups also manifest attitudes that are important in politics, and notable among these are attitudes of trust and distrust.

Obviously, political parties themselves are groups. But this is only the beginning of the story. There are many other significant groups: social movements in the areas of peace, environment, and feminism; cultural groups; groups defined by ethnic and racial identity; interest groups of labour, small business, veterans; and many more. Such groups play a significant role both in civil society and in party and electoral politics.

SOME ILLUSTRATIONS OF DISTRUST AND TRUST AS ATTITUDES OF GROUPS

The issue of supplying needles to drug users provides a telling illustration of distrust between groups – in this case between educated urban blacks and white medical professionals in the United States.[1]

When drug users share needles, the risk of AIDS is high. In some jurisdictions needles have been supplied to drug users in order to avoid sharing, and rates of AIDS infection among drug users have decreased. The policy of supplying needles to users is controversial, however, because it entails admitting the extent of the drug problem and seems to implicate government and social agencies in supporting drug use. Yet the humanitarian, medical, and financial benefits of free needles are substantial. The policy of supplying needles has been recommended for some troubled city areas and is favoured by many doctors, officials, and activists. However, the supplying of needles to addicts has become an extremely controversial issue within the African-American community in the United States.

In many urban areas of the United States a high preponderance of drug users are African-American. Some resistance to supplying needles on the part of African-American leaders and community workers is due to pride and an unwillingness to acknowledge the high rate of drug use. But distrust of white professionals, especially those in the medical community, is another important factor. Remembering the scandal of Tuskegee, wherein white doctors testing anti-syphilis drugs deliberately left black men with syphilis untreated for decades, allegedly as part of a medical experiment, many African-American community leaders simply do not trust white doctors and liberal professionals to have the interests of black people at heart. Such phenomena as the experimentation of Tuskegee have stained the memory of educated African-Americans and contribute to a distrust of white medical interventions purporting to benefit blacks.

Another poignant tale of distrust between groups is that of the Mohawks in the Montreal area and various segments of the white Canadian population. In *People of the Pines* Geoffrey York and Loreen Pindera describe how distrust among the Mohawk Indians for the Catholic church, French Canadian settlers, the Quebec Provincial Police, the federal Department of Indian Affairs, and the Canadian and Quebec governments grew over a period of two hundred and fifty years.[2] In 1718 the Mohawk Indians left their home territory in the centre of the developing city of Montreal. Catholic priests in the Sulpician order advised them to move west to the Lake of Two Mountains area, where they were told they would have land deeded to them by the French king. Instead, the governor of New France granted that land to the Seminary of St Sulpice for the use and benefit of the Indians. There was no written deed. A land dispute began, and ran through the eighteenth century. When the British conquered New France, the Treaty of Paris and Royal Proclamation of 1763 stipulated that the Indians were to be protected in their lands unless these were formally surrendered to the Crown. The Mohawks believed that these treaties guaranteed their land. But in 1840 the Sulpician claim was legally recognized by the British.

During the nineteenth century the Mohawks in the Lake of Two Mountains area lived in poverty under the dubious protection of the Catholic church. They had to pay for the upkeep of the church and presbytery, and many constraints were imposed upon them. The natives came to see the priests as hypocritical and false humanitarians; the priests in turn regarded the natives as barbaric savages. Distrust and animosity grew to the point that in 1869 the native people converted *en masse* to Protestantism. In the same year the federal government denied Mohawk land rights in the area. When a native leader appeared at the presbytery with forty armed men and told the Sulpicians they had eight days to leave, he was arrested. Eventually released on bail, he was advised to respect law and property rights and "trust the Government, which has your welfare at heart."[3] Between 1870 and 1873, criminal charges were brought against one-third of adult male Mohawks in the area of Lake of Two Mountains for refusing to ask permission from the Sulpicians to chop wood.

In the latter part of the nineteenth century the Sulpicians began selling land in the area to white French Canadian settlers. The town of Oka was populated by these settlers and became a municipality in 1875. The Mohawks protested the settlements. The Sulpicians and the Department of Indian Affairs encouraged natives to move elsewhere.

The government set aside 25,500 acres at Gibson, in the district of Muskoka, Ontario. The seminary, eager to get rid of the recalcitrant Mohawks, agreed to buy the land and pay 9000 dollars ... Each family would receive 100 acres in the new location, as well as a log house, paid for by the seminary. Thirty-five of the 120 Mohawk families made the move to Gibson in the fall of 1881, assured by the government's promise to provide them with provisions for one year. But when they arrived, they found no food or supplies waiting. Worse yet, with winter only weeks away, there were few jobs to be had and the log houses they were promised by the seminary had not been built. They also found many white squatters already living on the reserve; neither group welcomed the presence of the other ... Contrary to what they had been promised, the land was greatly inferior to the land they had cultivated at Oka, and several families decided to return there – only to discover that the Sulpicians had already sold their homes and property to French Canadian settlers.[4]

Though the white squatters were bought out by the federal government, which brought some supplies and built houses, the move to Gibson was not a success. The whole episode encouraged the

Mohawks near Oka to stand their ground, and aggravated distrust between natives and whites.

Most natives remained in the Oka area, where there were barricades, protests, arms, unrest, and arrests over many years. In 1945 the Canadian government purchased land on behalf of the Mohawks, but the area constituted only 1 per cent of the original total. The Mohawks, who had not been consulted about these arrangements, were bitterly disappointed. A key area of land called The Commons was not purchased. In 1961 the federal government established a committee to consider the matter, and the Mohawks engaged lawyers to appear before it. By this time the town of Oka had allowed part of the disputed Commons to be ploughed over for a golf course. The land issue was two hundred and forty years old. The federal committee recommended resolving the issue and acknowledged that the natives had got a bad deal. Its advice was ignored.

In the summer of 1990 the Oka issue blew up. The municipality wanted to extend the golf course, and a non-violent protest by natives had had little effect. One Quebec policeman was killed when the police tried to break through a native barricade. A summer-long stand-off followed, featuring stone-throwing by whites, looting by natives, and intervention by the Canadian Army, including deployment of tanks on Canadian soil. Extensive violence was barely averted by the replacement of Quebec Provincial Police by disciplined personnel from the Canadian Army.

The land issue in the area remains unresolved. Given the long history of embittered relationships between natives and whites at Oka and elsewhere, what is surprising is not that this intense and dangerous conflict occurred but that it did not occur earlier. Mohawks identify themselves as a nation with a history of hardship, mistreatment, and betrayal by whites. Many individuals involved in the 1990 confrontation were descendants or relatives of leaders and victims of earlier events. Recollections of poverty, arrest, jail, hiding, fights, and demonstrations were not distant history but their own family lore. Given this history and its importance for the people who lived and still live it, natives understandably had little trust in the Sulpicians, the Quebec Provincial Police, the Quebec government, the municipality of Oka, the federal Department of Indian Affairs, or the federal government. That distrust made negotiations during the Oka affair extremely difficult. It seems likely to persist for decades to come.

Although groups do not have a mind or consciousness, these cases vividly illustrate that there is a crucial sense in which groups have a memory. They have a lore and history – oral and documented – of events in their collective past, and a shared interpretation of what key events mean. Tales of the past, of victory and mistreatment, are told and retold. They are remembered, and a history of the group is constructed and cultivated by its members. Attitudes of victory or resentment, love or hatred, trust or distrust, are expressed and cultivated in the telling and re-telling of the history. The humiliation and betrayal of the Mohawks in the eighteenth and nineteenth centuries is not forgotten by Mohawks today, because members of the group recall it, talk about it, write about it, and teach it to the young. Distrust of whites, which was warranted in the past, is warranted not only by events today but by these long-ago betrayals and injustices. Whether any Mohawk living today was ever personally arrested for failing to ask the Sulpicians permission to cut wood, it is undeniable that the dependency and humiliation of past centuries contribute to present-day attitudes, prominent among which is distrust of French Canadians, the federal government, and the Catholic church. In conflict situations that attitude of distrust is a crucial factor making collaborative negotiated solutions far more difficult to achieve than they otherwise could be.

The same is true of many other groups, especially those organized around racial or ethnic identity. The memory of slavery remains vivid among African-Americans more than a century after the abolition of slavery. Whether the last ex-slave has died or not does not crucially affect the issue. The collective history of a group includes its relations with other groups, especially those to which it has been vulnerable. Thus whites figure large in black and native history, Christians and Arabs in Jewish history, Israelis in Palestinian history, men in women's history, management in labour history. Past injuries and insults do not disappear with the passage of time. When groups have suffered at the hands of others, the fact is recalled not only by the victims and their direct descendants but by members of generations to come because there is a tendency to emphasize such events and build a collective history and identity upon them. In group memory, harms and injustices gain mythic proportions, and the attitudes they shape are a central element in the dynamic of politics. As wars in the Balkans illustrate so painfully, the effects can be disastrous.

Many feelings and attitudes, including the attitudes of trust and distrust, characterize whole groups or nations of people and affect their relations with each other. When groups of nations distrust each other, they tend to interpret each other's actions, words, and policies in a negative way – just as individuals do when they distrust each other. They are fearful and suspicious, ready to take offence, and hesitant or unwilling to co-operate. Negotiations between groups whose relationship has been characterized by suspicion are likely to be difficult, more difficult than those between groups that have generally been inclined to trust each other. As is the case with individuals, distrust between groups tends to build on itself. When doings and sayings are negatively interpreted and co-operation is difficult and rare, it will be hard to build a better relationship and easy to find further grounds for distrust. Attitudes of trust and distrust between groups constitute powerful undercurrents in political and social affairs.

When we think of issues of trust arising between social groups, we tend to think first of cases of conspicuous distrust. Here as elsewhere it is cases of harm and injustice that come first to mind. Trust between groups also exists, of course, and tends to facilitate communication and co-operation. But, as is the case with individuals, groups are vulnerable when they trust. A too-complete and too-ready trust can be a grave mistake. In some cases people have trusted too readily and too completely, and come to significant harm as a result.

An example is the politically conservative and pro-military populations of Nevada and Utah. During the first decades of the atomic age these people had a very trusting attitude towards the American government. Knowing that these states were populated by such loyal and uncritical people, the American government used large tracts of Nevada for nuclear-weapons testing, taking little care to protect the people and livestock of Nevada and neighbouring Utah. It was not until the late seventies that high rates of cancer and birth defects among humans and sickness among livestock revealed the serious harm imposed on this conservative population.

Other examples of too much trust in political leaders and authorities are readily found. In the 1930s communists around the world put their faith in the Communist Party of Stalin's Soviet Union, dismissing bad news and evidence of purges as propaganda or as of little significance in the grand course of history. They trusted Stalin and the Communist Party of the Soviet Union far too much, as became painfully obvious later.

LOGICAL QUESTIONS ABOUT TRUST, DISTRUST, AND GROUPS

As these examples illustrate, we quite naturally ascribe attitudes of trust and distrust to various groups. Historians and journalists do not give a second thought to the matter. They write with no critical qualms about the various attitudes of various groups. African-Americans and Mohawks distrust whites; the Mormons trusted the u.s. government; the communists in the 1930s trusted Stalinist Soviet government. Distrust and trust are attitudes. In common usage, from the point of view of common sense and ordinary language, we do not hesitate to attribute trust, distrust, and many other feelings, beliefs, and attitudes to groups.

Yet some critical minds balk at this point. How can groups have mental states? To be sure, we speak of group memory, or groups resenting or believing things, of groups trusting and distrusting each other. But perhaps this is only loose talk. Does it make sense, from a logical point of view? Groups are not individuals, and they are not conscious. How can it make sense to attribute mental states to groups? Standard central cases of trust and distrust are those in which individual persons have these attitudes. Persons are conscious; they deliberate and choose and have expectations, emotions, dispositions, and various other mental states required for trust. Does it make sense to think of groups doing these things? Do groups like the Mohawks or the French Canadians or Mormon farmers in Utah have beliefs, values, feelings, dispositions, determinations, degrees of willingness to trust?

When we say "Susan trusts her father" and "The Dutch trust the Danes," can the word "trust" mean the same thing in both cases? For an individual to trust, she must have the confident expectation that the other, whom she trusts, will act well towards her because she is well motivated and competent. There is a possibility that the other will not do as she expects. There is, then, some risk in a situation of trust, and the one who trusts is vulnerable. But she accepts that risk. Trust affects her interpretation of the other's actions and attitudes.

Groups are composed of individuals. When we speak of groups deliberating, choosing, and acting, we must in some sense allow that they do only in so far as some or all of their individual members do so.[5] If a social-action group decides to hire a new staff member, at least some of its members must wish to do so and must have decided to do so. If farmers in Saskatchewan challenge a federal government decision, then similarly some or all of them must have decided the decision was wrong and resolved to do something about it. In this reductionist way we can easily make sense of attributions to groups. Groups can be said to do things and say things and believe things in the sense that some or all of their members do or say or believe these things.

To say that French Canadians trust English Canadians not to respond with violence in the event of an attempt by Quebec to separate from Canada is to say most French Canadians believe that most (and the prevailing) English Canadians would not act violently or condone violence in such an eventuality. That in turn means that most French Canadians would respond to and interpret what is said and done by English Canadians in the light of the belief that they are unlikely to resort to violence. Though aware that this is an uncertainty (after all, English Canadians, being free agents, could emerge from what has seemed to be stolid moderation to act in a vicious and unexpected way), most French Canadians do not take the risk of violence seriously; they assume there will be no violence and do not reflect much on the possibility that there might be. Clearly, in this case there is also a vulnerability, and people could be seriously hurt if the trust was misplaced. Trust ascribed to a group has the same sense and interpretation as it does for individuals, although the phenomena described are more complex, and it would be harder to gather evidence to confirm a statement to the effect that one group trusts another.

To say that French Canadians as a group have a particular belief or attitude is typically to mean that a majority of individuals among them have that belief or attitude, or at least that it is prevalent in the group. To confirm such a statement empirically would require a survey of some kind, or, for an organized group, a study of the attitudes of its leadership or of beliefs and attitudes assumed or expressed in key institutional documents or arrangements. But I would argue that there is no logical problem in ascribing beliefs or attitudes to groups. In general, if group A trusts group B, then most individual As have the requisite beliefs, expectations, and attitudes towards group B. That means either that they have them towards some, most, or all of the individuals in group B. There is no logical paradox or incoherence here.

Groups are not super-beings with a mysterious independent existence over and above that of their members. Were no individuals to be members of groups, there would be no groups. Still, there is a difference between a group and its members, and reductionist approaches that insist that groups are nothing but their members do not allow us to tell the whole story about groups. One reason that groups are not reducible to their members is that groups survive changes in their membership. If a member dies or leaves, a group such as the Mohawks, African-Americans, the Sierra Club, or the League of Women Voters persists all the same.

Not only are groups logically distinct from their members; they differ psychologically and sociologically as well. The properties and attributes of groups are not *simply* those of individuals. Thinking that we can reduce the sentiments of a group to those of individuals is not correct because it ignores the fact that some of the sentiments of individuals may arise simply because they are members of these groups and participate in groups activities, sharing the group's sense of its history and culture. When people live and work together, they develop collective sentiments arising from their social life; these characterize many members of the group and thus characterize the group. (That is, attitudes, sentiments, and beliefs arise, in many cases, from group activity and not from individuals atomistically understood.) For instance, when the Oka Mohawks remember their former dependency on the Sulpician order, that memory supports, and is supported by, beliefs and sentiments learned from others in family, community, and school. Individuals have some of the attitudes they have because the group believes and values certain things, and makes certain events and themes central in its history and identity. From these common memories and interpretations, attitudes of trust and distrust towards individuals and other groups emerge.

Some have argued that since groups are composed of individuals and can only act and think in so far as their member individuals do so, speaking of the beliefs and attitudes of groups as such is merely a loose and sloppy metaphor. On a thoroughly reductionist interpretation, to say that Quebec Mohawks as a group or collectivity distrust the Sulpicians would be to say only that all or most of the Quebec Mohawks as individuals do so. Such a view has been advanced by the philosopher Anthony Quinton. Quinton grants the existence of groups and is willing to acknowledge that individuals depend on groups, just as groups depend on individuals. But he insists that, from a strictly logical point of view, actions, intentions, reasons, and decisions can be attributed *only* to individuals: "Groups are said to have beliefs, emotions, and attitudes and to take decisions and make promises. But these ways of speaking are plainly metaphorical. To ascribe mental predicates to a group is always an indirect way of ascribing such predicates to its members." Quinton's position in this passage amounts to the reductionist one that group attitudes can be reduced to the attitudes of member individuals. They exist only metaphorically. But Quinton does not explain just what he means by "metaphorical" in this connection. If he means that a group cannot have a belief or attitude unless some or all of its members do, then he is obviously correct. But if he means that a group as such cannot in a literal sense have a belief or attitude, he is too hasty. His own follow-up statement shows why: "To say that the industrial working class is determined to resist anti-trade union laws is to say that all or most industrial workers are so minded. Where groups are said to decide or promise, the statements in question are *institutional*; the reference is to a person or persons authorized to take decisions or enter into undertakings on behalf of the group."[6] Significant limitations of individualist reductionism are implicitly recognized here in Quinton's reference to *institutional* undertakings. Institutions are social, products of social organization.

The institutional or organizational framework of deliberation and decision-making is an important factor here. There is a crucial difference between organized groups and others. Take, for instance, Quinton's example of the industrial working class. If the industrial working class were purely and simply a class of workers with no collective organization, then the reductionist view would seem to fit. The industrial working class as such could not have "determination" except in so far as all or most of the individuals within it had that attitude. But suppose that the industrial working class has been organized to generate a collectivity (call it the Workers Lobby) representing that class. If the Workers Lobby has institutions and clear procedures for decision-making and represents the industrial working class, then the "determination" of that group will be manifested, and constituted, by the statements and actions of its leadership. When such institutionalization exists, attitudes can be attributed to *the group as such*. The industrial working class can be said to *have determination to resist*, even if most of its individual members do not share the attitude, because that attitude is reflected in official pronouncements of the authorized decision-makers.[7]

Thus the reductionist model does not apply well to organized groups. When there are clear procedures for making decisions, stating reasons, intentions, and policies, and undertaking actions, the group itself may be said to deliberate, to undertake actions, and to have attitudes such as trust and distrust. For a peace group to decide to hire a staff person is not the same as for all, some, or most of its members to decide to hire a staff person. In fact, if the group has a duly elected executive and democratic procedures, no single member can make that decision. It must be taken by the authorized executive. To take another example, suppose that the authorized leadership of the Mohawks were to decline an offer of land from the Canadian government, stating as its reason that government assurances are not to be believed. In such a case the leadership would indicate its distrust of the government authority. Granting that this is an organized collectivity in which the leadership represents the membership, the distrust expressed by the leadership may be said to constitute the attitude of the group as such.[8] It is likely, though not certain, that most or all members individually share this attitude. Given that an executive or leadership represents the group and can make decisions on its behalf, it makes sense to attribute the attitudes underlying those decisions to the group. The decision and reasoning in such a case are collective and cannot properly be reduced to attitudes of individuals.

Frequently, when an attitude characterizes the leadership, and thereby the group, it will also characterize all or most members. But this connection is not a strict logical one. It is possible that the leadership will differ significantly from many or most individual members. The leadership may have different information, or may have given more thought to a matter, and may work out beliefs and attitudes that *represent* the members. Its decisions, policies, and attitudes can properly be said to constitute those of the collectivity, even in some circumstances in which many individual members do not agree.

Sometimes it is unclear whether an organized collectivity represents a particular group. If, for instance, a substantial number of industrial workers were publicly to criticize the Workers Lobby and insist that it did not represent them, then the relationship between the leadership and these individuals would be a contested one. But such indeterminacy does not show either that attitudes of groups reduce to those of member individuals or that they are merely metaphorical.

Reductionist accounts are not open only to logical objections. They are historically and sociologically misleading because they neglect the role of group dynamics in forming individual beliefs, emotions, and attitudes. They presuppose that individual beliefs and attitudes simply exist at a rock-bottom level and that group attitudes are an additive product of individual ones. There is such a thing as the social atmosphere of knowledge and attitudes. The point is well stated by the French philosopher Michele Le Doeff: "Contemporary culture is extremely contradictory on this point; it insists on the atomistic model of the person, although, in practice, it knows that ... individuals are 'atoms' only in very particular conditions and partially ... It takes as much technical precision to isolate a person as it does to isolate a chemical substance." Le Doeff uses advertising as an example. Advertisers typically show one or more people using their products. Clearly advertisers have discovered that we are affected by the idea that other people have found a product valuable. Ideas, opinions, and desires among the public are the social background of individual choices and affect our sense of reasonableness and value. The "social whole," Le Doeff argues, affects private decision-making and everyday life. If there is much discussion favouring some practice – for instance, giving up smoking, or equitably sharing domestic work – private deliberations about it are considerably affected.[9]

If one asks why a Mohawk has strong feelings about the relationship between his people and the Sulpicians or French Canadian settlers, the answer will be that he has learned from parents and elders or from prominent leaders or thinkers within the group. The same can be said of Serbs and Croatians, Turks and Kurds, blacks and whites, Arabs and Jews, French and English Canadians. In such cases it is the cultivation of beliefs and attitudes within a group that causes them to be acquired by individuals. There is group consensus on the significance of key events. Such consensus has not been established because many individual interpretations and assessments just happen to coincide. Beliefs, expectations, feelings, valuings, and attitudes – including those of trust and distrust – emerge from interactions within a community in which central stories are preserved and treasured.

We can distinguish between aggregates and organized groups.[10] An example of an aggregate would be a mob in a square; an example of an organized group would be the Sierra Club. In an essay on group action, Robert X. Ware notes that there are many different kinds of groups. Even the distinction between aggregation and organization admits of degrees. According to Ware, a "pure class," such as Protestant bachelors, cannot act as a group because it has no means of undertaking collective action. But it has the potential to act because it has the potential to organize. (If the federal government were to propose a special tax on Protestant bachelors, that would almost certainly inspire an organized response.)

Ware argues that groups can, in various ways, be collective agents of action. If five people lift a piano, each does something, but a slightly different thing – one may lift from underneath, while another grabs the side. If eighty people sing in a choir, they all sing, but are divided into parts; the tenors sing and the sopranos sing the same piece, but not the same notes. Each individual does something, and the group thereby does something. But just how the action of the individual contributes to the group varies from case to case. The action may be *distributed* among members; each member does something, and the total of their actions results in the group's doing something. There is also group action that is not distributed among individuals, as when a policy decision is taken on behalf of group members by an authorized executive. Here the action is undertaken *collectively*, in a way made possible by the organizational structures of the group – as would be the case if the Workers Lobby delivered a brief to the government.

Ware argues persuasively that social theory cannot be entirely individualistic. The problem is, there are just too many groups doing too many things. Groups *act*; they are *agents* in political and social life, and social theory will have to allow for that fact. Ware stops short of attributing mental characteristics to groups. Groups cannot, he says, be collective thinkers.

At this point, Ware strikes me as suddenly too cautious. In so far as we attribute intentions, reasons, beliefs, and attitudes to individuals, on the basis of their statements and actions, we can do the same for groups – as can be seen when a leader rejects a peace proposal because many of the people he represents distrust the other party and believe that it will not abide by a ceasefire agreement.

The common-sense idea that groups can trust or distrust makes sense in this way. Such attitudes can either be distributed among the members or they can collectively characterize the group as a whole by virtue of its organizational structures. In many cases it will be true both that individuals distributively have a certain belief or attitude and that the belief or attitude is characteristic of the executive or leadership.

PRACTICAL IMPLICATIONS

It is not mere logical nitpicking to reflect on what might be meant by attributing attitudes such as trust and distrust to groups. The various interpretations can be of real practical significance. Though the rigorous reductionism expressed by Quinton goes too far, I believe that there is a sound impulse behind reductionism when it warns us not to think of groups as monolithic "things." It is by virtue of the fact that individuals trust and distrust that groups and nations trust and distrust. The practical warning we can read from reductionism is that we should not oversimplify and think of groups as whole chunks of reality without distinguishable parts. It is all too easy to make cavalier attributions of beliefs, emotions, and attitudes to large groups of people without seriously thinking either about what we mean or about what the evidence warrants. Though groups can properly be said to trust and distrust, attributions of attitudes to groups are often based on stereotypes and poorly grounded on evidence.

It is all too easy to decide that the Germans do not trust the Russians; that "natives" do not like "whites"; that "women" oppose military development; or that "labour" distrusts management. Such attributions need to be carefully considered. Is the attribution distributive, meaning that *all or most* individual members have the attitude? Or is it collective, meaning that given the organizational structures of the group, those *authorized* to speak and act for it have this attitude? If it is collective, what is the relationship between leadership attitudes and those of members? In either case, what is the evidence for the attribution?

Sometimes group attitudes are obstacles to necessary collaboration or reform. We would like to change them, if only we could, and the practical significance of reductionist questions is that they may suggest a route towards constructive change. When one group distrusts another, there are nearly always some individuals who do not share the attitude. Some of these may be in positions of significance and may be approached constructively. It is all too easy – and apparently all too natural – to infer fallaciously that all members of the group have the same attitude, which is timelessly fixed – that Mohawks distrust whites, or Indians distrust Pakistanis, and that is just it. Attitudes within groups are variable and changeable, and for practical purposes these points are of considerable importance. Trying to look beneath the attribution, asking just who may hold this attitude and who does not, can suggest valuable routes to change. If leadership has one attitude and most of the membership another, important possibilities open up. If an attitude is distributed among individual members, some of whom do not share it, other approaches are suggested. The variability of individual attitudes within groups is extremely important when we come to consider cases in which those attitudes could constructively be changed.

The attitudes of trust and distrust that groups take towards each other are of central importance. Groups can act and take decisions, and they can, either distributively or collectively, trust and distrust. But groups are not monoliths; as reductionists remind us, they are ultimately composed of individuals. And the variety within them merits attention. Affecting key individuals or making use of dynamic tensions in a group can lead to constructive and creative shifts in collective attitudes, both in the realm of domestic politics and in international affairs.

10 Negative and Positive Pictures of International Life

There are people in all countries who feel allegiance to a community that in one sense does not exist – the community of humankind. It is this allegiance to a community that we are calling species identity. The community of humankind is a country without borders, with no capital city and with only one law – to avoid doing harm to any fellow human being.

Elise Boulding, *Building A Global Civic Culture*

The modern Leviathan is not a solitary beast. It swims in a school, and it is a member of an international community.

Haskell Fain, *Normative Politics and the Community of Nations*

In many respects the world has become smaller and more closely interconnected. Yet despite globalization in diverse areas of life, some still think of the international arena as one of anarchy. The United Nations is active in many areas but does not amount to a world government. Though there is international law, there are no international police to enforce it. Is there any workable basis for trust between states? Does an international community exist?

REALISM AND SUSPICION

For generations, scholars of international relations have been preoccupied with the problem of war. So-called Realists follow the seventeenth-century philosopher Thomas Hobbes, who argued that without a central authority, human beings would exist in a disorderly condition of competition, fear, and insecurity. This Hobbes termed the *state of nature*. Hobbes believed that people are greedy, self-interested, and desperate for power. Without a supreme authority to control their behaviour they would struggle in a "war of all against all," where life would be "nasty, brutish, and short." When critics asked for evidence, reminding Hobbes that nowhere in the world had a state of nature been observed, Hobbes pointed to relations between states. He regarded the disorderliness of international relations and the frequency of war and violence as a corroboration of his theory of the state of nature. What would human beings be like without a tough government to keep down their aggressive behaviour? Look at the international realm, at relations between states, and you will know.

Modern Realist commentators follow Hobbes, seeing human nature as greedy and competitive. Central authority is lacking in the international arena: there is no global cop. Thus, Realists conclude, there is no reliable international order. States cannot count on each other to keep treaties, abide by international law, or refrain from attempts at domination, invasion, and outright violence. International politics is a game of alliances, conflicts, balances, imbalances, spheres of influence, and the like – an arena with no respect for moral and legal norms. Though it may operate with a certain predictability, the international system is one in which the possibility of war looms as a constant threat. Sceptical and pessimistic about human nature, Realists approach international issues from a standpoint of distrust.

On the Realist model, *nation-states* are the essential actors in international affairs.[1] Individuals, transnational corporations, international institutions, non-governmental organizations, and subnational groups undertake many actions, but it is the actions of nation-states that really count. They have roughly equal power, are in continuing competition, and could attack each other at any time. Governments, contrived to handle the problem of internal order between unruly individuals, are aggressive in their interactions with each other. The so-called international order is really an international *disorder*, featuring conflict, violence, and perpetual insecurity. Violent conflict, Realists warn, will always be a feature of human life. In the absence of norms, effective law, and a central authority backed by military force, violence will be the inevitable outcome of disputes.

Realists distinguish themselves from moralizing Idealists, whom they regard as naïve. From a Realist point of view, those who attempt to impose moral norms in international relations only reveal their failure to understand the power dynamic of international relations. Any attempt to import morality into this realm will lead only to crude "moralism" – a dogmatic stance that will bring more harm than good. Realists see themselves as outside morality, not moral or immoral but amoral.[2] Realist scholars and analysts regard themselves as neutral, as merely describing the inevitable pursuit of interest and power and competition in interstate relations. Interests are there, power is there, states will contend, and that is all there is to it. Supposedly this sort of strategic analysis leaves the world as it is and does not take sides. Realists explain and advise from the point of view of *realpolitik*, and their prominence among experts in foreign policy has enabled them to affect the behaviour of states accordingly.

Realists see little or no meaningful sense in which there is, or could be, an *international community*. Trust has scarcely any valid role to play, even in such areas as the making, breaking, or keeping of treaties. That distrust is the basic, standing attitude in relations between states is, in effect, an axiom of Realist theory. Issues of trust and distrust are central in international relations because they construct a key dividing-point between Realist models and alternatives to them.[3] According to Realism, those who are not adversaries at a given moment are nevertheless potential adversaries. Each state naturally is, and should be, in a state of wariness and distrust towards every other. States are naturally contending, and what looks like peace is an unstable prelude to war. Over the long run the interests of states are necessarily opposed.

On this account the international arena is a level unto itself where states interact in quest of interest and power. States, not individuals, are the agents of action. Scarcely a human world, the international arena is surely not one in which personal emotions, beliefs, or attitudes affect the fundamental dynamic of events. Realist theory insists that relations between states are entirely different from relations between individual people. Individuals are individuals; small groups are small groups; and nation-states are something else again. The system of states is seen as an autonomous political realm distinct from the interpersonal realm of family, friendly relationships, collegiality, and community life. There is no effective legal system backed up by central authority; there is little predictability; there are no reliable sanctions against violence. The agents of change are not individual persons. In this abstractly turbulent world the intentions and emotions of individual people are of little significance. Political and economic interests, not psychological conditions, define the terms of international conflict. Thus domestic models for resolving conflict – based on such things as understanding, empathy, and co-operation – are deemed by Realists to be irrelevant to international relations and foreign policy.

Realists do not deny that states sometimes have common interests. But even when this is the case they hesitate to counsel co-operation. Preoccupied with power and security, predisposed towards conflict and competition, realist advisers to the state counsel suspicion that other states will cheat on agreements. Even if agreements are kept, opposing states can reap greater benefits from the agreement and enhance their competitive position. States that fail to protect their interests may pay dearly: today's ally could be tomorrow's enemy. War is possible at any time. Realists sardonically advise that states have no friends, only interests: "If it is irrational to rely upon the goodwill or desire for cooperation of one's adversary when one is at war with him, because doing so may mean not merely the loss of a battle but the war itself, and the fundamental national and human values for which the war is fought, then is it also not equally irrational to do so in the period *before* actual armed hostilities break out?"[4] Any period at all could be the period before armed hostilities break out, so there is a kind of standing distrust that is appropriate between nations. For the Realist it is irrational to rely on the goodwill of an "adversary" during a war or even "before a war." A period of normal peaceful relations is construed as one that is "pre-war." In the pre-war phase a state should distrust its neighbours and ready itself for the war that is likely to come. Generalized suspicion is a Realist axiom. States that pursue co-operation, trusting that commitments will be kept, make themselves dangerously vulnerable.

Realism sees itself as an objective kind of theory and international politics as a realm governed by objective laws that have their roots in human nature. These laws have always governed the relations between peoples and states; using Reason, we can understand them.[5] Assuming that the pursuit of interest is the underlying motivation for all state action, a Realist can readily "explain" what happens. Whatever is done can be interpreted as the pursuit of state interests and thereby interpreted according to Realist theory. On this view the "rational" state is like the "rational actor," and its policies should be based on an accurate assessment of state interests and a quest to maximize them. The irrational policy either misconstrues state interests or seeks to further them by ineffective methods. There is no room for ideals or moral principles in such appraisals. For Realists the only feasible perspective for judgment in international politics is that of state interest. The only question that can reasonably be asked is: how well do policies serve the interests of the state?

In international relations the agents of action are states, not individuals. And yet morality was designed for individuals, not states. Thus, Realists conclude, morality has no proper role in international relations. In any event, attempts to apply moral principles internationally have too often resulted in moralizing, prejudice, ethnocentrism, and holy wars. Far better to pursue state interests calmly and reasonably using the concept of interest and avoiding moral categories.

REASONABLE NUCLEAR STRATEGY?

To an astounding extent, Realist thinking dominated respectable Anglo-American discourse about nuclear weapons during the Cold War period. Anatol Rapoport, a mathematician and strategic theorist who later became a professor of peace studies, attributed this domination to the fact that Realists seem to speak in the voice of reason. From a Realist perspective, one could reasonably, deductively, calculate the costs and benefits of various nuclear strategies and (apparently) predict what opponents would do – on the assumption that they were rationally pursuing their own power and interests. In comparison, alternate modes of thinking seemed emotional, effeminate, unscientific, fuzzy, and lacking in credibility. Though the use of even a few nuclear weapons would result in hundreds of thousands of deaths and horrendous environmental damage, strategic thinking about nuclear policy was not burdened by sentiment. Even plans for fighting and winning a nuclear war could be made to sound sane and reasonable in the abstract discourse of strategic studies. Apparently, strategic studies was a science yielding precise discriminations between reasonable and unreasonable ways of relying on nuclear weapons for defence.

As early as 1964 Rapoport rejected such ideas. At the same time he rejected the fundamentally competitive interpretation of international life stipulated by Realists. Arrangements in which both parties can benefit are clearly possible between states – as when they exchange prisoners of war or arrange an anti-pollution treaty that they then work together to enforce. Rapoport insisted that whether it makes sense for a state to enter into a co-operative arrangement with another depends on the specific historical and psychological nature of the parties involved. It cannot be deduced from the abstract axioms of decision theory or abstract propositions about the state as a rational agent.

As in military thinking generally, strategic thinking tended to concentrate on the worst case. Rapoport characterized worst-case thinking as follows: "It is not necessary to ask what the enemy wants to do; but only what the enemy can do. If he can blackmail us, he will. If he can do us in, he will."[6] Worst-case scenarios make extreme distrust an axiom of planning. If "the enemy" will do the worst because that is predicted in worst-case reasoning, then military strategy must be based on countering that possibility. One expects the worst from the other party, regarding "him" as the enemy even in peacetime, because war is a permanent possibility. The worst "he" could do is what he might do, and this horror is the basis of strategy. Regarding every other state as an actual or potential opponent will select for certain types of information and certain interpretations of it. Realists claim that the international realm, wherein states are the primary agents, is completely different in logical level from the national or local realm, in which individual human beings are the primary agents.

But the distinction is overdrawn. Individuals and non-state groups undertake actions that have a significant impact on international relations; and within nations and communities, groups as well as individuals are active agents. International relations do not form a distinct realm of their own, sealed off from human emotion and psychology. Significantly, in international affairs it is still individual human beings who collect and interpret information, which is then used by other human beings to make decisions about action and policy. Those human beings really are just that: human beings, and as such they are not exempt from the truths of social psychology. People who are leaders and agents in international affairs can win friends, work passionately towards goals, and benefit from positive thinking, just as can politicians who work in a national society. The same can be said on the negative side. Stereotypes, prejudices, closed-mindedness, and the tendency to favor one's own hypothesis will apply to the human beings who conduct international relations just as they apply to human beings in the course of daily lives and national politics. Trust will build on trust; distrust will build on distrust. Realists, who characteristically brand their critics as idealistic and naïve, are themselves naïve if they presume that people can dispassionately collect and interpret information to describe and predict the behaviour of "enemy" states.

Rapoport concluded that, in the nuclear age, strategy had become "a plan of genocidal orgies." It was bitterly ironical that the founding assumption of strategic rationality appropriated for itself the name of Realism, because planning for limited or winnable nuclear wars was anything but realistic. When questions of foreign policy are turned into problems of maximizing the interests of our own state in dealings with others whom we conceptualize as actual or potential opponents, we will find security precarious and co-operation impossible.

CAUTIONARY TALES AND SALUTARY STORIES

Cautionary Tales

Distrust between states can go to extremes, as happened in some phases of the Cold War. Consider, for instance, the following comments by J. Halle, an American observer: "For Moscow to propose what we can accept seems to us even more sinister than for it to propose what we cannot accept. Our instinct is to cast about for grounds on which to discredit the proposal instead of seizing it and making the most of it. Being distrustful of Greeks bearing gifts, we are afraid of being tricked."[7] Halle points to a dangerous dilemma argument common in some circles during the Cold War. If the Soviet Union proposed what the United States could not accept, then there was no deal. But if the Soviet Union proposed what the United States could accept, this was a problem too. Some ruse must underlie the proposal. The offer would have to be rejected, else they would be tricked. Clearly this sort of entrenched distrust would make co-operation impossible. During the Cold War arms-control agreements were made and verified, and various other agreements were workable. That these things happened proves that even during these dangerous times Realist precepts were not always followed.

Arms control and disarmament presuppose a degree of trust. When each party fears that the other will attack some day, each has a powerful incentive to cheat, to hope for compliance from the other while continuing to build up its own arms. From an external point of view the best situation would be one where both states cut arms; the worst, one where neither does so. From the point of view of both parties, however, the best situation would seem (superficially at least) to be to continue arming while the other side cuts back on its armaments. In this way a state could seek to ensure its own military security while its opponent cut armaments; apparently, this would make it better off in the competition between the two. Casting arms competition as this kind of Prisoner's Dilemma may, however, be criticized as superficial because it ignores the economic and social cost of building up armaments instead of spending state money on social and economic development. In any event, parties pursuing their own interest and power as Realism advises will not be inclined to keep agreements in circumstances of distrust. The likely consequence is arming by both states and mutual defection, even if they have made an agreement. Applying Realism to a situation of arms control or disarmament and thinking of security and state competition in purely military terms, we arrive at a clear case of the Prisoner's Dilemma.

Each party will seem to have compelling reasons to pursue its own individualistically defined security interest. As a result both are worse off – even in terms of military security – than they would be if they trusted one another to abide by agreements. Generalized distrust and a conception of security based on a narrow military definition will lead to continued arming, reluctance or refusal to enter into agreements, and defection from any agreements that are made.

In a 1985 article on verification and trust in arms control, Allan Krass described the problem of trust between the United States and the Soviet Union during the Cold War period. The United States did not believe that the Soviet Union would comply with arms-control agreements; Americans were distrustful, suspecting cheating. The Soviet Union, by contrast, expressed a belief that states that signed treaties would live up to them, avowing an attitude of trust towards its partner in negotiation. Soviet negotiators found the explicit distrust of American negotiators insulting in both personal and national terms. They professed trust and urged that great nations working out important agreements should assume that both would abide by them. However, this avowed trust was largely rhetorical. The Soviet Union was often unco-operative about verification arrangements because it was intensely concerned about espionage by the United States. The Soviet Union professed trust and the United States did not. In this regard the United States was more honest, because neither side trusted the other.

What the United States saw as verification, the Soviet Union regarded as attempts to spy. The Soviets could perhaps have understood that there is a spectrum of cases between verification and espionage; they were, however, so afraid of American intrusion into areas of state secrecy that they were unable to accept this. For their part, the United States might have made some effort to understand Soviet politics and culture instead of simply branding the whole society "closed" and pontificating about how no one in a closed society could be trusted.

Krass commented: "From a purely logical point of view, it is clear that some initial degree of trust must be present if verification [of arms-control agreements] is to serve as a confidence-building measure. If one starts from the premise of total distrust, then one is demanding that the other side provide enough evidence to prove its innocence. But in all but the most blatantly unconcealable activities, this is a logical impossibility. No amount of evidence of compliance, for example, with a treaty banning possession of chemical weapons, could prove the absence of non-compliance."[8] The last sentence is especially important: no amount of compliance could prove the absence of non-compliance. If we feel a deep and entrenched suspicion that the other party will cheat and we find out on many occasions that he has not cheated in that particular case, that does not always overturn our suspicion. There could always be some other case of cheating, one we have not been able to discover. Distrust is not refutable by an accumulation of evidence. Krass might have added that without some degree of trust one would not enter into negotiations in the first place. If one party *completely* distrusted the other, it would fear even to send negotiators to a meeting-place – after all, the meeting itself might be some kind of ruse. Delegates might be killed or taken hostage, or deceptively manipulated to the advantage of the host party. In the end, no matter what the verification procedures are, no agreement can work without trust: suspicious minds can always find something to suggest cheating.

Innocence in such a context is impossible to prove. To be innocent, a party must do *nothing* wrong; to be innocent of cheating, a party must do *nothing* that constitutes cheating. The failure to find an instance of cheating does not prove there is no cheating; a clever cheater might have cheated in some way one could not detect. Thus someone who is deeply suspicious and does not want to change his attitudes can always hypothesize some cheating not yet discovered. If two states agree not to make chemical weapons, one can always suspect that the other is doing it somehow, somewhere – even when monitoring has shown no evidence of deviation.

Even in a context where there is intrusive monitoring of an agreement – as, for instance, when foreign inspectors arrive without notice to inspect facilities – evidence is almost certain to be incomplete and somewhat ambiguous. If one assumes at the outset that the other side cheats, one is likely to discover all sorts of evidence that seems to confirm one's suspicions. Even evidence of compliance with the agreement can be interpreted as a trick. Krass quotes one American observer who argued that the failure of American monitoring efforts to reveal any deviations from the accord only showed that the Soviets were especially clever cheats. Unaware of the irony, this man *complained* that "We have never found anything that the Soviets have successfully hidden!"[9] He was so suspicious that he failed to notice the logical truth that what has been successfully hidden has not been found. The tautology can hardly be cited as evidence of diabolical Soviet cleverness!

The verification of arms-control, disarmament, and other agreements is workable only if each side is committed and flexible, believes that the other side is committed to the agreement, and is willing to have its compliance monitored and deal with uncertainties and ambiguities in a business-like fashion. Given a practical and co-operative attitude, parties to an agreement can resolve technical disputes in a quiet and workmanlike manner instead of assuming the worst and screaming "cheating" and "defection" to the press and the public. In the context of arms control and disarmament, trust entails a willingness to give co-operation some benefit of the doubt. In the context of arms-control agreements, verification can be only part of the solution to problems of distrust because verification itself is unworkable without some degree of trust. Working out procedures to verify compliance with treaties itself presupposes trust. The implementation of these procedures also presupposes trust – in the authorizing of inspections, the gathering and interpretation of evidence, and many other areas. And without some willingness to give the other party the benefit of the doubt, no evidence will count as establishing compliance.

In international relations as in practical life, distrust can have its costs. Ironically, these appear even in contexts where states are trying to be *untrustworthy*. Michael Handel, a war historian, has written an essay on intelligence and deception in which he argues this point.[10] Handel, who adopts a broadly Realist perspective, expresses no scruples about the use of deception in international relations. He claims that in war deceiving one's enemies about one's capabilities or intentions is accepted standard procedure and can be effective. Ironically, though, even from this perspective there are advantages to more open, trusting, and trustworthy states when it comes to deceiving the enemy.

Like individuals, states come to have reputations in the area of truth-telling, and agents and spokespersons for a state are more likely to be believed if the state is reputed to be honest. In addition, those who deceive frequently may become unreceptive to new information, arrogant, and too trapped in their own world-view to grasp the opponent's situation. Thus they cannot deceive effectively. They are caught in their own web of disinformation. Leaders who are highly dictatorial and impose brutal penalties on their domestic enemies are protected from hearing unwelcome truths. This syndrome was probably the basis of Saddam Hussein's absolute failure to understand the reaction of the rest of the world to his 1990 invasion of Kuwait. Being closed to new information protects dictators from challenges to their favoured views of the world, but at the same time it precludes their understanding the reality in which they must operate. Dictatorial leaders whose tyranny spares them having to consider negative information tend to be ineffective in deception because their understanding of the world is gappy at best.

Anticipation of deception leads a person to be more sceptical of evidence. To the extent that he deems evidence from outside sources unreliable, his own preconceptions play a greater role in his decisions about what to accept and believe, and his sources of information are limited. As Philip Knightley demonstrates in his history of spying, when people are generally suspicious of all evidence, they find it easy to give reasons for dismissing or ignoring new evidence, and they are not receptive to new information. They have, then, little basis for reflecting critically on their view of the world. They cling to their own preconceived views, applying them in a biased and self-indulgent way. Dishonesty, distrust, and suspicion may have their uses, but they also have costs.

In an intelligence agency, a person disoriented by persistent distrust and suspicion works with others with the same basis for mental confusion. People know that they are constantly playing roles and deceiving others and their colleagues are doing the same. A whole institution, advisory to the state, is based on role-mandated deception and fraudulence. What is to be believed? Anything or anyone might be deceiving, betraying, about to attack at any time.[11] Reliable information and effective functioning become unlikely at best.

Salutary Stories

Relations between Israel and the Arab states were at an impasse in November 1977. There had been three wars since the establishment of the state of Israel. Little progress had been made towards peace. In a personal initiative the Egyptian president, Anwar Sadat, announced on 9 November 1977 on radio that he would go anywhere in the world, even to the Israeli Knesset, to seek peace. On 15 November Israeli Prime Minister Menachem Begin extended a formal invitation for Sadat to visit Israel. On 19 November Sadat arrived in Jerusalem. His widely televised visit was an extraordinary event in modern history. In his address to the Israeli Knesset, Sadat applied principles of international law to the Arab-Israeli conflict and made an eloquent call to the Israeli people for a better world where people could live in brotherly love, peace, joy, and prosperity. His initiative was a crucial turning-point in relations between Israel and Egypt. It showed a willingness by a major Arab state and past enemy to acknowledge Israel's existence and to negotiate directly.

It is not entirely clear why Sadat made this dramatic move.[11] It appears that he wanted a breakthrough and believed that u.s. President Jimmy Carter could be moved to see the justice of the Arab cause and help the Egyptians against the Israelis. He was becoming impatient with other Arab states, who struck him as indulging in fan-tastic rhetoric and impractical and unrealistic in their approach to Israel. The troubled Egyptian economy could certainly benefit from a reduced military budget, and Sadat wanted to regain control of the Sinai Peninsula, which had been occupied by the Israelis. Perhaps in addition Sadat wanted to ensure his own place in history.

Whatever the factors underlying Sadat's gesture, the ultimate effects of the Jerusalem initiative included the Camp David Accords of 1978, in which Egypt achieved a separate and lasting peace with Israel. Sadat's foreign minister Ibrahim Kamel believed that Egypt had become too isolated from the other Arab states and that the accords would harm inter-Arab relations and do little good with regard to the Palestinian situation. An unhappy member of the nego-tiating team at Camp David, Kamel resigned in disapproval just before the accords were signed.

There were others who felt as Kamel did. Eventually, Sadat paid for the peace with his life. He was assassinated in 1981 by soldiers in his own army, who believed that he had betrayed Islam and Egypt. But the peace between Israel and Egypt outlived him.

Sadat's Jerusalem initiative is an example of what some theorists have called a self-binding commitment. By going to Jerusalem, Sadat made himself politically and physically vulnerable, taking personal risks to meet the Israelis, acknowledging Israel's existence, and mak-ing a direct bid for peace. By making his visit so public, he indicated a firm commitment. The move was highly effective in terms of posi-tive publicity. In effect, world public opinion became a third party in the negotiations to come, and Sadat's move gave Egypt the moral upper hand. The initiative gave Israel little alternative but to co-oper-ate in future efforts towards peace. The Jerusalem initiative illustrates the possibility of breaking cycles of distrust in international relation-ships by a trusting gesture of self-commitment.[12]

Another striking peace initiative was that of F.W. de Klerk of South Africa. With blacks, East Indians, and people of mixed racial heritage denied the vote and access to many facilities and public institutions, South Africa was for decades an ostracized state. It had for many years incurred economic sanctions from major world powers. Many inside and outside South Africa had long feared that the struggle by South African blacks for equality and political power could only end in a bloodbath. But there were factors making peaceful change attrac-tive. By the late 1980s, South Africa was in difficulty economically. When the Berlin Wall came down in November 1989, the Cold War was declared officially over, and "winds of peace" began to blow in areas where superpower rivalry had been a factor in keeping conflicts alive. Links between the African National Congress (ANC) and communist parties in the Soviet Union and East-Central Europe had served to rationalize white Afrikaaner fear of black communism in southern Africa. The collapse of East European communism and the defeat of Soviet-style communism as a viable ideology and social system lessened that fear – and at the same time terminated Soviet-bloc financial support for the ANC. Within South Africa and in the world at large, it was increasingly clear that apartheid was untenable.

Willem de Klerk, a political analyst and older brother of F.W. de Klerk, wrote of seven fallacies of apartheid, several of these being moral:

The immorality of apartheid avenged itself on the system: the immoral basic philosophy that minorities could dominate majorities through a conspiracy of power and discrimination; the immorality of the lie that apartheid merely gave others what one claimed for oneself; the immorality of the arrogant hypocrisy that claimed to have designed a system that safeguarded civilized values and represented custodianship over the less privileged. Step by step, these immoralities were exposed as self-assertion and egotism, as self-advancement at the expense of others, as uncharitable and unjust ... apartheid had been feeding on evil. It was darkness masquerading as light. *Since apartheid was essentially criminal, it could not prevail.*[13]

Apartheid was based on the simplistic and insulting presumption that blacks would be happy enough if they had full stomachs and roofs over their heads.

Forces for change included pressure from South African blacks, East Indians, and people of mixed race; the English-language press; liberal whites of both English and Afrikaaner descent; foreign states; international non-governmental organizations; and would-be investors abroad, to name a few. The National Party, predominantly Afrikaaner, had invented apartheid. F.W. de Klerk had been a loyal member of the National Party and an active member of Parliament for many years. He seemed not to be a visionary, not a zealous reformer; if anything, he was rather conservative.

Yet it was de Klerk who undertook imaginative peace initiatives and began the rapid dismantling of the laws and institutions of apartheid. In a key speech to the South African Parliament on 2 February 1990 de Klerk called for negotiations among *all* South Africans as the only alternative to growing violence in the country and the basis for a new democratic constitution. He sought to end South Africa's isolation, citing the dramatic changes in East-Central Europe as a source of inspiration. He acknowledged the importance of respecting individual and minority rights and the need for sound economic development for all racial groups. He ended the ban on black political groups, including the African National Congress, the Pan-Africanist Congress, and the South African Communist Party, and released prisoners serving terms in virtue of their membership in these organizations. Nelson Mandela, the ANC leader who had served nearly twenty-eight years in jail, was to be released. De Klerk appealed to all individuals and groups to negotiate in order to work out procedures and institutions. Negotiation was the path away from confrontation and generalized violence, towards reconciliation and peaceful progress.

Following his release from prison on 11 February 1990, Nelson Mandela adopted an astounding attitude towards the white South Africa that had imprisoned him for most of his adult life. He spoke not of hatred, revenge, white wrongdoing, and black power but of reconciliation and the need to bring all races together in a new South Africa that would respect the rights of blacks, whites, and other minorities. De Klerk and Mandela began to work closely together. Key measures of apartheid were abolished by the South African Parliament. In 1990 the government opened hospitals, beaches, parks, and other facilities to all races, and in 1991 blacks were allowed to enrol in previously all-white schools. The first multi-racial elections were held in April 1994, and Mandela was elected president.

Mandela and de Klerk were joint recipients of the Nobel Peace Prize in 1993. The initiatives undertaken were imaginative, generous, and dramatic. They created hope for a relatively non-violent South African future, something that had seemed impossible just a few years earlier. An especially moving aspect of the political dynamic in South Africa was the way that Mandela and de Klerk were able to work together and, to a considerable degree, trust each other. De Klerk had the confidence to take the initiative, Mandela the generosity to forgive those who had been his jailors and white oppressors and to call for a positive and creative response from his people. These two men were determined to persevere to build an atmosphere of trust in which workable negotiations would lead the country away from terrible alternatives.

REALISM AS UNREALISTIC

The Realist model of international politics assumes that states are the essential actors in international affairs; that they have roughly equal power; that they control their internal affairs; and that there is no reliable compliance with moral or legal norms in international relations.

But not one of these four key assumptions is true, a basic fact acknowledged even by some who defend Realism.[14] In international affairs there are many agents as well as nation-states, and some undertakings by non-state agents have important and long-standing implications. As the examples of Sadat, de Klerk, and Mandela illustrate, individuals take important initiatives. Regional organizations like the European Community act; the European Parliament can rule adversely on practices and legislation of member states. The UN Security Council can send peacekeepers or authorize measures against aggression in cases of disputes within or between nations. Non-governmental organizations lobby around the world and at the United Nations for changes in policies on refugees, children, whaling, disposal of toxic and nuclear wastes, nuclear-weapons testing, and the international legality of nuclear weapons. Subnational groups launch publicity campaigns, carry out guerrilla operations, or take hostages. And multinational corporations move capital around the globe at the push of a button, with dramatic effects on currency values and the economic status of nation-states.

The assumption that states control their internal affairs is incorrect, as is obvious from the tremendous power of transnational corporations. In attempts to maintain viable economic life, many states must attend to conditions in neighbouring states when setting interest rates, currency levels, taxation policy, social, health, and welfare policies, and environmental legislation. Domestic economic life is tied to economic circumstances in other countries and by no means under the firm control of the national government.

Nor can the assumption that the international realm is one of anarchy, lacking central authority and devoid of operative norms, stand up to logical scrutiny. If the term "anarchy" simply means "lacking central government," then international relations are anarchistic by definition. However, the word "anarchy" also implies the absence of operative legal or moral norms, resulting in disorder. From the lack of central government we cannot logically infer these further features unless we assume that *only* an effective central government can establish order. This is to presume, in effect, that agents cannot restrain themselves or each other.[15]

As noted earlier, Hobbes appealed to international relations to confirm his ideas about the desperate precariousness of the state of nature and the selfish characteristics of human beings. Ironically, though, the very facts of contemporary international life tend to count against a Hobbesian assumption. The international sphere is by no means one of chaos and disorder: there is such a thing as scatter trust at the international level. If there were not, multinational corporations, the United Nations, countless non-governmental agencies, tourism, travel, and international trade and communications would not exist in their present form. Though there are no international police, most states abide by international law most of the time. The reasons are many but important, and among them is the fact that disobedience brings costs. States mostly abide by international norms, though there is no world cop or world government with the authority to enforce them. They abide by international norms and laws because they control themselves and each other and because they have good reason to do so. The absence of a central controlling authority has not produced a situation of anarchy in the sense of chaos and disorder. Large areas of international relations are relatively ordered and reflect degrees of trust and co-operation among states, based upon long-standing norms and expectations.

Hobbes and many other Realists tend to assume a false dichotomy between anarchy and centrally imposed order. They see two possibilities: a brutal state of anarchy in which no one is safe, and a world ordered by a central authority. The dichotomy is incorrect and misleading because there are many intermediate possibilities between total anarchy and absolute order; in addition, there are many different ways, apart from central authority, in which order can be established. It is hasty and simplistic, then, to infer anarchy in international relations from the absence of a world government that serves as a central controlling power. We cannot starkly contrast the single state as an ordered environment in which morality and trust make sense with the international system of states as a disordered environment where morality cannot apply and distrust is an axiom.

Virtually all states include various ethnic or national groups, the term "nation-state" being in this sense a misnomer. One author estimated that only 10 per cent of the world's states in the mid-1980s were ethnically unitary.[16] Since 1989 the ethnically constituted nation or people within the state has become increasingly significant in world events. Such nations have dramatically decreased the order and central authority in successor states of the Soviet Union and Yugoslavia. Their increasing power and frequently virulent nationalism has contributed to conflict and violence. But it should not be thought that these appalling ethnic conflicts confirm the Realist view of the world. To the contrary, they count against it because they constitute a potent demonstration of the limitations of the simplistic contrast between *order* within states and the *disorder* between them. There is appalling disorder within some states, and there is tremendous order in the relations between some other states. In 1995 there were thirty-nine wars in the world, and not one of them was a war between nations; these were civil wars. There is far more predictability and order in relations between Australia and New Zealand than there is within Russia or the former Soviet republic of Georgia.

In peace there are accepted norms – even in the absence of a super-state to enforce them – and we can rely on these norms. There is little point in adopting a war mentality as a basis for negotiating in peace. Rather, we should rely on the most likely predictions about what others will do in normal times. Assuming the worst and acting competitively is only likely to make things worse. While rightly warning that misplaced trust can be dangerous, Realists forget that unwarranted distrust has risks of its own. We can miss opportunities to engage in collective tasks, with resulting hazards for the human race and the planet itself.

In international relations as in everyday life, by far the preponderance of interactions are peaceful. There are conflicts, to be sure, but most of these do not lead to violence. International and transnational organizations play a key role in many important areas of human life; thousands of treaties are kept; there is considerable co-operation in international life; most states abide by international law. In the face of all this it is hard to understand why Realists cling to their Hobbesian model. Their negative picture of international life is still promulgated to many thousands of students of international relations, who carry their bleak picture to the voter's booth, the law courts, the civil service, and the legislature. If we take the Realist model literally, we disregard some basic and obvious facts about order, reliability, and co-operation, and look gloomily on prospects for a collective approach to global problems that are fundamental to human welfare.

A STRANGE DEFENCE OF REALISM

One thoughtful analyst of theories of international relations, K.J. Holsti, sets out the fundamental assumptions of Realism, then straightforwardly admits that all are false. Admitting that there is considerable interdependence and co-operation between states, Holsti nevertheless says: "The fact of interdependence has to lead to a *problem* before it warrants serious attention, just as concern with war, peace, order, and power led to our field centuries ago."[17]

In other words, the interdependence and co-operative activities of states often do not constitute a problem. So scholars and analysts are correct in disregarding them.

No wonder the Realist analysis of international life is bleak! Co-operative successes and interdependence in international relations are wilfully ignored; then Realism stipulates that co-operation is a risky business. Clearly, if we attend only to problems, we will describe reality on the basis of unrepresentative situations and events. We are wilfully ignoring non-problematic cases. For peace, co-operation, and issues of trust, this focus is seriously misleading. It will necessarily exaggerate the grounds for distrust and minimize the basis for trust. Distrust, pessimism, and cynicism will result.

Holsti readily acknowledges that there are many trends that could be interpreted as evidence that there is an international community or developing global society. In addition, there are global problems that can only be addressed by governments working in concert: resources of the seas, the earth's atmosphere, the use of Antarctica, airborne pollution, the movement of peoples ... There are sensational increases in personal contacts between people across international frontiers.

But the rosier picture that could emerge from attending to these phenomena constitutes only a "modest" challenge to the Realist tradition, according to Holsti. Peace between states, and the ongoing problems that face states in times of peace (trade, pollution, human rights, immigration, and so on), are just "not interesting" to those who study international relations, he says. A lecture on a topic like interstate co-operation in agriculture will put people to sleep, whereas a violent international conflict is something exciting. What is interesting (and, by implication, important) about international affairs is war and its permanent possibility. Concentrating on "interesting topics" pulls us right back to Realism: "Journalists do not report 'non-events.' Conflict, catastrophe, scandal, crime, and vice always precede achievement because they are assumed to be deviations from the norm. Likewise, medical research seldom focuses on the healthy person. And so, faced with the cataclysmic and sudden possibility of war anywhere on the earth, international politics and theory as fields of inquiry have always revolved around this problem."[18] Although war is exceptional, it cries out for attention – and receives it. But solid theory cannot be built on a preoccupation with the unusual. To the extent that Realists concentrate on war and its permanent possibility while ignoring peace and co-operation, they will generate a negatively biased picture of international life, perpetuate suspicion, and undermine the prospects for trusting relations between nation states.

We may also wonder whom Holsti has in mind when he says that people do not find non-conflictual topics interesting. To some people such matters as international law, peaceful conflict resolution, defence of human rights, treaties on the ozone layer, and UN programs for children and refugees seem interesting and important – more interesting and important, in fact, than war and war-preparedness. If such people are not among Holsti's colleagues, the explanation could just be that international relations has been dominated and defined by Realists preoccupied by power politics and military security. (This dominance seems to be lessening.) In any case, the (supposed) fact that violence strikes "people" (men?) as more interesting than peaceful relationships and co-operation provides no guarantee that Realism will produce a balanced, accurate, or constructive depiction of relations between states.[19] A negative picture inspired by the "fact" that violent conflict is more interesting than peaceable relations is counter-productive and misleading.

ROSIER PICTURES

Obviously, it is possible to view international relations differently, and many theorists and agents have done so. Recent alternatives to Realism include original and positive accounts by three women scholars: Elise Boulding, Sissela Bok and Dorothy Jones.

Elise Boulding on Global Civic Culture

Decidedly not a Realist, sociologist Elise Boulding argues in a recent work that a global civil society is developing.[20] In *Building a Global Civic Culture* Boulding emphasizes that human beings are of one species, more alike than different. A civic culture, according to Boulding, is the sharing of a common space, resources, and opportunities. In every society there are patterns of interactions, styles, and expectations that characterize public space and create a framework for events and a sense of public interest. We create and share a social space that is, in effect, a "company of strangers." There are more than 5 billion human beings on the planet, nearly two hundred states, and thousands of cultures and ethnic groups. Obviously these billions of human beings cannot be seen as living in a community like a village or city. To be sure, most of these people are total strangers to each other. The metaphor of the "global village" is only a metaphor, and in significant ways it is a misleading one. Nevertheless, there are literally millions of linkages between people in different cultures and states.

Elise Boulding defines the global sociosphere as "the sum total of social networks across national borders on the planet." This sociosphere, she submits, is far more extensive than we realize. In reflecting on the development of a global civic culture, Boulding emphasizes the role of international non-governmental organizations, of which there were some eighteen thousand when she described them in 1988. These organizations are composed largely of volunteers, and their activities vary widely, from humanitarian concerns to scholarly and cultural activities, children's programs, sports and games, and concern for women, peace, refugees, health, and environment. They cross borders, and many have long-term commitments to the welfare of human beings around the planet. Their members have loyalties that extend beyond the borders of nation-states.

International non-governmental organizations are comparable to the social movements that play a key role in civil societies within states. They are of key importance in the development of world affairs because many are idealistic, future-oriented, and based on a vision of the earth as a common space for peoples of all cultures, nations, and states.

Such organizations facilitate encounters between peoples across borders and lobby national governments, both at home and at the United Nations, with regard to interests transcending borders. The network spans the globe: every country on the earth has some international non-governmental organizations operating within it. In their daily lives many people participate directly or indirectly in international organizations, a fact that gives concrete evidence of the increasing linkages between citizens of different states. Some meaning can be given to the notion of world community because international non-governmental organizations (INGOs) and the United Nations provide contexts for conversation and co-operation between citizens of different cultures, nations, and states. In the process, social learning occurs and the channels of communication are kept open.

Elise Boulding speaks of the other side of history, that part of the human story that tells not of statesmen and war but of the mostly peaceable day-to-day activities of ordinary people. In daily life most interactions between people are non-violent. Similarly, most encounters between citizens of different states are non-violent, and at the interstate level most dealings between states are non-violent. Conflicts arise, of course, but proportionately few lead to violence or war. Even wars nearly always end by negotiation, not by knock-out conquest. Although global culture is still something of an abstraction, with artists, literature, film, and art moving rapidly around the globe it is moving towards reality. A global civil society can affect the international order, just as civil societies within states have affected them. Through international non-governmental organizations and other means the 5 billion people of this world collaborate and co-operate both within and across borders.

Sissela Bok on Strategy, Morality, and Peace

Sissela Bok, a moral philosopher and professor of peace studies, wrote extensively about the importance of trust in her 1978 book, *Lying*. Bok's 1989 work, *A Strategy for Peace*, treats issues of trust in an international context, offering a novel synthesis of themes from Immanuel Kant's "Perpetual Peace" and Carl von Clausewitz's classic Realist theorizing about war. Kant believed that there was an implicit direction in human history, towards an international order in which people would be citizens of the world, war would be outlawed, and competition between individuals and states would be conducted within peaceable limits. Clausewitz thought that war was a natural political means employed by states seeking their own survival above all else. Sissela Bok argues that, given the precarious situation of mankind, the perspectives of morality and survival ultimately coincide. The language of morality must ultimately join with that of strategy; the interests of humanity and those of any single state both presuppose survival.[21]

In areas of environmental and economic co-operation, as in areas of disarmament and peace, agreements between states are not workable without trust. Yet many areas of international relations are fraught with distrust. The way to counter distrust between states is to appreciate the significance of basic moral norms, without which no community can survive. Different cultures and communities have different moral practices, but for all this there are common elements at the core. These common elements are basic for the establishment and continuation of trust between people, whether in the community or nation or at the international level.

For Bok these basic moral norms are truth-telling and non-deceptiveness; promise-keeping; constraints on violence; and limits on secrecy. Norms of truth-telling, promise-keeping, and non-violence are fundamental for civil life in any community. Similarly, they are necessary for reliable and workable relations between states in the international community. People who deceive each other, break promises, and attack each other are not going to be able to work together. Nor are states that violate the basic norms of non-deceptiveness, promise-keeping, and non-violence. And if there are no limits on secrecy, we cannot tell whether the norms are being respected or not.

Breaches of trust will be extremely harmful to relations between states, and it is short-sighted to imagine that violations of fundamental moral standards have no long-term effect. Over the long term, respect for basic moral precepts is in the interests of states. Many conflicts of interest are merely apparent and result from taking a partisan and short-term point of view. Like so many theorists of war, Clausewitz assumed that war will always be a feature of human existence. Bok's response is to counsel that we cannot know this without first making every practical effort to eliminate war. War is, after all, a human institution. If we human beings decide not to support and construct it, it will disappear.

Clausewitz might have thought differently about war as a tool of national policy had he lived through the twentieth century. Given the dangers of war in the nuclear age, no prudent statesman would gamble with the results. Nuclear risks put orthodox strategy in serious question. What will serve survival is not war, not military equipment and strategies, but a stable international environment based on mutual confidence between states. That in turn will emerge from compliance with basic moral norms, as was argued long ago by Immanuel Kant. We can be as idealistic or as cynical about international ethics as we like, but the bottom line is that an atmosphere of trust between states is essential for survival. Thus Bok speaks of a "strategy" (Clausewitz) for "peace" (Kant).

The values of truth-telling, promise-keeping, constraints on violence, and limitations on secrecy are not culturally relative, Bok argues. They are central in virtually every religious and moral code, and operative in every human community. The fact that various cultures and communities do not agree on *all* aspects of morality does not show that they agree on *no* aspects of morality. And the fact – stressed by Realists – that moral appeals can be cynically manipulative does not show that such appeals are always manipulative or that they should be abolished altogether. For a viable international community to persist, states must abide by fundamental moral norms. Because there are formidable forces working against trustworthy behaviour, it may seem to be in our collective or individual interests to violate moral norms. But such understanding results from a limited perspective and a lack of imagination.

There are many agents, and many types of agents, whose actions affect international life and international relations. Because of the importance of an atmosphere of trust, all have good reason to abide by moral norms. Far from being irrelevant to international relations (as Realists urge), respect for morality is utterly fundamental.

Dorothy V. Jones on the Code of Peace

In her prize-winning book *The Code of Peace* Dorothy V. Jones offers a survey of international declarations and treaties between 1919 and

1989 to support her conclusion that there are legal and ethical norms for state action. States themselves have agreed that there should be limitations on their behaviour, and there is considerable consensus on what those limitations should be. The Code of Peace, as Jones calls it, includes the following nine basic principles:

- the sovereign equality of states
- the territorial integrity and political independence of states
- the equal rights and self-determination of peoples
- non-intervention in the affairs of a state
- the peaceful settlement of disputes between states
- abstention from threats of force and the use of force
- fulfillment in good faith of international obligations
- co-operation with other states
- respect for human rights and fundamental freedoms

In addition, there is considerable consensus supporting the creation of an equitable global economic order, human rights, and protection of the environment.

Dorothy Jones comments on how much of this international code protects states instead of people. Although people around the globe suffer more abuse from the hands of their own government than from other people's governments, most international law and declarations assume that the interests of *people* are those of their *state*, as represented by its *government*. The fact that during the period following the Second World War many previously colonial territories had just achieved state status and were anxious to protect their state autonomy contributed to this emphasis on state sovereignty in international law. At the same time, though, Hitler's regime had made it terribly clear that a government could grossly abuse its own people. There was pressure from private individuals, non-governmental organizations, and states themselves for declarations prescribing states duties to their citizens and citizens rights against the state. Dorothy Jones includes an extended discussion of declarations on human rights, such as the Universal Declaration of Human Rights (1948), the Convention on the Rights of the Child (1989), and the Helsinki Accords (1975). Curiously, she does not include such declarations within her Code of Peace.

Of course, state behaviour does not always conform to the principles, treaties, and declarations described by Jones. In stipulating principles for moral and legal state behaviour, those who devised and signed these declarations have, in the author's words, "dreamed an imaginary world of peace and justice." Although the Code does not describe the actual behaviour of states in our present world, it offers a bridge to a better world. And that bridge was constructed by states themselves.

Jones says that states have been "warlords" but have aspired to make themselves into something better. For Jones there is no mystery about the source of international law and the international ethics on which it is largely based. International law emerges from what the states themselves have said and done, from their own multilateral agreements and declarations. Scholars and analysts may be Realist about international relations, insisting that morality has no proper role to play in international life, but key state representatives have not adopted that view. On the contrary, they have taken considerable care to articulate many declarations and conventions about norms of behaviour within nation-states and in international relations.

The persistent quest by states themselves for basic norms with which to regulate their behaviour has received less attention than it deserves. Why? Jones answers with an analogy: "Part of the reason lies in the simple fact of dramatic impact. The movement of the earth by an earthquake makes news; the movement of the earth by an earthworm does not, although in the long term it may be more important because of its effect on the productivity of soil. This search [for internationally binding norms] by the states is intellectually exciting both for what it reveals about the states and because of its long-term potential. It does not, however, have the immediate impact of an earthquake." The trend by nation-states to declare and establish international laws by which their relations will be governed is slow and undramatic, like the movement of an earthworm in the earth. It has little or no immediate impact, but it may be highly significant in the long term: "What is remarkable about this endeavor by the states is their recognition of their own warlordish tendencies, and their persistent attempts to devise an ethical code and an international system in which the rewards that go to force – and they are frequently handsome – will be so overbalanced by other considerations that force will no longer mean war in the traditional sense."[22] In the area of international law, there is a constant sliding between is and ought. Here the "ought" is a *moral* ought. International law is not scientific, not descriptive of fully operative conventions, but moral and philosophical. It has a bearing on the actions and motivations of states and citizens. Its declarations are not irrelevant to the ways of the world, and they can become more relevant than they are. To the extent that they do, trust between states will increase, as will the confidence of citizens in their own governments.

MODELS OF HUMAN NATURE AND PICTURES
OF INTERNATIONAL POLITICS

Realists see human nature as fundamentally aggressive, competitive, and greedy; each person is out for himself or herself. These pessimistic assumptions about human nature contrast with the assumptions of other models, according to which human beings are fundamentally social, develop through interaction, and are naturally disposed to trusting and trustworthy collaboration and co-operation. Clearly, our degree of faith or trust in people influences our views about politics, domestically and internationally. Realists follow Hobbes and Machiavelli; liberals, idealists, and proponents of world order are more like Kropotkin, who stressed humanity's social nature and capacity for co-operation. The Hobbesian view stresses strength, force, and power, dismissing the role of morality in international affairs. Assuming a more social view of human nature, a decidedly non-Realist stance towards international relations will emerge, recommending peaceful co-operation for common benefit, friendship, respect, and non-violent conflict resolution.

Human beings are capable of all sort of things, ranging from spectacular generosity and self-sacrifice to reasoned collaboration based on interest, habitual co-operation, routine compliance with norms, wilful disobedience, reflective rebellion, blind self-interest, greed, brutality, and vicious violence. There is no one thing that human nature is. Culture, context, and institutions make a tremendous difference in the way human beings feel, think, and act and how they theorize about their own nature and motivations. A fixed notion of human nature makes a shaky foundation for a theory of international politics. In addition, promulgating a negative conception of human nature is bound to be counter-productive. If we expect greed, aggression, and competition, teach our youth that that is what human nature is and ever must be, and construe security and policy on these assumptions, we will evoke responses that confirm our expectations. Rosy spirals and blue spirals can emerge in international affairs just as they do in our personal lives.

The Hobbesian state of nature is a philosopher's fiction, one that is useful only if it is plausible and fruitful, which, as I have argued, does not seem to be the case. Anthropologist Mary E. Clark argues for a markedly non-Hobbesian conception of human nature. On her view, the deepest human need is for social bonding.[23] Human beings could not be what they are without large brains, and this physical feature requires that infants be born with relatively large heads and helpless bodies. These fragile human infants need maternal care for a long time, and this fact encourages parents to co-operate in providing it. Biologically, human beings need each other. The notion of a state of nature involving isolated human beings in unco-operative anarchistic circumstances is a biological contradiction in terms. Clark argues: "Hobbes was quite wrong. Our earliest ancestors did not evolve as calculating individuals, assessing how others might forward their own interests, but as entities programmed to seek out and enjoy the company of others of their own kind. The earliest humans were biologically designed to trust one another, and to become an intimate member of a group." Human infants can develop into human adults only if they receive sustained attention and care from their mothers, and this basic fact in turn puts conditions on the ways human beings can live. Mothers did not do the work alone, for others helped to ward off predators and fetch food, often from long distances, when necessary.

Social bonding to a group is an inescapable biological necessity for developing human beings. Contrary to Hobbesian mythology, prehistoric human societies do not seem to have been brutal and barbaric. They provided for social bonding, arguably far better than does modern industrial society. In that regard they were more humane than many contemporary societies because social practices better filled the basic human need for community and meaning. Human beings are deeply social animals; the need for social bonding is far more basic than the tendency to assert one's individual self and compete. As a species, we were social even before we were human.

All the facts of infant development and human capacity suggest that a Hobbesian state of nature was never a possibility for human beings. It makes little sense to ground a theory of the state and international life on this unfounded philosophical assumption. Humans live and have lived together in families and communities: they are interdependent; they are vulnerable to each other; they bond; they co-operate in order to survive. And in many areas of life, they trust each other.

No state ever emerged from a contract made in a state of nature because there never *was* a state of nature. Even if one had existed, the separated and suspicious people in it would not have been able to make and keep promises so as to establish a state by contract. Modern states exist for a wide variety of historical reasons. If we seek to justify the existence of states, referring to a state of nature and a social contract will not do the job. Many alternative arguments could be given, an especially plausible one being that people live in communities that experience problems and need a structure within which they can work to address their common problems. A group of people becomes and remains a community because those people face common tasks.[24]

The commonality of tasks is establishing an analogous basis for a world community. There are global problems that must be addressed. No state can do this alone; hence we move towards international community. In human and practical terms that peaceful other side of international life so underemphasized by Realists is extraordinarily important. It reveals capacities and possibilities that we ignore at our peril. Disregarding the interdependence of human beings and our capacities for trust, reliability, and co-operation, we may infer incorrectly that the human future is closed, that collective problems cannot be solved, and that war – potentially of a cataclysmic nature – is inevitable. To solve our problems, we must believe that fruitful trust and fruitful co-operation are possible. We must live and act in the world in a non-cynical way, trust other people unless there are specific reasons not to, and actively hope and work for solutions to our common global problems.

11 Cynicism, Pessimism, Optimism, and Hope

I am not cynical. I am only experienced, and that's pretty much the same thing.

Oscar Wilde

Many people adopt an attitude of tired cynicism, especially in their attitudes to politics. To contemporary cynics, human nature and society are not worth much. Official stories about the virtue or proper functioning of institutions are bound to be false, and appearances suggesting the contrary are mere illusions. All must be left as it is: the bleak aspects of human nature and society prove that, in any sense relevant to action, things are all right after all. With no confidence in the possibility of change, cynics renounce any idea of trying to improve things; reality, though sordid, is as good as it could be. In a perverse and unexpected way, mocking cynicism of this sort results in legitimation by disbelief.[1] Things are bad, but they could never be otherwise, so it is futile to try to change social and political institutions. Paradoxically, what is beyond reform turns out to be all right.

Generalized mocking cynicism is based on a systematic distrust of human beings and human institutions. A trusting attitude is rejected as naïve and gullible. To mocking cynics, human beings are power-hungry, greedy, and out for themselves, and morality is only a veneer. The correct interpretation of human actions and institutions will reveal a seamy reality under the glossy appearance, and anyone who thinks otherwise shows only that she is not too bright. This cynicism, which one recent author referred to as "chic bitterness," is a prominent mood in our time.[2]

CYNICISM AND RELATED ATTITUDES

Though related to distrust, doubt, and despair, cynicism has a tone all its own. The mocking cynic is suspicious of human nature and looks negatively upon people and institutions. This generalized cynicism is not distrust, for distrust is based on relevant evidence and good reasons, and can on occasion be practical and constructive. Distrust need not presume a broad theory of human nature and society according to which hypocrisy and corruption are inevitable. Cynicism is also quite different from scepticism. Sceptics express doubt, whereas cynics go beyond doubt to imply a broad theory of human nature and society and a sense of inevitability that no careful sceptic would endorse. Nor is cynicism is the same as despair: cynics feel disdain and bitterness, not sadness and grief. Fully convinced that the seamy aspects of life are inevitable, cynics do not grieve that there is no possibility of change for the better.

Mocking cynicism has some relation to pessimism. Like the cynic, the pessimist looks on the bleak side of events, and when making predictions will foretell a negative future.[3] But there is a central difference of emotional tone. Pessimists are depressed, cynics sardonic. Cynics do not feel sorrowful or fearful about what is happening or what is to come because they are above it all. Unlike pessimism and despair, sardonic cynicism is a top-dog attitude.

EARLY CYNICISM

The mocking cynicism prevalent in contemporary culture is quite different from the early cynicism of classical Greece and Rome. The cynicism of ancients like Diogenes, Crates, and Hipparchia in the fourth century BC was a radical, cheeky sort of thing. Early cynicism was anti-materialist and anti-establishment. The Greek Cynics sought to abridge their needs so as to remain spiritually and materially secure in a turbulent world. They ridiculed work that would extend wealth and power but, in the end, leave people more vulnerable to calamity. They taught and practised a simple lifestyle, their sole possessions being a cloak, wallet, and staff. "The privilege of the gods is to want nothing, and of those like the gods to want but little," Diogenes said. Human beings should live in a simple way, like animals – spurning luxury, eating lentils instead of oysters. The Cynics sought to expose the artifice of social conventions, the pomposity of wealth and power, and the meaningless abstractions of overly theoretical philosophers. Diogenes and fellow Cynics such as Crates and Hipparchia lived simply, teaching and preaching and begging for food. They wanted to care for their own souls while exposing the pretensions of social life.

When we compare the Greek Cynics to the mocking cynics of later times, the most conspicuous difference is that the Cynics professed radical ideals of how life should be lived, and actually lived according to those theories, often at considerable personal sacrifice. Like the mocking cynics who were to follow them, these cheeky ancient Cynics liked to point to pretensions and illusions. They offered a trenchant critique of social and political life, but it was not only a critique. Though some of their public behaviour was gross and tasteless, the early Cynics were radical reformers seeking to improve their own souls and society at large.[4] They were committed social critics with a definite mission. Although they thought wealth, political power, and social conventions were largely sham, they did not think life itself a sham.

Peter Sloterdijk, author of *The Critique of Cynical Reason*, calls Diogenes a low theorist, one who can smell the swindle of idealistic abstractions and the schizoid staleness of a thinking limited to the head.[5] The low theorist knows that it only takes a little brute fact to upset an awful lot of pretentious theory. Cheeky cynicism sought to bring abstractions, vague generalities, and pretensions down to earth. Vividly displaying humankind's animal nature in public is one way to do so; the man who would describe the beginnings of the universe still has to urinate and defecate like everybody else. From a position of poverty and simplicity, the cheeky Cynics satirized grandeur and social pretensions, emphasizing the omnipresence of the human body with all its needs and embarrassments.

The cheeky cynicism of the ancient Greeks was fundamentally a plebeian attitude. The plebeian cheeky Cynic laughed at the trappings of power and sought to expose them. He was not afraid to feel. He wanted to live simply and laugh from the belly, and ensure that behind all this lay clear reflection and understanding. Though some early Cynics were of noble birth, the stance they took was that of the outsider. They saw the broader culture as artificial and corrupt. Contemptuous of mainstream wealth, power, and influence, early Greek Cynics parodied power and screamed for reform.

By the second century of the Common Era, Cynics were more numerous, more scandalous, and less dedicated than they had been in the days of Diogenes. Many had begun to abuse the lifestyle of cheeky cynicism. Epictetus the Stoic found Cynics proud, self-righteous, abrasive, and not a little ridiculous. The Cynic, he remarked sarcastically, has a wallet and a staff – and a great jar to swallow the things he wants. The Cynic seeks happiness, yet is so afraid of attachment to other people that he has no friends or family. What is left in life? Only a great brawny arm, which the Cynic needs to protect himself.

Cynics sought to avoid fear and unhappiness by limiting their desires. If a person limits his desires and lives off as little as possible, he is minimally vulnerable to unpredictable fortune. Both Cynics and Stoics distinguished between events we can control and those we cannot. As individuals we can (or so they assumed) largely control our states of mind, our attitudes, beliefs, and emotions. But we cannot control the physical world, the gods, or human institutions. Cynics and Stoics recommended limiting desires and detaching the self from conventional social life so as to depend minimally on anything outside one's own individual power.

In Greek and Roman times cynicism was most conspicuous and influential in the time of Diogenes (the fourth century BCE) and then again in the second century CE, when Epictetus gave his lectures. The latter period was one of Roman imperial domination. Many people felt alienation from the imperial powers and from the city-states whose power had been diminished in the Roman Empire. There were swarms of wandering philosophers of many persuasions and also a great variety of religious sects, one of which was early Christianity. Though a ragtag lot on the whole, philosophers enjoyed the protection of the emperor and became a kind of non-establishment establishment. Cynicism was beginning to degenerate. It is not clear when, in the history of thought, mocking cynicism came to predominate over cheeky cynicism, but the disagreement in the second century between Peregrinus Proteus and Lucian is often identified as a crucial moment in the transition.

Peregrinus, sometimes called Peregrinus Proteus, was a Cynic and mendicant preacher of the second century CE. He had gone into voluntary exile as a young man and was for a time a member of the Christian sect in Palestine. When he was imprisoned in Syria, Peregrinus was cared for generously by the Christians. Upon his release he adopted Cynic garb and was for a time both a Christian and a Cynic. Eventually he was expelled by the Christians. Peregrinus lived for a time in Rome, where he spoke out against the emperor. Eventually he became so offensive in his criticisms that he was expelled from Rome. He went to Greece, where he lived the remainder of his life in a hut near Athens. A religiously inclined cynic, Peregrinus had mystical inclinations. Like many spiritually minded people today, he was fascinated by wise men from the East. After living to a fairly advanced age, Peregrinus announced that he would immolate himself at the Olympic Games in order to demonstrate that humankind had nothing to fear from death. In 167, clad in a white linen robe, he turned to face the rising moon, jumped into the flames of the pyre that had been prepared for him, and burned himself to death.[6]

Committing suicide when old was a fairly common practice among Cynics, but doing it in such a painful and public way was not. The self-immolation of Peregrinus provoked much thought and commentary, and considerable speculation about what his real motives were. Did Peregrinus kill himself so painfully to show that human beings had nothing to fear from death? That would be a philosophical demonstration of an extraordinary sort. Or did Peregrinus die by fire in order to purify his soul so that it would be better equipped for immorality? Was he trying to gain admirers? To make a lasting reputation for himself? To found a new religious cult? In anticipation of the event Peregrinus had sent testaments to all the principal cities of the empire. He did not want the deed to go unnoticed. Was this an early case of a media event? Hostile observers were suspicious of the publicity.

One observer was sure he knew what Peregrinus was up to, and the verdict was not flattering. Lucian was a skilled writer and a Cynic, definitely not of the plebeian sort. He defended common sense against religion, superstition, and façile or hypocritical philosophy. Lucian's attitude to the beggarly philosophers of the day was negative. He satirized wandering Cynics and other philosophers, criticizing them for betraying their profession with lust, quarrelsomeness, and greed. Mendicants had become exploiters of other people's work, enjoying special privileges such as protection from the emperor, free food, wine to make them drunk, and favours from gullible women who thought they were wise. Wearing Cynic garb and uttering generalities about human nature and existence was a poor basis for claiming the status of philosopher. Lucian thought Peregrinus and others like him were fuzzy-headed, feeble-minded, or worse. Cynicism was becoming a kind of cult.

Lucian attended the Olympic Games and witnessed the dramatic suicide of Peregrinus. To him the suicide gave not a hint of courage or sacrifice and constituted no philosophical demonstration. To Lucian, the urbane writer, the self-immolation merited only mockery. He referred to Peregrinus as a paragon of virtue turned into cinders and a drivelling old fool:

There was no call to pity anyone that desperately in love with being in the limelight, more so than all others hounded by the same curse. In any event, he went off with a mob at his heels and was getting his fill of public attention as he surveyed the ranks of his admirers; the poor devil didn't realize that criminals headed for the hangman or the cross draw even bigger crowds.

... This is how poor Proteus ended. To put it briefly, he was a man who never once looked truth in the face, whose every word and deed were for public attention and the plaudits of the crowd – to such a point that he leaped into a fire where, deaf to them forever, he was never to enjoy the cheers.

Lucian found nothing in the suicide save a quest for vainglory. He wrote mercilessly against Peregrinus, even claiming that Peregrinus would have felt no pain because he would have died quickly.[7]

This ancient story illustrates the contrast between cheeky and mocking cynicism at a time in human history when the latter was beginning to predominate over the former. Peregrinus was an out-sider, an underdog, with a radical message about how people should live and die. He sought to express this message in his life, in teach-ings and writings, and – or so it would appear – in his death. Lucian was a successful writer and rhetorician who did not forswear world-ly comforts in order to write and teach. He had no positive message about how life should be lived. Lucian "knew" just what Peregrinus's motive was: Peregrinus sought vainglory. No special examination of the case was needed to prove this. And Lucian was apparently confi-dent that he personally needed no reforming or illumination. A top dog, he was all right; common sense was all right; society was all right. Death, even by fire, was all right too. To Lucian, Peregrinus's suicide was clearly tasteless, unnecessary, and vainglorious. It did not move him. There was no need to feel anything but disdain in response to the event.

Both cheeky and mocking cynicism seek to expose illusions and pretensions, stressing the seamy side of social status, power, and practices. Both criticize social practices and norms, often falling into bitterness and misanthropy when doing so. But where underdog cheeky cynics laugh, feel, and seek to reform themselves as well as others, top-dog mocking cynics offer only an unfeeling grimace. The superior complacency that underlies Lucian's critique of Peregrinus is characteristic of mocking cynicism.

Ancient Greek and Roman Cynics explored questions about virtue and convention, power and corruption, nature and simplicity. Did Diogenes' obscenities prove anything about human nature and social artifice? Did Cynics and Stoics succeed in isolating themselves from social breakdown by living simply according to nature and control-ling their own states of mind? Did mendicant Cynics become as cor-rupt and hypocritical as the establishment they rejected? Why did

Peregrinus commit suicide in such a painful way? These questions are fascinating and absorbing. I find that they have a poignant appeal, possibly because they are located in the distant past. The worlds of Diogenes, Epictetus, Lucian, and Peregrinus feel *safe* because those worlds no longer exist. However tumultuous and fearful those times might have been for the passionate men and women who lived then, they cannot touch us now. In the days of Lucian and Peregrinus city-states had been robbed of power by an empire that was itself in decline; poverty and exile were real threats; travellers risked capture by pirates who would sell them into slavery. Bizarre sects and cults flourished. People did not know what to believe.[8] But whoever suffered, and however painfully, it was all long ago. Contemporary cynicism is another matter.

MOCKING CYNICISM

The attitude of mocking cynicism is one of generalized distrust in human nature and behaviour. Virtually any aspect of life can be mocked and dismissed for pretensions of virtue. No matter what might seem to be the case, things are bound to be rotten underneath. The mocking cynic laughs bitterly at the very idea that people might be altruistic, idealistic, or even just plain conscientious. Cynical laughter is not hearty, not an expression of enjoyment or fun, but rather a bitter amusement at the very idea that people could be good and institutions properly conducted. Such notions merit only ridicule.

In his recent book *The Cynical Society* Jeffrey Goldfarb describes cynicism as a prominent malaise in Western societies. Cynicism, Goldfarb argues, is especially prevalent in electoral campaigns, where reporting emphasizes image, personality, and gimmicks, even when substantive issues could be highlighted. Politicians and their backers seek victory at the cost of substance and rely on the quick snippet that will convey a positive image. After the 1988 election, Goldfarb remarks, Americans had "a cynical president elected in a cynical campaign reported by a cynical press to a cynical society." Democratic practices, ideals, and positions still exist, but press coverage and political strategies during campaigns do not call attention to them. Statements are interpreted as mere manifestations of interest. Cynical culture attacks and rejects reasoned substantive discourse, thereby undermining the meaningfulness of political campaigns. When façile solutions to complex problems are proposed, few can believe that the suggestions are serious. Many people come to see policy proposals as mere rhetoric, thinly disguising contending interests. Cynicism becomes a substitute for substantive reflection and commitment to meaningful values.

Cynicism can take many forms. A prominent one, as Goldfarb notes, is the reduction of substantive claims and committed actions to expressions of interest. Another style of cynicism uses the economic bottom line: if something is profitable it is true, real, and good; if not, it is without meaning or value. Democracies may have a tendency to produce cynical attitudes because in a democracy various interests are constantly competing. Observers come to suspect that actions alleged to be in the public good actually serve specialized interests. They come to reject official stories and, eventually, the very concept of the public good. "The mocking cynic knows that life is a sham, but the knowledge is so universal that alternatives no longer exist ... And in fact everywhere ideals are but facade for ugly realities." But critics and analysts of mass society dismiss its ideals too easily, Goldfarb argues. Democratic societies have had many accomplishments and continue to share such ideals as freedom, democracy, and egalitarianism. By appreciating these, we can avoid overwhelming cynicism.[9]

Mocking cynics see human beings as by nature greedy, aggressive, hungry for power and reputation, competitive in pursuit. Anyone who expects otherwise is set up for disappointment. Better to be above it all, to "know" human beings for what they "really" are, and disdain the activities of would-be reformers and the corrupt alike. The cynical attitude is accompanied by disdain and a sense of being above it all; it is a top-dog attitude. All this is joined with a profound sense of inevitability. Greed, corruption, hypocrisy, competition, and the like are permanent and pervasive in human affairs. Cynical analysis can be given different twists to fit special topics or contexts. A cynic about academic life, for instance, may insist that scholars are always pursuing reputation, status, money, or travel opportunities, not truth or intellectual understanding. Things go on this way: inevitably people pursue low, selfish goals. No matter: cynics themselves will be all right. They can show that they are worldly-wise by demonstrating that they understand the way things are and must be. The attitude of mocking cynicism is one of irony, sarcasm, and bitterness. Mocking cynics do not hoot, cheer, scream, or weep. They do not rage or despair but rather express sardonic disdain for the shabby state of human affairs and those naïve enough to think they can do something about it.

A more pointed sense of mocking cynicism may be gained by looking at examples. Consider the cynical saying, "In God we trust. All others pay cash." The saying "In God we trust" appears on American coins – originally, one would suppose, to express a common faith and commitment. In the cynical saying religious faith and patriotic commitment are reduced to mundane economic transactions. What does one want from God? The goods. God merits trust, but only because God is divine and not subject to human failings. Human beings must pay cash. Here we see the distrust in human nature characteristic of mocking cynicism.

Another example: in 1990 several American mediators went to Moscow to explain their ideas and techniques. One man had received funding from an American foundation to make contacts and do workshops. He believed that conflict-resolution techniques had much to contribute to a political culture in which open disagreement had long been difficult or impossible. Well received in Moscow, he returned to a conference in the United States to describe his work. "What's the matter," one listener asked. "Can't you make enough money at home?" This cynical response assumes that the mediator would not have gone to the Soviet Union had things gone well for him in the United States, and that the main thing he lacked at home and sought abroad was money. These cavalier assumptions were made automatically by the listener. She did not know the speaker or his financial situation – or, for that matter, the situation in Russia.

Clearly people do sometimes deceive themselves and others about their competence and motivation. Clearly they may be wrong when they credit themselves with altruistic and generous motives. Perhaps this mediator was short of money and did go to Russia solely out of self-interest. That is not the issue. What is notable and objectionable in the cynic's interpretation of human actions, motivations, and institutions is its automatic quality, its knee-jerk assumption that motivation must be self-serving and can never be otherwise.

Goldfarb cites Tom Wolfe's *Bonfire of the Vanities* as a paradigm of mocking cynicism. Though the book could have been written as a tragedy, it is comic in tone. The young black man who is the victim of the traffic accident is surrounded by "schools without learning, courts without justice, journalism without the pursuit of truth, churches without morality, and politicians who operate without the common good or collective interest in mind."[10] He is injured by a rich white man, who is then, for the wrong reasons, prosecuted by an unhappy lawyer functioning in a context of fear, greed, and deceptive love. The whole crazy sequence is ruthlessly exploited by press and politicians.

An author who felt genuine human concern or had any reformist instincts could have written the same story as an impassioned critic of the status quo in contemporary New York. But Wolfe takes no character or activity seriously. All is sham. Marriages and love affairs are empty of feeling and commitment; journalists are only out for themselves; black community leaders are manipulative and greedy; lawyers and judges seek self-protection, not justice. By implication, the author and his readers are superior beings who see through the façade and stand apart from the characters who suffer through these events. The top-dog aspect of mocking cynicism could not be clearer. *Bonfire of the Vanities* is written in a disdainful voice. It offers not sorrow, not sympathy, not even reasoned substantive discourse, only mockery. The book was promoted, celebrated, and consumed as "a good read"; thus advertised and consumed, it sold well, and the author made a lot of money. The circle is complete: in a cynical culture *Bonfire of the Vanities* was cynically written, cynically promoted, and well received by an audience to whom cynicism was perfectly normal. Could one expect more from a best-selling novel? Only noncynics would say yes.

A play greatly contrasting in tone was presented at the Edmonton Fringe Festival in 1991.[11] *Lily Truehart, MP,* by George Rideout, depicts the trials and victories of an idealistic political candidate out to save Canada from the ravages of big business. Heroine Lily is a "true heart" but has trouble communicating her ideas because cynical reporters plague her with questions about her husband's psychiatric problems. Heroic Lily pretends to be her husband's psychiatrist (it's the only way she can talk to him) and with the aid of two elderly aunts fends off two "bad guys" masquerading as CBC reporters. Lily and her family join 300,000 protesters who are surrounding Mount Rundle in an attempt to overcome a plot to sell Banff National Park to foreign interests. They succeed in their endeavour and, joined by the audience, sing a rousing "O Canada."

Staged in the form of a melodrama, *Lily Truehart* is a deliberately unsophisticated play. In melodrama, lines between good and evil are stark; emotions and characters are exaggerated; plots are hectic, often absurd; happy endings arrive implausibly. Melodrama as a theatrical form suggests the rural past. In adopting it, a playwright would seem to be making implicit reference to a simpler pioneer time of vaudeville and amateur theatrical productions. Because *Lily Truehart* adopts an obsolete theatrical form, one might suppose that the author is distancing himself from its explicit message. But such an interpretation is not plausible: the singing of the national anthem at the end of the play is a clear call to action. The form of melodrama distances the playwright from some of the more madcap details of the plot but not from the play's central message: there are caring and committed people, and they can accomplish worthwhile things when they work together. In contrast to *Bonfire of the Vanities*, the tone of *Lily Truehart, MP* is straightforward and sincere.

Mocking cynics characteristically think of themselves as *realists* who are above it all, not as true-hearts who plunge to intervene in events. The way to cope in life is not to try to help each other, not to try to improve institutions and abuses that make life worse, but rather to display one's superior awareness of the seamy aspects of life and pursue one's own interest, seeking to exploit people and institutions for purposes of one's own. The cynic wants to get what he can for himself and use his supposed knowledge and detachment to demonstrate his superiority to poor sods who take life seriously.

In its most insidious forms, mocking cynicism combines *description*, *prediction*, and *recommendation*. Motives and actions are *described* in categories of interest, greed, and competition, so that whatever people do is negatively framed. Actions that appear to be altruistic or virtuous will be reinterpreted as selfish. If someone donates money to a charity, she wants to be known as generous, or is trying to make herself feel good, or gain influence in some political quarter. If an establishment club opens its doors to women and visible minorities, it is merely trying to recoup financial losses. And so on and so forth. By imputing motives and emphasizing negative aspects of situations while neglecting more positive ones, a cynic can interpret any action or event so as to confirm his bleak picture of the world. It is a small step to make *predictions* in the same conceptual framework. People will always be self-promoting, competitive, greedy, and so on. Generalized mocking cynicism will not be falsified. Anything may be described in its terms, which will be defined as "realistic." Cynics also make recommendations about human action and policy. Machiavelli's *The Prince* is a prime example. According to Machiavelli, we should not trust other people. We should manipulate them, trying all the while to get their trust without deserving it. We should be constantly on our guard. And we should be out for ourselves, trying to get the best for ourselves in the smartest way possible. Certainly we should not try to abide by canons of old-fashioned morality, a sham to which no one is seriously committed and which will lead at best to risk and at worst to useless sacrifice.

Journalistic practices contribute considerably to cynical attitudes. A journalist must distance himself from events and avoid identifying with the feelings and goals of social and political actors. If he were to take people and events at face value, objectivity would be lost. Objectivity in journalism is understood as requiring an aloofness that can lead to cynical detachment. The objective journalist is disengaged. By imputing ungenerous motives and intentions, a journalist can distance himself while at the same time presenting himself as worldly-wise. In one striking case, Mother Theresa was interviewed on CBS by a young reporter who inquired persistently about the motivation behind her work. Unable to accept that the alleviation of suffering, disease, and poverty were her goals, he pushed to determine what she was "really" trying to do. Eventually (you could sense a barely repressed pat on the head) she told him that he would not understand, and steered him to another topic.

Non-profit groups pursuing idealistic goals such as weapons reduction and environmental preservation are characteristically represented by journalists as special-interest groups pursuing goodies for themselves – quite on a par with those lobbying for special rights and entitlements. Dedication, commitment, and altruism disappear, and the volunteer ethic, which plays a large and essential role in civil society, receives little attention in the press. Meanwhile, stories of murder, corruption, and struggles for power are commonplace. In investigative journalism, cynicism is virtually an axiom. Reporters assume that there is something rotten at the core and set out to find it. Not surprisingly, they usually do.

Cynicism in the public and cynicism among journalists can build upon each other. The public is suspicious; journalists express cynicism and distrust; the public becomes more suspicious; journalists seek to cater to public attitudes to give people what they want; further cynical journalistic coverage strengthens cynical attitudes in the public at large. Eventually cynicism is entrenched.

One journalist concerned about cynicism is Susan Delacourt, who has written several articles about cynicism in Canada in the context of constitutional proposals. After the failure of the Meech Lake Accord, which would have granted the province of Quebec status as a distinct society within Canada, the Conservative government of Brian Mulroney was criticized for not having permitted sufficient public participation. Critics said that the Meech proposal had been worked out by "eleven men in suits." In response the government made various arrangements for public consultations. But by this time the Canadian public was suspicious that the government wanted only to *appear* to be listening to people. The Mulroney government resented public criticism of Meech and resisted the "lesson" that public participation was necessary. When the Mulroney government established the Beaudoin-Dobbie Commission as a forum for public discussion, the public was already disillusioned, and the government warned testily that those who had insisted on public consultations might not like what the public had to say. People feared that they were being manipulated by a government that had tried to manipulate them before.

Then media cynicism came into play. According to Delacourt, "The media have been on the lookout for any signs of trouble for this unity initiative. An empty room, an anti-Quebec outcry, and angry, ill-informed citizens have all set off alarms that may have been premature or excessive ... The media reports also did not distinguish between problems of organization and problems of substance for the unity initiative. A poorly attended meeting had come to be translated as a near-fatal blow for the whole package of proposals." The opposition parties, who had at first supported the commission, began to attack it. The female co-chairperson, Dorothy Dobbie, came under attack as an incompetent patronage appointment: "Manitoba MP Dorothy Dobbie, co-chairperson of the committee, has become a mirror of all its problems. She is, in many ways, a creation of cynicism and a victim of it. Mrs. Dobbie's appointment was seen in some circles as the ultimate in cynical postings. The government needed a counterweight for Quebec Tory Senator Claude Castonguay so it chose a woman, an anglophone, from anti-Meech Manitoba. Mrs. Dobbie, in turn, gave her own display of cynicism when she got into a controversy over hiring her Tory friends and colleagues to help with the committee."[12] Dorothy Dobbie was later blamed for the failure of the commission, Beaudoin, the male co-chairperson, being ignored. That irritated the feminists to whom Dobbie's appointment had been a token offering. The government's insincere efforts to consult with the public were cynically received by ordinary people and major players, and cynically interpreted by the press. Delacourt concludes that a credible constitutional debate would require breaking away from "the rampant cynicism that nearly derailed the entire unity campaign." That did not happen.

Mocking cynicism is primarily an interpretive framework. Although there are variations in cynical frames of reference, these can be subsumed under some version of a bleak theory that human nature is degeneratively self-interested. People pursue their own interest in whatever way they can, though they often seek to represent themselves as doing otherwise. A willingness to trust in the benign appearances of things amounts to gullibility pure and simple. Cynics have the "smarts" and know that the *real story* must be something else. The mocking cynic practises an interpretive strategy that is fundamentally suspicious and negative. He imposes this interpretation on events, often with no specific evidence or reason for doing so, and feels confident that he is smart enough to see beneath the façade while others, less worldly-wise, are deluded.

There are, of course, many actions and situations in which a cynical interpretation has no natural fit. A man in New York City planted corn in street dividers because he wanted to see its beautiful green growth and recall his rural youth, relieving the hard grey of the city's concrete jungle. Fellow New Yorkers seemed to love the plants, and many tenderly helped to care for them. There was no vandalism. In the summer of 1991 two Alberta teenagers worked all summer growing potatoes and carrots to donate to a Calgary food bank. A newspaper pictured them radiant with health, pride, and a sense of accomplishment.[13] Asked why they undertook the project, the young men said they "wanted to help people."

Vast numbers of similar examples can be found. In addition to villainy, aggression, and greed, human beings throughout history have displayed courage, heroism, dedication, altruism, commitment, and a passion for reform. Human experience provides grounds for distrust and despair but also grounds for trust and hope. One might think that the generalized distrust that is presumed in mocking cynicism can be refuted by counter-examples, on empirical grounds. Cynics are saying everyone is out for himself. We can readily find examples of people who are not out for themselves. So isn't cynicism refuted? Unfortunately, matters are not so simple. The underlying attitude of cynicism emerges not from experience itself but rather from a particular *perspective* on it, from a way of interpreting experience. Die-hard cynics are not going to have their attitudes altered by events. It is always possible to impose a negative interpretation on events. The teenage farmers, for instance – cynics might say they just wanted their picture in the paper. Or couldn't get jobs and needed something to do. Or wanted to feel superior, patronizing poor people. One can sustain cynicism by looking bleakly at the context of their efforts, imputing motives, and emphasizing the negative. Generalized cynicism cannot be decisively refuted by counter-example because it is not the result of empirical generalization. It amounts to a perspective on the world, a style of interpretation imposed without any need for specific evidence and information.

As a general attitude issuing in a universal interpretive frame, mocking cynicism can protect itself against any proposed counter-example. It is a kind of *a priori* grid imposed on the data. Some people and institutions display pretence, hypocrisy, and pomposity and are naturals for cynical interpretation. The Beaudoin-Dobbie Commission was an example. But even people and actions that are on the surface generous and well-intentioned can be interpreted cynically. For the die-hard mocking cynic, nothing good will ever happen, nothing inspiring will ever be done. This sour result is guaranteed *a priori* to be true because everything will be interpreted so as to confirm his embittered attitude.

MOCKING CYNICISM DISPUTED

Counter-examples provide no ready refutation of mocking cynicism because negative interpretations, serving the cynic's view of humanity, can always be constructed and imposed on events. But this very fact provides another route to refutation. The spurious universality of cynicism is just what proves it to be incorrect. Because the mocking cynic can impose his interpretation on any action or event, his superficially persuasive interpretation shows nothing illuminating about any particular event. The whole exercise is too façile. Cynical interpretation and commentary may seem to be the result of informed analysis by a sophisticated person, smart and alerted to the realities of power, savvy and worldly-wise. But it is no result at all, only tendentious interpretation. Cynics may think they have exposed our deepest motivations, but they merely impose a model on actions and events. Cynics have no special insight into human nature, merely a bleak and bitter attitude that holds them captive.[14] Mocking cynicism is too simplistic to be credible.

Mocking cynicism mocks the official story, the appearance, insisting that it is not reality but only a misleadingly benign appearance. In every case, reality is more sordid. Like most reductionistic accounts, this one depends on making a logical exception of itself. If mocking cynicism and its mode of interpretation were to be applied universally, it would defeat itself. The cynic understands other people's professions of truth and insight as manifestations of bias and interest, all the while presuming that his own insights should be taken seriously. The cynic distrusts human beings. He is himself a human being. But he does not distrust himself. Contemporary mocking cynics exempt themselves from criticism, and this exemption is arbitrary and inconsistent.

There are, then, decisive objections to generalized cynicism. Cynical interpretation is too façile and rigid, open to logical objections, and too insensitive to detail and alternate possibilities. Its claims of deep insight and wisdom are mere pretensions. Ironically, the cynicism that represents everything else as a sham turns out to be a sham itself. Mocking cynicism is simplistic, cavalier, *ad hoc*, and insufficiently sensitive to evidence. In addition, completely generalized cynicism is self-refuting.

But these intellectual problems pale in significance when compared with the practical perils of cynicism. Like despair, cynicism discourages effort and encourages depression. It offers no hope and counsels helplessness. The cynic interprets everything negatively, imposing his bleak picture on even those claims that would appear to be substantive and even those actions that would appear generous and altruistic. This interpretive pattern blocks communication and limits analysis. The inevitabilism that is so often a feature of cynicism leads to paralysis in action. The cynic is sure that corruption, greed, lust for power and reputation, pursuit of interests, and the like are inevitable aspects of human affairs. When he detects them, he only finds what he expected. So there is no point in acting. Cynics have learned inaction and helplessness because their fixed and negative interpretations leave no opening for meaningful action. There is just "nothing one can do." Enjoy the Vanity Fair. Watch the spectacle. Look down from above. Do not engage.

One might wonder why cynicism is so popular if it is so objectionable. Part of the answer, I think, is that there are superficial benefits to maintaining a cynical attitude. A cynical analysis comes easily, requiring no detailed knowledge or sensitivity to alternate interpretations. It gives a person a sense of certainty and superior wisdom. And it relieves him of any responsibility to act. But overall, mocking cynicism is a harmful attitude from a practical point of view. It is based on negativism, lack of imagination, and tendentious interpretation. It inhibits insight, energy, optimism, and effort. A world viewed with a distrustful glare confirms the suspicions of the viewer and offers no invitation to action. Generalized mocking cynicism is superficial, intellectually flawed, psychologically unhealthy, and politically dangerous.

Today's world is a hazardous one, its dangers disturbingly real and present. In the face of what seem overwhelming hazards, mocking cynicism offers no positive norms, no program for action, and no hope. It presumes a false invulnerability and counsels only supercilious dismissal. Worse yet, its perverse legitimation by disbelief counsels passivity, making mocking cynicism downright dangerous. Clichés about "corrosive cynicism" and cynicism being a "malaise" do not exaggerate. Cynicism is a malaise, a sickness, because it robs us of hope, energy, and power.

For every action, institution, and person, there is a variety of readings, a plurality of interpretations and causal and motivational possibilities. The cynic who allegedly "knows" just what human nature is like, just how things work, and what inevitably must happen is not, in the end, credible. Just as Lucian discounted many possible interpretations of Peregrinus's suicide, opting unquestioningly for "vainglory" as a motive, the contemporary cynic is sure he understands the deepest motivations of fellow human beings. Against such unreasonable confidence, an antidote of scepticism and pluralism is needed. A little cheekiness might help too.

By imposing a negative interpretation, mocking cynicism distorts relationships and situations and hides possibilities from us. It works against positive expectations, optimism, and hope. As in so many other contexts, we risk lapsing into self-fulfilling prophecy. If people are going to be regarded as manipulative exploiters *whatever* they do, they will conclude that they might as well enjoy the benefits of living down to their negative reputation. If anyone who proposes what he takes to be a constructive change and runs for political office will be regarded as corrupt and power-hungry, few well-intentioned people will enter politics, and thus the corrupt and power-hungry will be ever more present.

ANTIDOTES TO MOCKING CYNICISM

How to resist mocking cynicism? Sloterdijk believes that cheeky cynicism can serve as an antidote. We should let ourselves feel, and laugh, realize how ridiculous many pretensions are, and abandon any sense of occupying top-dog position. Goldfarb sees moral relativism as the deep philosophical mistake underneath mocking cynicism. People assume that they hold no common values, and this makes them cynical when others profess values instead of interests. Goldfarb argues that people do share basic values and that autonomous cultural voices can recall and appeal to those values to create a meaningful and believable public discourse: "Autonomous authentic voices constitute a pluralistic democracy; manipulated mass culture produces a cynical society."[15]

Even when a cynical interpretation is partially correct, that does not rule out other meanings and values. Events and policies can have multiple causes, meanings, and values, as was the case with Peregrinus's suicide long ago. An automatically cynical attitude is no more wise and accurate than one of utter gullibility. Whether an action, person, or event is as it appears on the surface varies from case to case. Mocking cynicism is too slick and confident. An element of its dangerous appeal is that it can make the ignorant appear wise. Part of the solution to the malaise of cynicism lies in sensitivity to alternative interpretations and to detail.

The mocking cynic feels distanced from the human beings damaged by recession, violence, pollution, and poverty and lacks any sense of solidarity with suffering humanity, assuming he will never be in its midst. But in fact his top-dog position is insecure; he is not so immune as he thinks. Most of today's hazards are democratic in nature. Even the rich and powerful breathe polluted air and succumb to cancer. Like other human beings and like his ancient predecessors, the cynic is a human animal, a creature of nature, vulnerable to earth, water, and atmosphere. To assume invulnerability is to deceive oneself.

Cynicism counsels passivity because it implies that human corruption and greed are inevitable. To *hope*, one must envisage a future that is open, that contains unrealized possibilities, positive outcomes that might be the product of human effort and energy. Hope is linked to time, to a sense that the present is not everything and the future holds new possibilities. Although human beings in the past faced problems parallel to those that trouble us today, the present is not like the past. And from this we can infer that the future will not be like the present. The openness of the future is a basis for hope. To hope, we must go beyond ourselves to a conception of human beings as beings who have potential for vision and change, to a sense of unforeseen events and unseen possibilities. Cynics fix on a single interpretation of human nature and human affairs. Hope preserves a sense of openness in events and people, an awareness of the lack of fixity that is an antidote to the immobility of despair.

HOPE AND POSSIBILITIES

Strange as it may seem, logic itself is on the side of hope. Not only is a hopeful attitude more respectful and positive than a cynical one, it is, in the final analysis, more accurate. Hope sees an open future, recognizing that there are innumerable tendencies and possibilities in people and events. To reach important goals, we must act, and to act, we must preserve a sense that what we do can make a difference. Before the days of Diogenes, Heraclitus, the philosopher of change, said, "He who does not expect what cannot be expected will not make the unattainable attainable."[16] He meant, I think, that we can achieve what might seem to be unattainable only if we look at the future with the attitude that unexpected things do happen sometimes. Throughout natural and human history unexpected things have happened; we can, then, assume that there is a sense in which we should expect the unexpected. From this lesson we can derive an attitude of openness, a sense that even when things appear gloomy, happier possibilities may lie ahead. To make the unattainable happen, to act in hope, we must see the future as open, retaining our knowledge that beneficial change can come in unpredicted ways. We know that the world will change and that different things will come; we do not know what they will be; we strive for a positive vision.

Hope sees the future as latent with desired possibilities and human action as a central element in making these possibilities real. The ancient Cynics and Stoics drew a firm line between those things that are within our power and those beyond it. They counselled restricting our desires and adapting our life so as to minimize dependence on things beyond our own control. They saw hope as based on foolish illusions, urging that it would only disappoint us. Ancient Stoics and Cynics placed trust in the self, sought control of their feelings and beliefs, and tried to detach themselves from the tumultuous and unreliable external world.

Contemporary knowledge argues against a firm distinction between what is within our control and what is outside it. The distinction does not even apply in the hard science of physics. Modern physics teaches that those physical states that exist in the universe and how we observe and measure them are interdependent, not independent facts. Still less can this distinction be upheld in human affairs.

What we feel and believe affects our context and situation, which affect our possibilities for action. These in turn reflect back on our attitudes, actions, and beliefs and those of other people, which then help to determine future circumstances and states of affairs. Reflexivity and interaction appear at every level. Our very selves develop and are defined in relation to others, and those others are significantly affected by who we are and how we act towards them. Actions, circumstances, and events are interpreted negatively or positively, and these interpretations make a difference. We see ourselves differently, see our prospects for action differently, and, with different degrees of persistent effort, structure different realities.

When we hope, we actively anticipate the future, seeing that future as open and seeing ourselves as helping to prepare for it in various ways. To anticipate a better future, we should preserve our hope, respecting and trusting human capacity and dignity, and avoiding the facile dismissals of mocking cynicism.

Hope may have specific objects, some trivial in the grand scheme of things. We may hope for a warm evening on Hallowe'en, hope the daffodils will last until June, or hope to win the lottery. Hope may have more profound objects: we may hope our child will become a happy and conscientious adult, hope to save the Northern rainforests, or hope for world peace. Some hopes are almost entirely passive. Hoping for a warm Hallowe'en involves no action or commitment. But, characteristically, hope requires and informs action.

In addition to specific hopes, there is such a thing as *latent* hope, a general attitude of positive expectation about the future. Latent hope is hope about hope itself. It is a general underlying attitude that helps us to go on hoping even when we are disappointed in our specific hopes. Latent hope preserves our hope when we are disappointed. If a specific hope is not realized, we need not collapse in despair, thinking that all is over and done with and there are no better possibilities in the future.

A woman might work for years on an ambitious film, hoping when it is distributed to have an impact on public thinking, acquire a good reputation, and establish financial security. Then it fails. The world has changed rapidly; people are no longer interested in the subject, and audiences are small. Hope, energy, and confidence were necessary to complete the project, but they did not suffice for success. Still, failure will not counsel helplessness or hopelessness. If she has a fundamentally positive and open stance towards reality, she will not simply give up but will go on to work on something else. Latent hope affects how she responds to disappointment. She will try to learn from what happened, but also to look to the open future to go on to a new project. With latent hope she can respond positively and actively to her disappointment, to preserve a sense that the future is open and her efforts will not be futile.

If we were representing hope on a diagram, we might draw two arrows, one extending to states of affairs, the other to human agents.[17] A person who hopes for improvements in the ozone layer will hope both that human agents will devise the necessary environmental agreements and that states of affairs will make human action meaningful and possible. One aspect of this hope involves human agency, the other states of affairs. It is relevant to think of "other agents" because we have to hope for co-operative and appropriate action by other people. But human agency includes ourselves. In hoping that *we* will act rightly to protect ozone and other environmental goods, I must hope not only that *other agents* do so but also that *I myself* can do so. Hope, then, requires trust in ourselves and in other people. What happens socially and politically is both within our control and outside it. We have partial control: what we do affects reality in multitudinous and unpredictable ways, and that open reality reflects back on us. All of this sets the context for hope.

One may hope for a warm October evening, and actions of human agents have little to do with this. But with most profound hopes, human beings and institutions are involved and matters are otherwise. Without some notion that I and others – that *we* in solidarity – can make a difference, I am in a position of despair and helplessness.

Mocking cynicism is not just the same as pessimism; it is not distrust; it is not despair. But it will cause pessimism and inspire despair. At a time when change in human institutions and practices is desperately necessary, mocking cynicism counsels only supercilious passivity.

Although there is a charm in early cynicism, the mocking cynicism that is so prevalent in our age is truly a malaise. Cynics take a negative stance, impose a picture on human nature and society, and believe themselves to have revealed our deepest motivations. Through self-fulfilling prophecies they worsen our relationships and restrict our possibilities for action, all the while believing that human beliefs and actions do not fundamentally affect social reality. Deceived and misled, mocking cynics see themselves as worldly-wise and others as naïve. Mocking cynicism is a trap – logically, personally, ethically, and politically. We should escape from this trap with trust and hope.

Notes

CHAPTER ONE

1 Govier, "An Epistemology of Trust."
2 Govier, "How We Trust Ourselves" and "Self-Trust, Autonomy, and Self-Esteem."
3 See chap. 8.
4 Buber, *I and Thou*, 78, 85.
5 This discussion, like many others, avoids the question of how much inductive evidence does warrant. It is simply too large a topic to take on as a side theme.
6 Erikson, *Childhood and Society*.
7 For summaries see Rapoport, "Formal Games"; Pruitt and Kimmel, "Twenty Years of Experimental Gaming"; and Messick and Brewer, "Solving Social Dilemmas." Messick and Brewer refer to "an avalanche of research." They argue that two-person Prisoner's Dilemma research is irrelevant both to the understanding of basic psychological states and to the solution of policy dilemmas.
8 Deutsch, "Cooperation and Trust." The version of the Prisoner's Dilemma given here is taken from Robert Martin's popular treatment in *There are Two Errors in The The Title of This Book*. Good comments on the practice of deception in social- psychological experiments may be found in Bok, *Lying* and Kelman, "Human Use of Human Subjects."
9 Rotter, "A New Scale," "Generalized Expectancies," and "Interpersonal Trust."
10 Schlenker, Helm, and Tedeschi, "The Effects of Personality and Situa-

tional Variables on Behavioral Trust." Compare also Fisher and Brown, *Getting Together*. See especially the appendix on Prisoner's Dilemmas and the TIT FOR TAT strategy.

11 Isaacs, Alexander, and Haggard, "Faith, Trust, and Gullibility."

12 Wisdom, "Gods," 103.

13 Pearce, "Trust in Interpersonal Communication."

14 Rempel, Holmes, and Zanna, "Trust in Close Relationships," 101.

15 Horsburgh, "The Ethics of Trust."

16 Thomas, "The Duty to Trust."

17 Baier, "Trust and Antitrust," 236.

18 Hertzberg, "On the Attitude of Trust," 321.

19 Garfinkel, "'Trust' as a Condition of Stable Concerted Actions."

20 Henslin, "Trust and the Cab Driver" and "What Makes for Trust?"

21 Lewis and Weigert, "Trust as a Social Reality."

22 Sellerberg, "On Modern Confidence," 242.

23 Luhmann, *Trust and Power*. See also Luhmann, "Familiarity, Confidence, and Trust." I have tried here to give a relatively simple and clear outline of Luhmann's ideas, which are presented in a somewhat difficult style.

24 Ibid., *Trust and Power*, 46.

25 Ibid., 53. A similar view is argued by Steven Shapin in *A Social History of Truth*: "What counts for any community as true knowledge is a collective good and a collective accomplishment. That good is always in others' hands, and the fate of any particular claim that something 'is the case' is never determined by the individual making the claim" (5). Shapin later states that a world in common is built up through acts of trust, and its properties are decided through the civil conversations of trusting individuals. Shapin's work will be discussed briefly in chapter 3.

CHAPTER TWO

1 Thomas, *Living Morally*.

2 Compare Govier, "Distrust as a Practical Problem."

3 Isaacs, Alexander, and Haggard, "Faith, Trust and Gullibility."

4 Zand, "Trust and Managerial Problem Solving."

5 Fukuyama, *Trust*. The discussion of trust and lean manufacturing appears in in chap. 22.

6 Snyder, "When Belief Creates Reality." The specific examples given are my own.

7 Ibid. The point is also noted by Horsburgh in "The Ethics of Trust." Corresponding to my Rosy Spirals and Blue Spirals, Robert Putnam defines a Virtuous Equilibrium and Vicious Equilibrium, where trust and distrust each tend to buttress themselves in a societal context in much the same way as they sustain themselves as personal attitudes. See Putnam, *Making Democracy Work*, and compare chap. 6 following.

8 Michalos, "The Impact of Trust."

9 Ibid., 626.

10 Ibid.

11 For evidence of the partisan bias see Greenwald, "The Totalitarian Ego."

12 Rotter, "Interpersonal Trust;" Williams and Barefoot, "Coronary-Prone Behavior"; Hardin, "The Street Epistemology of Trust."

13 There are many possibilities, obviously.

14 Michalos, "The Impact of Trust," 631.

15 I address the issue of trust in negative societies in chap.6. Fukuyama's discussion in *Trust* argues for the significance of trust patterns in a culture and society for its corporate organization and worker-management relations.

16 Russell Hardin notes that we cannot simply decide to trust and then trust, all in an instant. However, Hardin claims that trust can be cultivated. Presumably we would cultivate trust in much the way we might cultivate belief – by deliberately exposing ourselves to the sorts of situations in which it would naturally arise. Hardin notes the possibility of this Pascalian approach. We could try to trust more, much in the way that Pascal argued that we should try to cultivate belief in God.

17 Fukuyama, *Trust*; see espec. chaps. 9 and 11. Compare also Putnam, *Making Democracy Work*.

18 We sometimes speak simply of trusting a person, without implying any relevance to a context or range of activities. One might, for instance, say, "I trust my brother absolutely." In such cases expectations of motivation and integrity count far more than expectations of competence, which count scarcely at all. But such claims tend to be overstatements. Even with a person whom we trust "absolutely" there are things we would not trust him to do, due to limitations of competence or personal eccentricities. (Russell Hardin makes the same point.)

19 In circumstances where scarcely anyone abides by moral norms there may be risks in trustworthiness. Even in normal circumstances, highly conscientious and trustworthy people do risk being taken for granted, being exploited. The point is, though, that the advice to "be trustworthy" makes more sense and is less risky than the advice to "trust more."

20 Hobbes, *Leviathan*.

21 Baier, "Secular Faith."

CHAPTER THREE

1 Coady, *Testimony*, 7.

2 Hardwig, "Relying on Experts." Emphasis is mine.

3 Shapin, *The Social History of Truth*, 17–18.

4 Coady makes amusing and apt comments about the implicit contradiction in the work of psychologists who have sought, on the basis of

observation and questioning, to discredit eyewitness testimony. See *Testimony*, 264–76.

5 Ibid., 42.

6 H.H. Price, in *Belief*, 122, notes that acceptance of testimony presupposes trust. James R. Ross, "Testimonial Evidence," 36, observes that "a large part of what we know has come to be believed simply because we have trusted various reporters." Michael Welbourne, describing what he calls the community of knowledge, says that what binds the members of an epistemic community is trust ("The Community of Knowledge," 305.) Elizabeth Fricker maintains that our ability to gain knowledge from testimony must be accounted for by "any sane theory of knowledge," noting the implication of trust ("The Epistemology of Testimony," 3). See also Govier, "When Logic Meets Politics," "Trust and Testimony," and "Needing Each Other for Knowledge."

7 Wittgenstein, *On Certainty*. 159, 160.

8 Shapin, *A Social History of Truth*, 303, 287.

9 Wittgenstein, *On Certainty*, 503. See alsoWalsh, "Knowledge in Its Social Setting."

10 The point is strongly argued in Sydney Shoemaker, *Self- Knowledge and Self-Identity*, and is implicit in virtually all accounts contrasting subjective impressions with objective knowledge.

11 Luhmann, *Trust and Power*. Quoted passages are on 51–3. Shapin takes the same view.

12 Welbourne, "The Transmission of Knowledge," 1–9.

13 Price, *Belief*, 114–15.

14 Shapin, *A Social History of Truth*, 307.

15 Wittgenstein, *On Certainty*, 450.

16 See, for instance, Philip Green's *Deadly Logic*.

17 Turnbull, *The Mountain People*.

CHAPTER FOUR

1 Barber, *The Logic and Limits of Trust*, chap. 7.

2 Apparently judges, lawyers, doctors, and dentists earn the highest annual incomes among occupational groups in Canada: *Globe and Mail*, 14 April 1993.

3 This point is well stated in a doctoral thesis by Michele Carter, "Ethical Analysis of Trust in Therapeutic Relationships."

4 All these examples are derived from things said either to me or to members of my family.

5 Pellagrino, "Trust and Distrust in Professional Ethics"; the quoted comment is on 84.

6 Veatch, "Is Trust of Professionals a Coherent Concept?"

7 These figures are taken from Barber.

8 Hardwig, "The Role of Trust in Knowledge." Hardwig cites J.P. Tangney, "Fraud Will Out – Or Will It?" for a recent survey of scientists at a "highly ranked American university."

9 Hardwig, "The Role of Trust in Knowledge."

10 Shapin, *A Social History of Truth*, takes essentially the same view. See, in particular, his epilogue.

11 V. Fabrikant, e-mail provided by Professor James Parker, Computer Science Department, University of Calgary.

12 *Maclean's*, Sept. 1992.

13 Arthurs, Blair, and Thompson, *Integrity in Scholarship*, 65.

CHAPTER FIVE

1 Garfinkel, "A Conception of, and Experiment with, 'Trust.'"

2 Ibid., 223.

3 The phenomenon has been described by various writers, including a number cited here. The term, however, is my own.

4 Sellerberg, "On Modern Confidence."

5 Frankl, *Money*. Simmel is quoted on 24.

6 Frankl, *Money*, 32.

7 Dannefer, "Driving and Symbolic Interaction," *Sociological Inquiry*. The quoted passage is on 36. Notably, one also has to trust *oneself* in order to drive.

8 Baier, "Trust and Antitrust." The quoted passage is on 237.

9 Thomas, *Living Morally*. The term "basic trust" is often used in a quite different sense to refer to the early trust between a baby or young child and its caretaker. See chaps. 1 and 2 above.

10 Thomas, "Trust, Affirmation, and Moral Character," 249.

11 Ibid., 250.

12 Interview with B.K., Aug. 1991. B.K. is a twenty-two-year-old Calgary man finishing the last year of his university degree. Note that this interview was given several years prior to government cutbacks that seriously affected the Alberta health-care system.

13 Interview with A.V., Aug. 1991. A.V. is a social worker in his mid-thirties, living in Cochrane, Alta.

14 Interview with S.R., Oct. 1991. S.R., in her late forties, is a mother of four grown children who works as an aide in a Calgary high-school English program.

15 Ibid.

16 Ibid.

17 Interview with H.S., Sept. 1991. H.S. is a Calgary psychology professor, about forty, father of two young boys.

18 Interview with B.S., Oct. 1991. B.S. is a seventy-year-old Calgary woman, mother of three grown children, who has volunteered with many community and political groups.

19 Among the many works discussing limitations of the rational-actor model is *Beyond Self-Interest*, ed. Jane J. Mansbridge.

20 For further detail about this study, see Govier, "An Epistemology of Trust."

21 Such issues look somewhat different from the viewpoint of a woman.

22 Thomas, "Next Life, I'll Be White." See also his "Statistical Badness."

23 Thomas, "Statistical Badness," 30.

24 The underlying assumption in this and similar work is that *general attitudes* about "people" or "human nature," as opposed to specific cues drawn from the other's dress, demeanour, age, race, or social class, or cues of context, would be the most pertinent factors on which to base a judgment. Compare Morris Rosenberg, "Misanthropy and Attitudes toward International Affairs"; the scale is given on 341.

25 Rotter, "Generalized Expectancies for Interpersonal Trust."

26 This lack of correspondence constitutes a significant objection to Rotter's overall account, as I argue in chap. 1.

27 Nevertheless, there would seem to be cogent conceptual criticisms. In addition to the fact that the items deal with concerns going beyond verbal commitment, which is the scope indicated by the definition, a number of items on the scale are logically vague or ambiguous. For example, in the statement "In these competitive times one has to be alert or someone is likely to take advantage of you" there is uncertainty whether there is a (small) possibility or a (substantial) probability of someone taking advantage of you. On the latter interpretation, a greater extent of distrust is indicated than on the former. The item "In dealing with strangers, one is better off to be cautious until they have provided evidence that they are trustworthy" is open to criticism on the grounds that it seems too context-free and vague to disagree or agree with.

28 Rotter, "Interpersonal Trust, Trustworthiness, and Gullibility." See 6.

29 Knightley, *The Oldest Profession*. See 341–2.

30. Rotter, "Interpersonal Trust, Trustworthiness, and Gullibility," 6.

31. Fukuyama, *Trust*.

CHAPTER SIX

1 See Robert Redfield, *Peasant Society and Culture*, for a useful overview.

2 Foster, "Peasant Society and the Image of the Limited Good," 296.

3 Ibid.

4 The aspect of jealousy regarding possessions and hiding one's material status for fear of provoking envy among others is also a theme of Barry Broadfoot's *Ordinary Russians*.

5 Banfield, *The Moral Basis of a Backward Society*. In *Trust* Francis Fukuyama notes that the name "Montegrano" was fictitious. The town was real, though; its real name was Chiaramonte. Extensive evidence that civic bonds are still loose or non- existent in southern Italy, and that this is a handicap materially and politically, is presented in Robert D. Putnam, *Making Democracy Work*.

6 Cited in Banfield, *The Moral Basis of a Backward Society*, 126.

7 Ibid., 164. Compare also Putnam, *Making Democracy Work*, and Silvermaln, "Agricultural Organization, Social Structure and Values in Italy."

8 Carlo Levi, *Christ Stopped at Eboli*.

9 Ibid., 122.

10 Ibid., 76.

11 Ibid., 234.

12 Ibid., 78.

13 Friedman, "The World of La Miseria," quoted by Canciun in "The Southern Italian Peasant." Fukuyama cites strong centralization as a factor that works against the formation, by strangers, of civic associations that can take on community tasks. Such associations presume some degree of trust but also serve as a place to build trust. The case that civic associations build social trust, which is then a form of "social capital" serving economic and political ends, is argued in detail by Putnam in *Making Democracy Work*.

14 Westacott and. Williams, "Interpersonal Trust and Modern Attitudes in Peru."

15 Aquilar, "Trust and Exchange."

16 Ibid. Aquilar cites a number of other scholars who have made similar observations.

17 Ibid., 10.

18 Ibid., 18.

19 A claim made by John Lux in *Adam Smith's Mistake*.

20 Godwin, "Trusting Behavior and Social Modernization."

21 See Almond and Verba, *The Civic Culture*. . Fukuyama cites Putnam, *Making Democracy Work*, as support for his claim that lower trust causes economic disadvantage, not the other way around.

22 Roniger, "Institutionalized Inequalities," 155.

23 This rather elegant distinction can be applied to a number of contrasting patterns as between modern and "pre-modern" societies.

24 Roniger, "Institutionalized Inequalities," 150.

25 Roniger, in the concluding chapter of *Democracy, Clientelism, and Civilized Society*.

26 Roniger, "Institutionalized Inequalities," 157.

27 There seems to have been an equivalent of the patron-client relation in the communist society of the Soviet Union, especially in the 1970s and 1980s. In this context, the disparity between rich and poor would be

replaced by a disparity in power. Instead of "rich" read "established and powerful in the nomenklatura." As a means of dispensing favours, the "patron" would helping his or her protégé to move through the system of offices and powers in the communist bureaucracy. See Tatiana Vorozkeckina, "Clientelism and the Process of Political Democratization in Russia," in Roniger and Gunes-Ayata, *Democracy, Clientelism, and Civil Society*.

28 Eisenstadt and Roniger, "Patron-Client Relations," 69.

29 Ibid., 70.

30 See Seligson and Salazar, "Political and Interpersonal Trust among Peasants," for criticisms of the view that peasants are more distrustful than urban dwellers.

31 Putnam, *Making Democracy Work*, 88.

32 Ibid., 99.

33 Ibid., 115.

34 Ibid., 164. Compare Coleman, *Foundations of Social Theory*, from which the concept of social capital is taken.

35 Putnam, *Making Democracy Work*, 171.

CHAPTER SEVEN

1 I am aware of the profound disagreement over whether Stalinist practices are a natural outcome of trying to run a state on Marxist-Leninist theory, and I take no stand on the issue here.

2 Adam Ulam, quoted in Tismaneanu, *The Crisis of Marxist Ideology in Eastern Europe*, 9.

3 Tismaneanu, *The Crisis of Marxist Ideology in Eastern Europe*, 24.

4 One could scarcely instal a revolutionary government and begin the otherthrow of social institutions without fairly wide public enthusiasm for the changes. The phenomenon is also confirmed in a number of writings by citizens and former citizens of Stalinist states. See, for instance, Rybakov, *Children of the Arbat*, and Posner, *Parting with Illusions*.

5 Stojanovic, "How Can We Explain the Changes in Eastern Europe and the USSR?" Lecture given at the University of Calgary, 15 Nov. 1991.

6 Havel, New Year's Address 1990, as printed in the Toronto *Globe and Mail*, 24 Jan. 1990. See also Havel, *Living in Truth*.

7 Ralf Dahrendorf, quoted in Tismaneanu, *Reinventing Politics*, 244.

8 Campeanu, "The Revolt of the Romanians." The young woman was one of a number of Romanian citizens interviewed on the CBC news commentary show "The Journal" during January and February 1990.

9 Elton, "East Germany: Crime and Punishment."

10 Tismaneanu, *Reinventing Politics*, 250

11 Dr Fritz Arendt, interview, Dresden, Germany, 21 Mar. 21, 1994. According to Belinda Cooper, an American expatriate who had been involved

with opposition groups in the GDR and was herself, in a minor way, a victim of Stasi efforts, there were fascinating differences between the role of men and women in Stasi activities. For a variety of reasons, an extraordinarily high proposition of Stasi agents were men. One estimate is that 90 per cent of agents were men, and men represented 75 per cent of the special agents implanted in opposition groups. The Stasi apparently tended not to recruit women, having fairly traditional ideas about female roles and finding it expensive to have two contacts to deal with each woman agent in order to protect their staff from sexual liaisons. Another explanation for the gender difference seems to have been that women, being busy with both work and children, simply did not have sufficient time to be agents. In addition, women seem to find it more difficult than men to compartmentalize their lives and pretend to have friendships and love affairs, all the while betraying their intimates to the police state. I owe this information to Belinda Cooper, "Women and the Stasi," and interview, Berlin, 18 Mar. 1994.

12 For pertinent reflections see Kramer, "Letter from Europe."

13 Dr Fritz Arendt, Wolfard Prehl, and Berndt Joop, interview, Dresden, Germany, 22 Mar. 1994. See also Elton, "East Germany: Crime and Punishment," and Rosenberg, *The Haunted Land*.

14 Bao Lord, *Legacies*.

15 Chen Jo Hsi, *The Execution of Mayor Yin and Other Stories*.

16 Heng and Shapiro, *Son of the Revolution*, and other sources describe how some people divorced their spouses to try to maintain a favourable class identification.

17 This character was a spy with some integrity. In East Germany many spies did not hesitate to take on the role of intimate friend.

18 Samir al-Khalil, *Republic of Fear*.

19 Ibid., 66.

20 Ibid., 117. My emphasis.

21 Some believe that the cry was planned and executed by a Securitate agent, that the Securitate itself had decided to dump Ceausescu. Even if this should be true, it does not refute the point that the response of the crowd made Ceausescu's apparent legitimacy disappear in an instant. When the crowd first responded, people believed that others were calling out against the dictator.

22 Tismaneanu, *Reinventing Politics*, 283. Laszlo Tokes is a bishop and leader in the Hungarian Romanian community whose courageous demonstration at Timisoara brought violent repression by the Ceaucescu regime and was a major force in inspiring the revolution of 1989. In a talk at the University of Calgary on 8 Nov. 1995 Tokes reported that many former communist officials were still in power; the Securitate was still active under another name; there were still many incidents of intimidation and terror and restrictions on journalistic freedom. Though

democratically elected, the regime preserves significant characteristics of totalitarianism.

23 Bellah, Madsen, Sullivan, Swidler, and Tipton, *Habits of the Heart*. *In Trust* Francis Fukuyama argues that the United States has traditionally been a high-trust society but currently exhibits features of a low-trust society. From a completely different perspective from Bellah et al., he reaches a similar conclusion.

24 This point is convincingly argued in Barber, *Strong Democracy*.

25 Cohen and Amato, *Civil Society and Political Theory*, 346.

26 Moyer, "The Movement Action Plan," 5. Similar accounts of people-power have been articulated by others, including, most notably, Mohandas Gandhi and Gene Sharp. See, for instance, his *Gandhi as a Political Strategist*.

CHAPTER EIGHT

1 Rotter and Stein, "Public Attitudes toward the Trustworthiness, Competence, and Altruism of Twenty Selected Occupations." Subjects were primarily college students but also included secretaries in public schools and teachers; 169 were male and 227 female.

2 Benjamin, *Splitting the Difference*. Compromise sounds negative to many people and is also criticized by some theorists of conflict resolution, who see it as *less* than what can be achieved by people who, in conflict, are willing to share their feelings and beliefs and maximize the satisfaction of their interests in creative conflict resolution. But this criticism of compromise presumes conditions that do not apply in all situations. Benjamin argues the case convincingly.

3 Barber, *The Logic and Limits of Trust*, chaps. 2 and 8.

4 See Coontz,. *The Way We Never Were*, 113–31.

5 I owe this expression to Professor David Taras, Department of Communication Studies, University of Calgary.

6 See, for instance, Barnet, "The End of Jobs," and Morris, "It's Not the Economy, Stupid."

7 Barber, *The Logic and Limits of Trust*, 89.

8 Reported on the "Facts and Arguments" page of the Toronto *Globe and Mail*, 9 Aug. 1993.

9 *In Context*, (Spring 1985): 24–6.

CHAPTER NINE

1 Kirp and Bayer, "Public Health: Needles and Race."

2 York and Pindera, *People of the Pines*. The account given here is based on this work.

3 Ibid., 93.

4 Ibid., 97.

5 There are many issues about collectives and individuals, falling broadly under the headings of ontology (what is real), methodology (what should be assumed to exist for the purposes of investigation), and ethics (what is morally primary.) The debate is too vast to explore here; I touch only on methodology. In addition to the articles mentioned in the text I have benefitted by studying Gruner, "On the Action of Social Groups"; Copp, "Collective Actions and Social Actions"; and French, "Corporate Moral Agency."

6 Quinton, "Social Objects," 17; my emphasis.

7 Of course this is an unstable situation. With regard to changing attitudes, such instabilities are important.

8 In fact, who represented the Mohawks at Oka was not clear; there were several different groups among which there were substantial differences.

9 Le Doeff, *Hipparchia's Choice*.

10 Ware, "Group Action and Social Organization." In this essay Ware notes that mental attributes (beliefs, attitudes, and so on) are ascribed to individuals by some who are philosophically sceptical about *minds* as such and that this possibility is relevant to the issue of what is ascribed to groups. But he does not take the point further.

CHAPTER TEN

1 Strictly speaking, the expression "nation-state" is a misnomer. The *nation* or people (a group typically sharing a history, territory, language, culture, and religion) is logically distinct from the *state* a legally constituted territorially based entity with a recognized place in the United Nations.

2 See Marshall Cohen, "Moral Skepticism and International Relations," for an excellent critical discussion of the amoral position.

3 A point stated clearly in Holsti, *The Dividing Discipline*.

4 From Brunk, "Two Paradigms of Conflict and Conflict Resolution."

5 Morgenthau, *Politics among Nations*.

6 Rapoport, "Critique of Strategic Thinking." See also, Green, *Deadly Logic*.

7 Halle, "The Struggle Called Coexistence."

8 Krass, "Focus On: Verification and Trust in Arms Control."

9 Ibid., 286.

10 Handel, "Intelligence and Deception."

11 Kamel, *The Camp David Accords*. This book offers an rather negative view of Camp David. See also Genner, *One Land, Two Peoples*.

12 Maoz and Felsenthal, "Self-Binding Commitments."
13 De Klerk, *F.W. De Klerk: The Man in His Time*, 60. My emphasis.
14 Most notably K.J. Holsti, in *The Dividing Discipline*.
15 Compare Fain, *Normative Politics and the Community of Nations*.
16 Connor, "Nation Building or Nation Destroying?"
17 Holsti, *The Dividing Discipline*, 47.
18 Ibid., 143.
19 We might certainly suspect a gender bias at this point, and I do. It is noteworthy that the three alternative accounts considered here were developed by women. For essays on feminist approaches to international relations and strategic studies, see Grant and Newland, *Gender and International Relations*.
20 Boulding, *Building a Global Civic Culture*.
21 Bok, *Lying* and *A Strategy for Peace*.
22 Jones, *Code of Peace*.
23 Clark, "Meaningful Social Bonding as a Universal Human Need," in *Conflict: Human Needs Theory*, ed. John Burton.
24 The notion that common tasks are the moral basis for community is defended by Fain in *Normative Politics and the Community of Nations*.

CHAPTER ELEVEN

1 Goldfarb, *The Cynical Society*.
2 Sloterdijk, *Critique of Cynical Reason*.
3 A relevant discussion of pessimism may be found in Seligman, *Learned Optimism*.
4 Information on the early cynics is drawn from Dudley, *A History of Cynicism*, and Malherbe, *The Cynic Epistles*.
5 Sloterdijk, *Critique of Cynical Reason*.
6 Information about Peregrinus is taken from *The Encyclopedia of Philosophy*; Jones, *Culture and Society in Lucian*; and Turner, ed. *Lucian: Satirical Sketches*.
7 Lucian, "The Death of Peregrinus," in *Selected Satires of Lucian*. See also his "Philosophers Going Cheap" in Turner, *Lucian: Satirical Sketches*.
8 Jones, *Culture and Society in Lucian*.
9 Goldfarb, *The Cynical Society*.
10 Ibid.
11 Rideout, "Lily Truehart, MP," presented at the Fringe Festival in Edmonton, Canada, 19 Aug. 1991.
12 Delacourt, "Nation United in Mistrust."
13 Clarkson, "Teens Harvest Hits the Spot."
14 The reference is to Wittgenstein's *Philosophical Investigations*. Wittenstein says "a picture held us captive," meaning that we have a model in our

minds, cannot get rid of it, and because we retain it, are blinded to significant details of reality.

15 Goldfarb, *The Cynical Society*.
16 As translated by H. Frankl and quoted in Dauenhauer, "Hope and Its Ramifications for Politics."
17 Dauenhauer, "Hope and Its Ramifications for Politics."

Bibliography

Adler, Jonathan. "Testimony, Trust, Knowing." *Journal of Philosophy* 91 (1994): 264–275.

Al Khalil, Samir. *Republic of Fear: The Inside Story of Saddam's Iraq.* New York: Pantheon Books 1990.

Almond, G., and S. Verba. *The Civic Culture.* Princeton, NJ: Princeton University Press 1963.

Anscombe, Elizabeth. "Hume and Julius Caesar." *Analysis* 34: 1–7.

– "What Is It To Believe Someone?" In *Rationality and Religious Belief,* ed. C.F. Delaney. Notre Dame: University of Notre Dame Press 1979. 141–151.

Aquilar, John. "Trust and Exchange: Expressive and Instrumental Dimensions of Reciprocity in a Peasant Community." *Ethos* 12 (1984): 3–29.

Arthurs, H.W., Roger A. Blair, and Jon Thompson. *Integrity in Scholarship: A Report to Concordia University.* Montreal: Independent Committee of Inquiry into Academic and Scientific Integrity 1995.

Ash, Timothy Garton. "East Germany: The Solution." *New York Review of Books,* 26 Apr. 1990, 14–20.

Axelrod, Robert. *The Evolution of Cooperation.* New York: Basic Books 1984.

Baier, Annette. "Secular Faith." *Canadian Journal of Philosophy* 9 (1980): 131–48.

– "Extending the Limits of Moral Theory." *Journal of Philosophy* 83 (1986): 538–45.

– "Trust and Antitrust." *Ethics* 96 (1986): 231–60.

Baker, Judith. "Trust and Rationality." *Pacific Philosophical Quarterly* 63 (1987): 1–13.

Banfield, Edward C. *The Moral Basis of a Backward Society.* New York: Free Press 1958.

- *The Unheavenly City.* Boston: Little Brown 1970.

Barber, Benjamin. *Strong Democracy.* Berkeley: University of California Press 1984.

Barber, Bernard. *The Logic and Limits of Trust.* New Brunswick, NJ: Rutgers University Press 1983.

Barnet, Richard. "The End of Jobs." *Harper's,* Sept.1993, 47–92.

Bellah, R., with R. Madsen, W. Sullivan, A. Swidler, and S. Tipton. *Habits of the Heart.* New York: Harper and Row 1985.

Benjamin, Martin. *Splitting the Difference: Compromise and Integrity in Ethics and Politics.* Laurence: University of Kansas Press 1990.

Blais, Michel. "Epistemic Tit for Tat." *Journal of Philosophy* 84 (1987): 335–49.

Bok, Sissela. *Lying.* New York: Pantheon 1978.

- *A Strategy for Peace.* New York: Pantheon 1989.

- "Can Lawyers be Trusted?" *University of Pennsylvania Law Review* 138 (1990): 913–33.

Boulding, Elise. *Building a Global Civic Culture.* Syracuse, NY: Syracuse University Press 1990.

Boulding, Kenneth E. *Stable Peace.* Austin: University of Texas Press 1978.

Brann, Peter, and Margaret Foddy. "Trust and the Consumption of a Deteriorating Common Resource." *Journal of Conflict Resolution* 31 (1987): 615–30.

Broadfoot, Barry. *Ordinary Russians.* Toronto: McClelland and Stewart 1989.

Brothers, Doris. "Trust Disturbances in Rape and Incest Victims." PhD, Yeshiva University, New York 1982.

Brunk, Conrad. "Two Paradigms of Conflict and Conflict Resolution in the Arms Control and Disarmament Debate." Paper presented at the Inter-University Centre, Dubrovnik, Yugoslavia, June 1987.

Buber, Martin. *I and Thou.* Trans. Walter Kaufmann. New York: Charles Scribner and Sons 1970.

- *The Knowledge of Man: Selected Essays.* Trans. Maurice Friedman and Ronald Gregor Smith. Atlantic Highlands, NJ: Humanities Press 1988.

Campeanu, Pavel. "The Revolt of the Romanians." *New York Review of Books,* 1 Feb.1990: 30–1.

Canciun, Frank. "The Southern Italian Peasant: World View and Political Behavior." *Anthropological Quarterly* 34 (1961): 1–18.

Carter, Michele. "Ethical Analysis of Trust in Therapeutic Relationships." PhD, University of Tennessee, Knoxville 1989.

Chen Jo Hsi. *The Execution of Mayor Yin and Other Stories from the Great Proletarian Cultural Revolution.* Bloomington: Indiana University Press 1978.

Cialdini, Robert B. *Influence: The New Psychology of Modern Persuasion.* New York: Quill 1984.

Clark, Mary E. "Meaningful Social Bonding as a Universal Human Need." In *Conflict: Human Needs Theory,* ed. John Burton. New York: St Martin's Press 1990.

Clarkson, Michael. "Teen Harvest Hits the Spot." *Calgary Herald*, 12 Oct. 1991.

Coady, C.A.J. *Testimony*. Oxford: Clarendon Press 1992.

Cohen, Jean L., and Andrew Amato. *Civil Society and Political Theory*. Cambridge, Mass.: MIT Press 1992.

Cohen, Marshall. "Moral Skepticism and International Relations." *Philosophy and Public Affairs* 1987: 299–346.

Coleman, James S. *Foundations of Social Theory*. Cambridge, Mass.: Harvard University Press 1990.

Coontz, Stephanie. *The Way We Never Were*. New York: Basic Books 1992.

Cooper, Belinda. "Women and the Stasi." Unpublished paper, Berlin 1994.

Copp, David. "Collective Actions and Social Actions." *American Philosophical Quarterly* 16 (1979): 177–86.

Dannefer, W. Dale. "Driving and Symbolic Interaction." *Social Inquiry* 47 (1977): 33–8.

Dauenhauer, B. "Hope and Its Ramifications for Politics." *Man and World* 17 (1984): 453–76.

De Klerk, Willem. *F.W. De Klerk: The Man in His Time*. Johannesburg: Jonathan Ball Publishers 1991.

Delacourt, Susan. "A Nation United in Mistrust." *Globe and Mail*, 8 Nov. 1991.

Deutsch, Morton. "The Effect of Motivational Orientation upon Trust and Suspicion." *Human Relations* 13 (1960): 123–39.

– "Cooperation and Trust: Some Theoretical Notes." In *Nebraska Symposium on Motivation*, ed. Marshall Jones. Lincoln: University of Nebraska Press 1962. 302–19.

Dizard, Jan E., and Howard Dizard. *The Minimal Family*. Amherst: University of Massachusetts Press 1990.

Downie, R.S. *Roles and Values*. London: Methuen 1971.

Dudley, Donald R. *A History of Cynicism*. New York: Methuen 1937; Gordon Press 1974.

Eisler, Riane. *The Chalice and the Blade: Our History, Our Future*. San Francisco: Harper Collins 1988.

Elon, Amos. "East Germany: Crime and Punishment." *New York Review of Books*, 14 May 1992, 6–12.

Erikson, Erik. *Childhood and Society*. New York: Norton 1950.

Fain, Haskell. *Normative Politics and the Community of Nations*. Philadelphia: Temple University Press 1987.

Farberman, Harvey A., and Eugene A. Weinstein. "Personalization in Lower Class Consumer Interaction." *Social Problems* 17 (1970): 449–57.

Fisher, Roger, and Scott Brown. *Getting Together*. Boston: Houghton Mifflin 1988.

Flanigan, Beverly. *Forgiving the Unforgivable: Overcoming the Bitter Legacy of Intimate Wounds*. New York: Collier Books, Macmillan 1994.

Foster, George. "Peasant Society and the Image of the Limited Good." *American Anthropologist* 67 (1965): 293–315.

Frankl, S. Herbert. *Money: Two Philosophies: The Conflict of Trust and Authority.* Oxford: Basil Blackwell 1977.

Franklin, Satya Bharti. *The Promise of Paradise: A Woman's Intimite Story of the Perils of Life with Rajneesh.* Barrytown, NY: Stationhill 1992.

French, Peter A. "Corporate Moral Agency." In *Ethical Theory and Business,* ed. T. Beauchamp and W. Bowie. Englewood Cliffs, NJ: Prentice Hall 1979. 175–86.

Fricker, Elizabeth. "The Epistemology of Testimony." *Aristotelian Society Supplement* 61 (1987): 57–83.

Friedlander, Frank. "The Primacy of Trust as a Facilitator of Further Group Accomplishment." *Journal of Applied Behavioral Science* 6 (1970): 387–400.

Friedman, Marilyn. "Feminism and Modern Friendship: Dislocating the Community." *Ethics* 99 (1989): 275–90.

Fukuyama, Francis. *Trust: The Social Virtues and the Creation of Prosperity.* London: Hamish Hamilton 1995.

Gambetta, Diego. *Trust: Making and Breaking Cooperative Relations.* Oxford: Basil Blackwell 1988.

Garfinkel, Harold. "A Conception of, and Experiments with, 'Trust' as a Condition of Stable Concerted Actions." In *Motivation and Social Interaction,* ed. O.J. Harvey. New York: Rival Press 1963. 187–238.

Geach, Peter. *The Virtues.* Cambridge: Cambridge University Press 1977.

Gellner, Ernest. *Conditions of Liberty: Civil Society and Its Rivals.* New York: Allen Lane The Penguin Press 1994.

Genner, Deborah. *One Land: Two Peoples.* Boulder, Colo.: Westview Press 1991.

Godwin, R. Kenneth. "Trusting Behavior and Social Modernization." *Studies in Comparative International Development* 11 (1976): 44–62.

Goetz-Stankiewicz, Marketa, ed. *The Vanek Plays: Four Authors, One Character.* Vancouver: University of British Columbia Press 1987.

Goffman, Erving. *The Presentation of Self in Everyday Life.* New York: Anchor Books 1959.

Goldfarb, Jeffrey. *The Cynical Society: The Culture of Politics and the Politics of Culture in American Life.* Chicago: University of Chicago Press 1991.

Govier, Trudy. "How We Trust Ourselves and What Happens When We Don't." *Cogito* 1991: 145–53.

– "Distrust as a Practical Problem." *Journal of Social Philosophy* 23 (1992): 52–63.

– "Trust, Distrust, and Feminist Theory." *Hypatia* 7 (1992): 16–32.

– "An Epistemology of Trust." *International Journal of Moral and Social Studies.* 8 (1993): 155–74.

– "Needing Each Other for Knowledge: Reflections on Trust and Testimony."

In *Empirical Logic and Public Debate: Essays in Honour of Else M. Barth*, ed. Erik C.W. Krabbe, Renee Jose Dalitz, and Pier A. Smit. Poznan Studies in the Philosophy of the Sciences and Humanities 35. Amsterdam: Rodolphi 1993. 13–26.

- "Self-Trust, Autonomy and Self-Esteem." *Hypatia* 8 (1993): 99–120.
- "Trust and Testimony: Nine Arguments on Testimonial Knowledge." *International Journal of Moral and Social Studies* 8 (1993): 21–39.
- "When Logic Meets Politics: Prejudice, Distrust, and Rhetorical Credibility." *Informal Logic* 15 (1993): 93–104.
- "Is It a Jungle Out There? Trust, Distrust, and the Construction of Social Reality." *Dialogue* 33 (1994): 237–52.

Granovetti, Mark. "The Strength of Weak Ties." *American Journal of Sociology* 78 (1973): 1360–80.

Grant, Rebecca, and Kathleen Newland. *Gender and International Relations.* Bloomington: Indiana University Press 1991.

Gratton, Carolyn. "Summaries of Selected Works on Social and Interpersonal Trust." *Humanitas* 9 (1973): 347–60.

- "A Theoretical-Empirical Study of the Lived Experience of Interpersonal Trust." PhD, Duquesne University 1975.

Grazziano, Luigi. "Patron-Client Relationships in Southern Italy." *European Journal of Political Research* 1 (1973): 3–34.

Green, Philip. *Deadly Logic.* Columbus: Ohio University Press 1966.

Greenwald, Anthony. "The Totalitarian Ego: Fabrication and Revision of Personal History." *American Psychologist* 35 (1980): 603–13.

Gruner, Rolf. "On the Action of Social Groups." *Inquiry* 19 (1976): 443–54.

Halle, J. "The Struggle Called Coexistence." *New York Times Magazine*, 5 Nov. 1959.

Hanen, Marsha, and Kai Nielsen, eds.. *Science, Morality, and Feminist Theory. Canadian Journal of Philosophy Supplement* 13. Calgary: University of Calgary Press 1987.

Hardin, Russell. "Trusting Persons, Trusting Institutions." In *The Strategy of Choice*, ed. Richard Zeckhauser. Cambridge, Mass.: MIT Press 1991. 185–209.

- "The Street Epistemology of Trust." *Politics and Society* 21 (1993): 505–62.

Hardwig, John. "Depending on Experts." In *Selected Issues in Logic and Communications*, ed. Trudy Govier. Belmont, Calif.: Wadsworth 1988. 125–37.

- "The Role of Trust in Knowledge." *Journal of Philosophy* 88 (1991): 693–708.

Harre, Rom. *Social Being.* Oxford: Basil Blackwell 1979.

Hart, Kerry Marshall, with H. Randall Capps, Joseph P. Cangemi, and Larry M. Caillouet. "Exploring Organizational Trust and Its Multiple Dimensions: A Case Study of General Motors." *Organizations Development Journal* 4 (1986): 31–9.

Havel, Vaclav. *Living in Truth*. Trans. Paul Wilson. London: Faber and Faber 1986.
– "New Year's Address 1990." *Globe and Mail* 24 Jan. 1990.
– *Summer Meditations*. Trans. Paul Wilson. Toronto: Knopf Canada 1992.
Held, Virginia. "On the Meaning of Trust." *Ethics* 78 (1968): 156–59.
Heng Liang and Judith Shapiro. *Son of the Revolution*. New York: Knopf 1983.
Henslin, James. "Trust and the Cab Driver." In *Sociology and Everyday Life*, ed. Marcello Truzzi. Englewood Cliffs, NJ: Prentice Hall 1968. 138–58.
– "What Makes for Trust?" In *Down to Earth Sociology*, ed. James Henslin. New York: Free Press 1972.
Hertzberg, Lars. "On the Attitude of Trust." *Inquiry* 31 (1988): 307–22.
Hitchens, Christopher, "Why We Are Stuck in the Sand: Realpolitik in the Gulf: A Game Gone Tilt." *Harper's*, Jan. 1991, 70.
Hobbes, Thomas. *Leviathan*. Ed. intro. by C.B. Macpherson. Harmondsworth: Penguin 1968.
Hoffman, Stanley. *Duties beyond Borders: On the Limits and Possibilities of Ethical International Politics*. Syracuse: Syracuse University Press 1981.
Holmes, John G., with John K. Rempel and Mark P. Zanna. "Trust in Close Relationships." *Journal of Personality and Social Psychology* 49 (1985): 95–112.
Holsti, K.J. *The Dividing Discipline: Hegemony and Diversity in International Theory*. Boston: Allen and Unwin 1987.
Holzner, Burkart. "Sociological Reflections on Trust." *Humanitas* 9 (1973): 333–45.
Horsburgh, H.J.N. "The Ethics of Trust." *Philosophical Quarterly* 10 (1960): 343–54.
Isaacs, K.S., James M. Alexander, and Ernest A. Haggard. "Faith, Trust and Gullibility." *International Journal of Psychoanalysis* 44 (1967): 461–9.
Jackson, James O. "State of Treachery." *Time*, 3 Feb. 1992, 16–20.
Jones, C.P. *Culture and Society in Lucian*. Cambridge, Mass: Harvard University Press 1986.
Jones, Dorothy V. *Code of Peace: Ethics and Scarcity in the World of the Warlord States*. Chicago: University of Chicago Press 1989.
Kaila, Paul. "Concordia's Trials." *Maclean's*, 9 Nov. 1992, 52–5.
Kamel, Mohamed Ibrahim. *The Camp David Accords*. London: Routledge Kegan Paul 1986.
Kapuscinski, Ryszard. *Imperium*. Trans. Klara Glowczewska. Toronto: Knopf Canada 1994.
Keeping, Janet. "Environmental Protection through Land Claims Processes: The Importance of Trust." Canadian Institute for Resource Law, Calgary, 1993.
Kelman, H.C. "Human Use of Human Subjects: The Problem of Deception in Social Psychological Experiments." *Psychological Bulletins* 67 (1967): 1–11.

Kimmel, M.J., and D.G. Pruitt. "Twenty Years of Experimental Gaming: Critique, Synthesis, and Suggestions for the Future." *American Review of Psychology* 28 (1977): 363–92.

Kinsella, Noel A. "Some Psychological Dimensions of the Trusting Attitude." *Humanitas* 9 (1973): 254–71.

Kipnis, K., D. Meyers, and C. Murphy, eds. *Kindred Matters: Rethinking the Philosophy of the Family*. Ithaca, NY: Cornell University Press 1993.

Kirp, David, and Ronald Bayer. "Public Health: Needles and Race."*Atlantic*, July 1993, 38–41.

Knightley, Philip. *The Second Oldest Profession: The Spy as Patriot, Bureaucrat, Fantasist and Whore*. London: Pan Books 1987.

Kohn, Alfie. *No Contest: The Case Against Competition: Why We Lose in Our Race to Win*. Boston: Houghton Mifflin 1986, 1992.

Kramer, Janet. "Letter from Europe." *New Yorker*, 25 May 1992.

Krass, Allan. "Focus On: Verification and Trust in Arms Control." *Journal of Peace Research* 21 (1985): 285–88.

Kropotkin, Pietr. *Mutual Aid: A Factor of Evolution*. London: Heinemann 1902.

Kymlicka, Will. *Liberalism, Community, and Culture*. Oxford: Clarendon Press 1989.

Lagerspetz, Eerik. "Money as a Social Contract." *Theory and Decision* 17 (1984): 1–9.

Le Doeuff, Michele. *Hipparchia's Choice: An Essay concerning Women, Philosophy, etc.* Trans. Trista Selous. Oxford: Basil Blackwell 1991.

Levi, Carlo. *Christ Stopped at Eboli*. London: Farrer Straus 1947.

Levi, Margaret. "Social and Unsocial Capital: A Review Essay of Robert Putnam's *Making Democracy Work*." *Politics and Society* 24 (1996): 45–55.

Levi, Primo. *If This Is a Man. The Truce*. Trans. Stuart Woolf. London: Sphere Books 1987.

– *The Drowned and the Saved*. Trans. Raymond Rosenthal. New York: Simon and Schuster 1988.

Lewis, J. David, and Andrew Weigert. "Trust as a Social Reality." *Social Forces* 63 (1985): 967–85.

Lindskold, Svenn. "Trust Development, the GRIT Proposal, and the Effects of Conciliatory Acts on Conflict and Cooperation." *Psychological Bulletin* 85 (1978): 772–93.

– and Han Guyseog. "Responsiveness and Conciliation in Conflict." Paper presented at the annual meeting of the Midwestern Psychological Association, May 1985, Chicago, ERIC doc. ED257763.

Loomis, Charles P. and Zona K. Loomis. "Social and Interpersonal Trust - Its Loss by Disjunction." *Humanitas* 9 (1973): 317–31.

Loomis, James L. "Communication, the Development of Trust, and Cooperation." *Human Relationships* 12 (1959): 305–15.

Lord, Bette Bao. *Legacies: A Chinese Mosaic*. New York: Ballantine Books 1990.

Lucian. "Philosophers Going Cheap." In *Lucian: Satirical Sketches*, ed. and trans. Paul Turner Bloomington: Indiana University Press 1961. 147–65.

Luhmann, Niklas. *Trust and Power.* Trans. H. Davies, J.F. Raffman, and Kathryn Rooney. London: John Wiley and Sons 1979.

Lux, Kenneth. *Adam Smith's Mistake: How a Moral Philosopher Invented Economics and Ended Morality.* Boston: Shambhala 1990.

Malherbe, Abraham. *The Cynic Epistles.* Missoula, Mont.: Scholar's Press 1977.

Mansbridge, Jane, ed. *Beyond Self-Interest.* Chicago: Chicago University Press 1990.

Maoz, Zeev, and Dan S. Felsenthal. "Self-Binding Commitments, the Inducement of Trust, Social Choice, and the Theory of International Cooperation." *International Studies Quarterly* 31 (1987): 177–200.

Martin, Robert. *There are Two Errors in The The Title of This Book.* Peterborough: Broadview Press 1992.

Messick, D.M., and Brewer, M. "Solving Social Dilemmas." *Review of Personality and Social Psychology* 4 (1983): 11–44.

Meyers, Diana T. *Self, Society and Personal Choice.* New York: Columbia University Press 1989.

Michalos, Alex. "The Impact of Trust on Business, International Security, and the Quality of Life." *Journal of Business Ethics.* 9 (1990): 619–38.

Miller, Jeffrey. *Naked Promises: A Chronicle of Everyday Wheeling and Dealing.* Toronto: Random House 1989.

Mirsky, Jonathan. "In a Cruel Country." *New York Review of Books*, 26 Apr. 1990. 23–6.

Morgan, George W. "On Trusting." *Humanitas* 9 (1973): 237–51.

Morgenthau, Hans. *Politics among Nations.* New York: Alfred A. Knopf 1966.

Morris, Charles R. "It's Not the Economy, Stupid." *Atlantic*, July 1993, 49–64.

Moyer, Bill. "The Movement Action Plan." *Dandelion*, Fall 1983.

Murphy, John W. "Talcott Parsons and Niklas Luhmann: Two Versions of the Social 'System.'" *International Review of Modern Sociology* 1982 (12): 291–301.

Noddings, Nel. *Caring: A Feminine Approach to Ethics and Moral Education.* Berkeley and Los Angeles: University of California Press 1984.

Nyberg, David. *The Varnished Truth: Truth Telling and Deceiving in Ordinary Life.* Chicago: University of Chicago Press 1993.

Oakes, Guy. "The Sales Process and the Paradoxes of Trust." *Journal of Business Ethics* 9 (1990): 671–9.

O'Hara, Bruce. *Working Harder Isn't Working.* Vancouver: New Star Books 1993.

Orbach, Susie, and Luise Eichenbaum. *What Do Women Want?* New York: Berkeley Books 1983, 1993.

Orne, Martin T. "On the Social Psychology of the Psychology Experiment:

With Particular Reference to Demand Characteristics and Their Implications." *American Psychologist* 17 (1962): 776–80.

Ostrom, Elinor. *Governing the Commons: The Evolution of Institutions for Collective Action*. New York: Cambridge University Press 1990.

Pearce, Barnett. "Trust in Interpersonal Communication." *Speech Monographs* 4 (1974): 236–44.

Pellagrino, E. "Trust and Distrust in Professional Ethics." In *Ethics, Trust and the Professions: Philosophical and Cultural Aspects*, ed. E. Pellagrino, R. Veatch, and John P. Langan. Washington, DC: Georgetown University Press 1991.

Pitt-Rivers, Julian. "The Stranger, the Guest, and the Hostile Host: Introduction to the Laws of Hospitality." In *Contributions to Mediterranean Sociology*, ed. J.G. Pvistiany. The Hague: Mouter and Co. 1963. 13–30.

Pizzerno. "Amoral Familism and Historical Marginality." *International Review of Community of Development*. 15 (1966): 55–66.

Poster, Mark. *Critical Theory of the Family*. New York: Seabury Press 1978.

Postman, Neil. *Amusing Ourselves to Death: Public Discourse in the Age of Show Business*. New York: Viking Penguin 1985.

Pozner, Vladimir. *Parting with Illusions*. New York: Atlantic Monthly Press 1990.

Price, H.H. *Belief*. London: George Allen and Unwin 1969.

Putnam, Robert D. *Making Democracy Work: Civic Traditions in Modern Italy*. Princeton: Princeton University Press 1993.

Quinton, Anthony. "Social Objects." *Proceedings of the Aristotelian Society* 76 (1976): 1–27.

Rapoport, Anatol. "Formal Games as Probing Tools for Investigating Behavior Motivated by Trust and Suspicion." *Conflict Resolution* 7 (1963): 570–9.

– "Critique of Strategic Thinking." In *International Conflict and Behavioral Sciences*, ed. Roger Fisher. New York: Basic Books 1964. 211–37.

Redfield, Robert. "The Primitive World View." *Proceedings of the American Philosophical Society* 96 (1952): 30–6.

– *Peasant Society and Culture*. Chicago: Chicago University Press 1961.

Reid, Angus. *Shakedown*. Toronto: Doubleday 1996.

Ricci, David M. *The Tragedy of Political Science: Politics, Scholarship, and Democracy*. New Haven: Yale University Press 1984.

Rideout, George. *Lily Truehart, M.P.* Play presented at the Edmonton Fringe Festival, August 1991.

Roninger, Luis. *Patrons, Clients, and Friends*. New York: Cambridge University Press 1984.

– "Institutionalized Inequalities, the Structure of Trust, and Clientelism in Modern Latin America." In *Comparative Social Dynamics*, ed. Erik Cohen, Moshe Lissak, and Uri Almager. Boulder, Colo.: Westview Press 1985. 148–63.

– "Coronelismo, Ciciquismo, and Oyabun-kobun Bonds: Divergent Implications of Hierarchical Trust in Brazil, Mexico, and Japan." *British Journal of Sociology* 38 (1987): 311–30.

– and Ayse Gunes-Ayata. *Democracy, Clientelism and Civil Society*. Boulder, Colo.: Lynne Rienner 1994.

– and S.N. Eisenstadt. "Patron-Client Relations as a Model of Structuring Social Exchange." In *Comparative Studies in Society and History* 22 (1980): 42–77.

Rosenberg, Morris. "Misanthropy and Attitudes to International Affairs." *Conflict Resolution* 1 (1957): 340–345.

Rosenberg, Tina. *The Haunted Land: Facing Europe's Ghosts after Communism*. New York: Random House 1995.

Ross, James. "Testimonial Evidence." In *Analysis and Metaphysics*, ed. Keith Lehrer. Dordrecht: Reidel 1975. 35–55.

Roth, John K. "On Losing Trust in the World." *Echoes from the Holocaust*, ed. Alan Rosenberg and Gerald Myers. Philadelphia: Temple University Press 1988. 163–80.

Rotter, Julian B. "A New Scale for the Measurement of Interpersonal Trust." *Journal of Personality* 35 (1967): 615–54.

– "Interpersonal Trust, Trustworthiness and Gullibility." *American Psychologist* 35 (1980): 1–17.

– and Donald K. Stein. "Public Attitudes toward the Trustworthiness, Competence, and Altruism of Twenty Selected Occupations." *Journal of Applied Social Psychology* 1 (1970): 334–43.

Rybakov, Anatoli. *Child of the Arbat*. Trans. Harold Shukman. Boston: Little Brown 1988.

Schlenker, Barry M., with B. Helm and J.T. Tedeschi. "The Effects of Personality and Situational Variables on Behavioral Trust." *Journal of Personality and Social Psychology* 25 (1973): 419–27.

Schmookler, Andrew Bard. *The Parable of the Tribes: The Problem of Power in Social Evolution*. Boston: Houghton Mifflin 1984.

Schoenfelt, Eugen. "Image of Man: The Effect of Religion on Trust." *Review of Religious Research* 20 (1978): 61–7.

Seligman, Martin E. *Learned Optimism*. New York: Alfred A. Knopf 1991.

Seligson, Mitchell A. "Unconventional Political Participation: Cynicism, Powerlessness, and the Latin American Peasant." In *Political Participation in Latin America*, vol. 2, *Politics and the Poor*, ed. Mitchell A. Seligson and J.A. Booth. New York: Holmes and Meier 1979.

– and Jose Manuel Salazar X. "Political and Interpersonal Trust among Peasants: A Reevaluation." *Rural Sociology* 44 (1979): 505–24.

Sellerberg, Ann-Mari. "On Modern Confidence." *Acta Sociologica* 25 (1982): 39–48.

Shapin, Steven. *The Social History of Truth: Civility and Science in Seventeenth-Century England*. Chicago: University of Chicago Press 1994.

Sharp, Gene. *Gandhi as a Political Strategist*. Boston: Porter Sargent Publications 1979.

Shoemaker, Sydney. *Self-Knowledge and Self-Identity*. Ithaca: Cornell University Press 1963.

Silverman, Sydel F. "Agricultural Organization, Social Structure and Values in Italy: Amoral Familism Reconsidered." *American Anthropologist* 70 (1973): 3–34.

Sloterdijk, Peter. *Critique of Cynical Reason*. Trans. Michael Eldred. Minneapolis: University of Minnesota Press 1987.

Smith, Anthony. *National Identity*. Harmondsworth: Penguin 1991.

Snyder, Mark. "When Belief Creates Reality." *Advances in Experimental Social Psychology* 18 (1984): 2247–305.

– and Seymour W. Uranowitz. "Reconstructing the Past: Some Cognitive Consequences of Person Perception." *Journal of Personality and Social Psychology* 36 (1978): 941–50.

Stojanovic, Svetoza. "How Can We Explain the Changes in Eastern Europe and the Soviet Union?" Lecture presented at the University of Calgary, 15 Nov. 1991.

Strub, Peter J. "Two Patterns of Establishing Trust: The Marijuana User." *Sociological Focus* 9 (1976): 399–411.

Szabados, Bela. "Wittgenstein on 'Mistrusting One's Own Belief.'" *Canadian Journal of Philosophy* 11 (1979): 603–12.

Tangney, J.P. "Fraud Will Out - or Will It?." *New Scientist* 115 (1987): 62–3.

Thomas, D.O. "The Duty to Trust." *Proceedings of the Aristotelian Society* 79 (1978): 89–101.

Thomas, Laurence. "Liberalism and the Holocaust: An Essay on Trust and the Black-Jewish Relationship." In *Echoes from the Holocaust*, ed. Alan Rosenberg and Gerald Myers. Philadelphia: Temple University Press 1988. 105–17.

– *Living Morally*. Philadelphia: Temple University Press 1989.

– "Trust and Survival: Securing a Vision of the Good Society." *Journal of Social Philosophy* 20 (1989): 34–41.

– "Next Life I'll Be White." *Toronto Globe and Mail*, 16 Aug. 1990.

– Trust, Affirmation, and Moral Character: A Critique of Kantian Morality." In *Identity, Character and Morality*, ed. Owen Flanagan and Amelie Oksenberg Rorty. Cambridge, Mass.: Bradford Books 1991. 235–57.

– "Statistical Badness." *Journal of Social Philosophy* 33 (1992): 30–41.

Thorne, Barrie, and Marilyn Yalom, eds. *Rethinking the Family: Some Feminist Questions*. Boston: Northeastern University Press 1992.

Tismaneaunu, N. *The Crisis of Marxist Ideology in Eastern Europe*. London: Routledge 1988.

Turnbull, Colin. *The Mountain People*. New York: Simon and Schuster 1972.

Turner, Paul, ed. *Lucian: Satirical Sketches*. New York: Norton 1968.

Turner, Roy. "Speech and the Social Contract." *Inquiry* 28 (1985): 43–53.

Ugresic, Dubravka. *Have a Nice Day: From the Balkan War to the American Dream*. London: Jonathan Cape 1994.

Veatch, Robert. "Is Trust of Professionals a Coherent Concept?" In *Ethics, Trust, and the Professions*, ed. E. Pellagrino, R. Veatch, and John P. Langan. Washington, DC: Georgetown University Press 1991.

Vendler, Zeno. "Telling the Facts." *Philosophical Quarterly* 31 (1981): 302–24.

Walker, Connor. "Nation Building or Nation Destroying?" *World Politics* 24 (1972): 319–55.

Ware, Robert X. "Group Action and Social Organization." *Analyse and Kritik* 10 (1988): 48–70.

Webb, Mark Owen. "Why I Know about as Much as You: A Reply to Hardwig." *Journal of Philosophy* 92 (1993): 260–70.

Welbourne, M. "The Transmission of Knowledge." *Philosophical Quarterly* 29 (1979): 1–9.

– "Knowing and Believing." *Philosophy* 55 (1980): 317–29.

– "The Community of Knowledge." *Philosophical Quarterly* 31 (1981): 302–14.

– *The Community of Knowledge*. Scots Philosophical Monographs no. 9. Aberdeen: Aberdeen University Press 1986.

Westacott, George H., and Lawrence K. Williams. "Interpersonal Trust and Modern Attitudes in Peru." *International Journal of Contemporary Society* 13 (1976): 117–37.

White, Caroline. *Patrons and Partisans: A Study of Politics in Two Southern Italian Communities*. New York: Cambridge University Press 1980.

Wight, Martin. "Why Is There No International Theory?" In *Diplomatic Investigations*, ed. Herbert Butterfield. Cambridge: Harvard University Press, 1966.

Williams, Redford B., Jr, and John C. Barefoot. "Coronary-Prone Behavior: The Emerging Role of the Hostility Complex." In *Type A Behavior: Research, Theory, and Intervention*, ed. B.K. Houston and C.R. Snyder. New York: John Wiley 1988.

Wisdom, John. "Gods." In *Philosophy and Psychoanalysis*, ed. John Wisdom. Oxford: Basil Blackwell 1953. Repr. in *An Introduction to Philosophical Inquiry*, ed. Joseph Margolis. New York: Knopf 1968.

Wittgenstein, Ludwig. *Philosophical Investigations*. Oxford: Basil Blackwell 1953.

– *On Certainty*. Oxford: Basil Blackwell 1969.

Wrightsman, Lawrence S., Jr. "Measurement of Philosophies of Human Nature." *Psychological Reports* 14 (1964): 743–51.

Yamagishi, Toshio. "The Provision of a Sanctioning System as a Public Good." *Journal of Personality and Social Psychology* 51 (1986): 110–16.

Yamamoto, Yutaka. "A Morality Based on Trust: Some Reflections on Japanese Morality." *Philosophy East and West* 40 (1990): 451–69.

York, Geoffrey, and Loreen Pindera. *People of the Pines: The Warriors and the Legacy of Oka.* Toronto: Little Brown 1991.

Yuan, Gao. *Born Red: A Chronicle of the Cultural Revolution.* Stanford: Stanford University Press 1987.

Zand, Dale E. "Trust and Managerial Problem Solving." *Administrative Science Quarterly* 17 (1972): 229–39.

Index